Internal Conflict in Nepal:

Transnational Consequences

Internal Conflict in Nepal:

Transnational Consequences

Editor

V.R. Raghavan

Published for
Centre for Security Analysis
Chennai, India

Vij Books India Pvt Ltd
New Delhi, India

Published   by

Vij Books India Pvt Ltd

2/19, Ansari Road, Darya Ganj
New Delhi - 110002
Phones: 91-11-65449971, 91-11- 43596460
Fax: 91-11-47340674
e-mail : vijbooks@rediffmail.com
web : www.vijbooks.com

© **2011, Centre for Security Analysis, Chennai, India**

Centre for Security Analysis
"9-B" Ninth Floor,
Chesney Nilgiri, 71, Ethiraj Salai,
Egmore, Chennai-600008
Tamil Nadu, India
+91-44-65291889
office@csa-chennai.org
www.csa-chennai.org

The views and opinions presented in this book are of the author(s) of the chapters in the book and not necessarily that of the Centre for Security Analysis, Chennai, India.

First Published : 2011

ISBN 13 : 978-93-80177-64-9

Acknowledgement

The Centre for Security Analysis (CSA) has undertaken a three year research project **Internal Conflicts and Transnational Consequences** supported by the John D and Catherine T MacArthur Foundation. This volume is part of the ongoing project and its publication has been possible by the project grant.

TABLE OF CONTENTS

FOREWORD

This book forms part of CSA's project titled *Internal Conflicts and Transnational Consequences.* The project was conceptualized to examine the relationship between the consequences of internal conflicts and how these in turn drive the conflict. These consequences are not always limited to the boundaries of a state and there are external implications of what is essentially an internal problem. Sometimes those who are a party to the conflict have a vested interest in creating external consequences which can then ensure the continuity of the conflict. The question, therefore, is whether consequences strengthen the conflict? Or does the conflict itself gain in strength from the effects its consequences has on the state? The focus on consequences in this light is a new approach to internal conflicts. The project analyses conflicts in four different states with four different forms of governance. The case studies include India (Kashmir, Northeast and Naxalism), Nepal, Myanmar and Sri Lanka. Nepal until recently was a constitutional Monarchy, Myanmar has a military dictatorship, India is a full-fledged democracy which has not been able to satisfy some of its own people and Sri Lanka has a different kind of democracy. The project looks at how these four different systems of governance have dealt with essentially similar causes of conflict.

There are two types of internal conflicts. There are some conflicts that threaten regional as well as global security, global economic stability and the vital interests of many countries. Afghanistan is a case in point. The events in Afghanistan threaten the interests of Europe, USA, India and most of all Pakistan. Palestine and Georgia are other such examples. US and EU are extremely concerned about the situation in these conflict zones lest they lead to a war which can potentially spread to a larger area. Former

Yugoslavia was another such conflict which evoked an international response. International interests are at stake in such conflicts and also the primary reason for the involvement of major powers. Hence the EU safeguards its interest by sending NATO troops to Afghanistan and the U.S. has a major interest in Pakistan as long as the Al Qaeda and Taliban continue to carry out their operations from that country.

There are other internal conflicts where the external impact is minimal. Major Powers are at best unaffected by these conflicts even if they continue for several decades. Darfur, Somalia, Sub-Saharan Africa, Chechnya and even Sri Lanka are examples. The international community hardly took notice of the conflict in Sri Lanka until the LTTE decided to up the ante by involving the Tamil Diaspora in the western countries. The LTTE was declared a terrorist organization once LTTE projected an external threat dimension in the western countries. Myanmar is another example. Several countries are interested in establishing a democracy in Myanmar but it has not evoked an international response on the scale of Afghanistan. As long as it does not affect the vital interests of major countries and threaten regional security such conflicts raise limited concerns. In 2009 there was an attack in northern Myanmar's Kokang region. This region houses thousands of Chinese and the scenario changed immediately once these Chinese started moving back into China. China was now concerned with the problem in Myanmar as it did not want to face the problems arising from the sudden migration of people. The response to internal conflicts which have little external impact is at its best, one of neglect.

Where does Nepal, which is the focus of this book, stand in this context? The instability in Nepal is in no way going to have an impact on Europe or for that matter on global security issues. It does not affect the vital interests of either the EU or the US. A diaspora, of the size of the Tamils from Canada to New Zealand, can lobby for the involvement of their host countries but there is no Nepalese Diaspora comparable to that of the Tamil Diaspora. There is no Nepal caucus in the US Congress. The only country that is immediately concerned with the situation in Nepal is India. The Chinese on the other hand may see this as an opportunity to expand their sphere of influence. The Indian response, on the other hand, is guided by significant security concerns. Instability in Nepal can overflow into the neighboring Indian provinces of Uttar Pradesh and Bihar. A demographic shift of even 50,000 or 100,000 people into India will be a serious issue. As far as the economic and political consequence is concerned, it would be marginal on India but very substantial on Nepal.

Looking at the security concerns, it is fascinating how China's role in Nepal is portrayed as something that is troublesome for India or even as leverage on Indian policies. The fact however is that India and Nepal share an umbilical relationship and India's inherent strength and stability cannot be threatened by the Chinese. Nevertheless, India does have genuine concerns. Indian border states will certainly be affected by the political instability and turmoil in Nepal. There are real concerns that terrorists may use Nepal's territory as in Afghanistan. India certainly does not want a situation where Nepal would lose control over its own territory. The Indian interest lies in ensuring that Nepal remains a stable state in control of its own situation.

The central lesson from Nepal is that all parties involved need to have clear objectives and a strategy to manage the consequences of internal conflict. The Nepal Maoists went into a revolution without a post revolution strategy. The Monarchy having been displaced, they are unable to form a government. The consequences were thus not visualized. Each consequence creates a new dynamic for the conflict and it is important to not only anticipate the consequence but also strategize its management. Both the objective and the consequence should be studied and understood carefully. The distressing part in Nepal is a situation where the Centre does not hold. There is no monarchy and the political parties are also unable to hold the Centre. The military, which is the only organized institution left in Nepal, cannot also hold the Centre.

We are living in an era where conflicts are perennial and it is going to be difficult to manage post-conflict outcomes. One cannot wait for the post-conflict phase to respond to the consequences. Parties cannot wait until the conflict is over to implement their post-conflict role. It is necessary to work within the conflict scenario. Nepal is in many ways going through this phase.

The Project is being supported by the John D. and Catherine T. MacArthur Foundation as part of its *Asia Security Initiative*.

V. R. Raghavan

President, Centre for Security Analysis (CSA)

INTRODUCTION

Brig K Srinivasan (Retd)

Nepal, the oldest nation state in the region has been a peace loving country with a friendly population, a tourist paradise with no ethnic, linguistic or religious disputes and associated struggles. However, deprivation, poverty, subjugation for years have given in to social and political upheaval resulting in Maoist insurgency, termination of monarchy and declaration of secular and federalist state full of hope and promise. The euphoria evaporated soon after. The hope that peace, democracy and development would take root and formally be consolidated stands belied. However, the issue of marginalization of the minorities and under privileged has been brought to the forefront for all to take notice. The political and social transformation of Nepal has begun. But, socio-political struggle seems stuck in the narrow grooves of self interest of the political outfits losing vision and hope.

Nine experts from different fields were engaged to study this conflict and its consequences and same were presented at the seminar held in Varanasi on 4- 5 June 2010. The observations, views and analyses are thought provoking and the same have been presented in this volume.

Yubaraj Ghimire in *Nepal: Impact of Internal Conflict on Security* discusses the post 2006 developments in the context of constitutional crisis, political uncertainty, national security and economy. Continued political instability and lack of consensus among the key political parties on several key issues have created a political vacuum in the country. This has lowered the credibility of political actors in the eyes of the people and the international community. He observes that the internal conflict, if allowed to linger, the impact would not necessarily remain internal as transnational forces blur the boundaries between national sovereignty and international security.

In his paper *Nepal's counter insurgency campaign:Impacts and Aftermath* Chiran Jung Thapa recounts the counter insurgency campaign of the State and the impact of campaign on the Monarchy, the State, political system, society, civil military relations and security institutions - Nepal Army, Police, Armed Police that were directly associated with the formulation and implementation of the counter insurgency campaign. State and political structures were altered. Monarchy was abolished and the Hindu identity was discarded. Nepal was declared a Federal Democratic Republic. With no constitution to guide, the structure of the political systems is still uncertain. Political polarizations, spread of culture of violence, lawlessness, destructive and disruptive activities by the militant youth wings of political parties have corroded the Nepali society. Newer fissures have emerged as demands on lines of federalism, ethnic nationalism and autonomy by different ethnic groups became more vehement. On the security front, the Nepal Army lost the Royal title and is no longer a ceremonial force. It has gained experience in asymmetric warfare, acquired new weaponry and formed a new elite force Mahabir Battalion (Rangers). Nepal police on the other hand, suffered the most causalities. After Armed Police Force was formed, the Nepal police was pushed to the third position in the hierarchy of security institutions in the state. The Civil military relation is still at infancy and is evolving. While the military claims that the state was not defeated militarily he makes an interesting observation. It is debatable as to whether it was the military campaign executed by the state or the insurgent's strategy of victory through alternative means that ended the insurgency resulting in abolition or monarchy and conduct of election.

Uddahab Pyakural and Indra Adihkari in their paper *Internal Conflict in Nepal after the Comprehensive Peace Agreement* examine the issues that came forth after the signing of the Comprehensive Peace Agreement (CPA). CPA was a turning point for many political and social movements in Nepal which resulted in Seven Party Alliance (SPA) signing of agreements with many ethnic groups with the main objective to have a political system based on ethnic identity. The paper also explores the growth and causes of armed and semi armed groups which mushroomed after the CPA. This development has resulted in increased culture of violence and intimidation all over the country. Political accommodation through dialogue that is inclusive, transparent, and institutionalized is the only way to ensure peace and social transformation easy.

The changing social structure, philosophy of life, cultural norms and values and the psyche of the society brought about by post conflict developments and political changes have also affected the army. Brig Gen (Retd) Keshar Bahadur Bhandari in his paper *Impact of Internal Conflict on the Nepal Army* explores the effects of the People's war on Nepal army particularly in the areas such as force structure, integration of Maoist cadres, morale and discipline, recruitments, human rights issues and civil-military relations. The Nepal Army witnessed major changes in the organizational structure during the conflict period. The number of the Maoist combatants to be integrated into Nepal Army (NA) has been the main issue of disagreement between the Maoist and other political parties. The upheavals in Nepali politics added confusion in the army regarding its role, allegiance and direction and also changed the relationship between the army, political parties and the society to a large extent. Civil-Military Relations (CMR) is a new subject in Nepal. The CPN (Maoist) led government tried to reduce the power of the military by establishing their party's army, like in a totalitarian regime, or at least tried to influence the national army, but lacked the capacity to bring about a shift in the overall power balance. As a post conflict development, CMR during the CPN (Maoist) led government further deteriorated in 2008, and reached the stage of an institutional confrontation between the government and the army. The relationship between the army, political parties and the society is in a state of transition. The democratization of the army reflecting the national and inclusive character has drawn a lot of attention, but the government has not been able to formulate an extensive work plan. He is of the view that civilian supremacy can prevail only when the new constitution of Nepal is drafted in time, law and order and stability in governance are reestablished.

Over 80 per cent of the Nepalese are dependent on agriculture and natural resources for their livelihood. B.C. Upreti in his paper *Conflict in Nepal: Impact on Environment and Its Cross-Border Implications* discusses impact of decade long insurgency on the biodiversity, community forests, land and land resources. The community forests, protected areas, national parks became target of the Maoist attacks due to the presence of army patrolling units there. The Maoists also assaulted the infrastructure of these areas by destroying outlying guard posts and forest offices. This resulted in decrease in tourism, a major source of foreign currency earnings. There was a decrease of 50 per cent in tourism since 2001. In Nepal, land and land resources were always exploited from time immemorial. Therefore, the Maoist slogan 'land to the tillers' had gained sympathy in tenants, poor farmers and the marginalized. Rich and medium commercial farmers faced continuous pressure to pay to the Maoists huge amount of money. Such extortion greatly affected commercial farming such as tea gardens, fruit gardens, livestock farming, cardamom growing, broom grass and ginger growing, etc. The impact of the Maoist conflict on the environment of Nepal also had its implications for India – Nepal relations. The sharing of the river water resources has been a complex issue between India and Nepal. The Maoist termed all the treaties concluded between India and Nepal unequal and hence demanded that these treaties be scraped. It adversely affected the water resources development cooperation between India and Nepal. Some of the ongoing projects got delayed due to the conflict situation.

Anjoo Sharan Upadhyaya in her paper *Conflict in Nepal and Transnational Ramifications* explores the impact of the internal crisis in Nepal on the security issues in general and with special focus on the southern region of Nepal – Terai region, its implication on the neighbouring states of India mainly Bihar, UP and West Bengal. A major outcome of the Maoist war has been the growing salience of force and violence among other militating groups. The rise of Youth Communist League (YCL) has provoked many political parties and ethnic groups to create their own militant wings. As many as 109 armed outfits operate in parts of the country, mainly in Terai. Impunity for past crimes has been one of notable features of the post conflict Nepal which has emboldened the members of party youth wings and armed groups to resort to extortion and intimidation and also political killings. The post conflict surge of militant regionalism in Terai undermined the already frail law and governance in the areas bordering India. Terai has long been a favourite spot for the Pakistani intelligence agencies to foment trouble for India. The unholy alliance between the illicit traders, criminals and terrorist in Terai thrives on a range of connected activities i.e. hawala system, fraudulent letters of credit and the distribution of counterfeit Indian currency. The illegal trading and the circulation of fake currency is protected by the transnational criminal syndicates which in turn facilitate their cross border operation including money laundering. The growth of gun culture in southern Nepal has led to undesirable cross border transaction including arms supply through the bordering states of UP and Bihar. She recommends for a need to look beyond nabbing the individual criminals and work in concert to reform the border management as well as develop a zero tolerance policy for corruption.

Padmaja Murthy in her paper *Internal Conflict in Nepal: Implications for India* says that a new politics of identity has come up to empower the marginalized and oppressed sections of the society. The marginalized majority effectively organized themselves and asserted their demands for direct participation in political process. This resulted in fresh eruption of the violence and conflicts within the State. India is an important external stakeholder which is directly influenced by this instability politically, socially and most importantly in terms of security. The post Constituent Assembly elections saw emergence of newer power equations within Nepal with United Communist Party of Nepal- Maoist (UCPN (M)) seeking closer ties with China at the cost of India. The protest movement by Maoists has drawn India into the divisive politics played within the state. The divisive politics played over the issues relating to Nepal Army, integration of Maoist combatants have derailed the fragile peace process. The fractured consensus, deep divisions and polarization of views have prevented the Constituent Assembly from drafting new constitution. She also brings out the impact of the conflict on the economy of Nepal and the India- Nepal economic relations. The continuing instability even after the Constituent Assembly (CA) elections does not create an environment conducive to foreign direct investment in Nepal. She is of the view that India and UCPN (M) should build cordial relations for the stability and peace of both the countries. This would also enable India to be constructively influential and have a meaningful role to play in Nepal. An Indian foreign policy towards Nepal which is not able to build constructive relations with the Maoists will have only limited success in fulfilling India's interests.

Dr Nihar Nayak in his paper *International Impact of Conflict in*

Nepal focuses on the involvement of external actors, in particular India, China, the United States, the European Union, the UK and UNMIN in Nepal since 2006. Nepal' strategic location has drawn external forces to engage directly and indirectly in Nepal's internal affairs. Growing triangular relations between China, Pakistan and some groups in Nepal and the anti – India feeling have been major concerns for India. These groups can have easy access to separatist and Maoist outfits operating within Indian territory and can foment anti-India activities. There are concerns that Chinese presence in Nepal may leverage Pakistan to carry out anti-India activities from Nepalese soil. On the other hand, China considers Nepal as extremely significant for its security along its vulnerable Tibet border. Since 2008, there has been enhanced political engagement, economic cooperation, people-to-people and cultural exchanges and cooperation in international and regional affairs between the two countries. The other actors like US and UK have tacitly supported the Monarchy during the people's war but following the demise of the monarchy in 2008, Washington worked to counterbalance the Maoists by supporting other political parties and their accession to power. The US and the UK provided valuable military assistance to fight the Maoists. Having a friendly regime in Kathmandu is therefore of highest priority to any US administration as US wants to maintain a psychological pressure on China. European Union countries were actively involved in conflict resolution and restoration of democracy in Nepal and also contributed to conflict mitigation through support to core legal institutions, improving peace research capacities and assistance programs to victims of Maoist insurgency.

The politicians in Nepal need to realize the seriousness of the situation, sit together and decide as to how they can overcome the difficulties and set up a constitution and a government for themselves. This would need give and take in a number of areas. They need to convince their constituencies and with out playing to the gallery, should start with constructive cooperation.

NEPAL: IMPACT OF INTERNAL CONFLICT ON SECURITY

Yubaraj Ghimire

Introduction

Internal conflict emerges from the unrealized rights, demands and aspirations of citizens within the institutional context of the state and society. Some times internal imbalances of power, unfulfilled basic needs, denial of rights, aggressive impulse of leaders and groups, sense of ideological supremacy, identity politics and absence of weak law-enforcing mechanism also contribute to internal conflict.[1] Unaddressed aspirations, if endorsed by organized voice, do have a tendency to snowball into a political movement and agitation. Given the scale of illiteracy, poverty and corruption in the Nepalese society, these aspirations and frustrations can fuel any movement if there is an alternative leadership, with proven or even perceived credibility. Such a movement often may take radical or militant course and tie the leadership in an expectation trap. Pervasive poverty, inequality and discrimination provide a sound recipe to radicalize the society and generate conflict against incumbent political classes representing the state. Obviously, "extreme poverty exhausts governing institution, depletes resources, weakens leaders and crushes hope, fuelling a volatile mix of desperation and instability".[2]

---

[1] John Mearsheimer, "Back to the Future: Instability in EuropeAfter the Cold War", in *The New Shape of World Politics* (New York:Foreign Affairs, 1999), 108-110.

[2] Lael Brainhard, Derek Cholleta nd Vinca LaFleur, "The Tangled Web: The Poverty-Insecurity Nexus," in Lael Brainhard and Derek Chollet eds, *Too Poor for Peace? Global Poverty, Conflict and Security in the 21st Century*, (Washington DC: Brooking Institution Press, 2007), 1

After all, it is far easier to sell a radical dream to the people who want a quick and magical relief from poverty and corruption and increased risk of uncertain future. In a country penetrated by international regimes such as Nepal, transnational ideological movements also make a common cause with local movements—peaceful or violent— and erode the capacity of the state to maintain national security and authority as well as muster the loyalty of people to the nation-state. National security in the context of global anarchy requires the management of conflict of interests with the neighbors and the resolution of security dilemma through balanced foreign policy. The central point of security dilemma is that an increase in one state's security decreases the security of others.[3] In Nepal, severe internal strains viciously feed one set of conflict to another and even unfold cross border connections and networks thus undermining the sovereignty of national space. The uncertain strength of the political forces in Nepal and inter and intra-party struggles are standing in the way to vitiate national security issues.[4] There are other unresolved constitutional issues that also serve as the motors of conflict.

Nepal is facing intense security challenges incomparable to any other time in the nation's history. The chapter will mainly delve into the political developments, from February 1996, the phase that witnessed the birth and rapid expansion of Maoist insurgency, up to April 2006 when it gave up violence and joined the political mainstream based on the 12-point agreement mediated by New Delhi. The Maoist conflict resulted in the loss of more than 15,000 lives, leaving several people disabled, causing devastation of development infrastructures and private property worth billions of rupees, and leading to internal displacement of more than 60,000 people. The mass movement of April 2006 against the Royal takeover and the direct rule by King Gyanendra for 15 months since February 2005 brought unexpected political outcomes. National Day of Nepal was suspended and many national

---

[3] Robert Jervis, "Offense, Defense and the Security Dilemma," in Robert J Art and Robert Jervis eds, *International Politics* (London: Longman, 2001), 84

[4] Sridhar Khatri, "Health and Human Security and Possible Trajectories for Nepal by 2015", *Non-Traditional Security Challenges in South Asia: 2015*, NBR-BEI Workshop, November 21-22, 2009, http://www.nbr.org/research/activity.aspx?id=58

icons were contested. Nepal's better known identity—Unitary Hindu Kingdom—changed into a Federal Democratic Republic (FDR) which was to be institutionalized by a constitution. The Comprehensive Peace Agreement (CPA) signed in 2006 has many national security components including normalization process, de-radicalization of politics, integration and rehabilitation of 19,600 UN verified Maoist combatants, democratization of Nepal Army and improved civil-military relations. This chapter discusses the issues of constitutional crisis, embedded links in political uncertainty, mechanism of political stability, national security and economy.

Constitutional Crisis

The Constitutional system seeks to settle issues of legitimate political order and internal security dilemma by reinforcing law-governed behavior. National interest and survival are best served by harmonizing the goals of the state, market, civil society and international community and capturing the synergy. "The appropriate state action is calculated according to the situation in which the state finds itself".[5]

In Nepal, when it was clear that the Constituent Assembly would miss the deadline of 28 May 2010 to draft a new Constitution, the polity extended its tenure by another year. The three big political parties—Unified Communist Party of Nepal-Maoists (UCPN-M), Nepali Congress and the Communist Party of Nepal-Unified Marxist Leninist (CPN-UML)—which together form more than two-third majority in the House which is required to frame and deliver the new constitution—reached an understanding to complete the assigned role within the new time frame. However, skepticism is growing as political parties are losing their credibility in achieving the urgent tasks. Are they serious and sincere about drafting and delivering the new constitution? Will the constituent assembly dominated by the three parties, with UCPN-M, the largest one, be able to manage the major differences they have on at least 20 contentious issues that range from the model of governance to federalism to the independence of judiciary?

In all probability, the political conflict will be intensified. Until and unless

---

[5] Kenneth Waltz, *Theory of International Politics*, (California: Addison-Wesley,1979), 134

Nepal has a properly drafted and adopted constitution, uncertainties may continue to prevail in the country. Continued political instability, and lack of consensus among the key players on several issues, will cause deterioration of the situation. In addition, non-political factors of insecurity are also becoming stronger. Nepal today is facing "shortages of the four basic agricultural sources—land, water, energy and fertilizer. No nation can isolate itself from these scarcities or their economic and political consequences".[6] Climate change has also led to scarcity of water. Issues like terrorism, globalization and transnational social movement are weakening the capacity of state to create public order, provide service delivery and settle problems and conflicts. "As political survival and internal peace are more often defined in economic terms, states have become responsible for economic transformation".[7]

Embedded Links in Political Uncertainty

On 28 May 2010, the three mainstream parties penned an accord in which then Prime Minister Madhav Nepal—who completed over one year in office - agreed to step down 'without delay'. The offer was in response to the longstanding demand of the Maoists to step down and pave the way for formation of a national unity government, preferably led by the UCPN-M as it is the single largest party in the Constituent Assembly that was elected in April 2008. The accord also stated that the Maoists will agree to honor the past commitments like returning the property the party had confiscated from political opponents and ordinary people during the decade long insurgency. In addition, they also agreed to transform the Young Communist League (YCL) into a civilian outfit and work earnestly for rehabilitation and integration of the Maoist combatants in the society and security agencies of the state.

But within hours, they began squabbling over whether the resignation

---

[6] Robert Johansen, "The Threat to Survival," in George A. Lopez and Michael S. Stohl eds, *International Relations: Contemporary Theory and Practice*, (Washington:Congressional Quarterly Press, 1989), 300

[7] Peter Evans, "States and Industrial Transformation," in Roe Goddard, Patrick Cronin and Kishore Dash eds., *International Political Economy: State Market Relations in the Changing Global Order*, (New Delhi: Viva Books, 2005), 122

offer was unconditional or linked to the Maoists implementing the past accords. The state and politics of Nepal are guided and dictated by this confusion and uncertainty because each top political leader wants to become Prime Minister and, therefore, each uses his leverage in other parties to bargain and weaken the opponents within the same party. Yet, the three parties agreed to extend the tenure of the constituent assembly for various reasons. One, they preferred collective survival than joint death. Second, people were feeling betrayed by the inability of the House to deliver the constitution and there was tremendous international pressure, from the United Nations, United States and the European Union to have the term extended so that a legitimate institution of the people does not disappear suddenly. Its absence, they feel, will aggravate the existing political authority vacuum. But there was neither an apology offered, nor a guarantee assured by the government as well as the signatories to the May 28 accord that they would address major contentious points that have come in the way of writing the Constitution. In brief, the post conflict situation continues to keep the political spectrum divided sharply and, therefore, muddling around than marching ahead.

Prime Minister Madhav Kumar Nepal complied with the accord in July 2010, but the promised politics of consensus could not be restored. The House could not elect its successor by consensus within the 12-day deadline that President Rambaran Yadav had set. The UCPN-M, through a Position Paper released on July 11, said the party was not in possession of land confiscated during the years of conflict, and that YCL was not a para-military outfit. Politics of 'understanding' is increasingly getting displaced by politics of deceit and history of betrayal of each other prevents the possibility for long term cooperation on national issues. What went wrong in Nepal in the past four years when there was so much euphoria and hope that peace, democracy and development would be firmly consolidated and take deep roots in the country? How safe and secure do the people feel now? This issue needs to be dissected and viewed from different dimensions as security presupposes not only freedom from fear but also from basic needs deficit.

Mechanism for Political Stability

Political stability and consensus factors need to be taken into account. The credibility of the political actors in the eyes of the people and the international community needs to be analyzed. The 12-point agreement that united the parties for the removal of monarchy is unraveling due to change in the internal political equation and political change in India. The conflict, of course, has left a deep impact on the security instruments of the state, and the post conflict scenario as well as the ongoing peace process—with a heavy dose of uncertainty—has visibly enhanced the role of external players. It will be too early to predict where Nepal goes from here, but the current developments do not make people optimistic as they were four years ago. The promised politics of consensus—that forms part of the interim Constitution which is still in vogue—has already fragmented thus undermining the constitutional and institutional mechanism of stability. In April 2006 under pressure of the mass movement, King Gyanendra not only handed over power to a conglomeration of the political parties led by G P Koirala, he also revived the parliament that was not only dissolved three years ago— and subsequently (that dissolution) upheld by the Supreme court—but it had also outlived its normal five year tenure by then. Political necessity dictated the situation rather than democratic choice. The political parties probably realized that not having an elected body would give any 'dictator' an ideal platform to take over power. Perhaps the parties were guided by the same logic and fear when they decided to extend the tenure of the constituent assembly on May 28, 2010.

The politics of consensus is almost dead already. G P Koirala who worked as interim Prime Minister heading a coalition government, made no attempt to relinquish the post for almost three months even after his party, the Nepali Congress, lost to the UCPN-M in the CA elections which secured 28.1 per cent votes with 238 members in a House of 601. Instead, the government headed by Koirala transacted major bills and decisions with larger political implications without even taking oath as the Prime Minister after the elections to the CA. Once Prachanda managed to get other parties support crossing the majority mark in the House, Koirala and the Nepali Congress, the main architect of the politics of consensus—refused to join the coalition giving almost an irreversible jolt to that process. The prevailing confusion and CA's failure to have Constitution delivered on time has its root in the collapse of the politics of consensus and the ability to attain collective action. This trend continued even after the change of government subsequent to the resignation by UCPN-M Chief Prachanda as the Prime Minister in May 2009 and takeover by UML's Madhav Nepal as the Maoists refused to join the government. The exercise to have the National Unity government sounds good in principle but there are doubts if at all it can be translated into action.

The collapse of political consensus also witnessed a parallel and equally damaging as well as negative trend of politics and politicians being discredited. Hopes had died, and leaders were fast turning into a breed that could not be and should not be trusted. Moreover, they failed to come to an understanding on what should a Federal Republic and Secular Nepal look like? Maoists want Nepal split into 12 provinces—mostly on the basis of ethnicity—with the right to self-determination while the two other parties fearing its consequences on national unity are still not clear about the basis of federalism. Similarly, Maoists want a judiciary accountable and servile to the legislature with the provision that judges could be hand-picked by the people's representative body. They also want an executive President while UML wants a directly elected Prime Minister. The Nepali Congress continues to harp on parliamentary democracy, something Maoists are rigidly against. Maoists have been insisting that they would want 'people's republic' in Nepal in which the competing parties would need the endorsement of only one national party i.e. the UCPN-M to operate legally. Their intermittent cry that they would capture state power only makes politics and future of Nepal uncertain as a democracy besides forcing pro-democracy parties to rely more on the security agencies of the state—mainly the Nepal army— to defeat such a move if and when it comes. That is why there are doubts and skepticism about the implementation of the May 28 accord and the politics of consensus being revived.

National Security and Economy

The 12-point agreement—initiated and mediated by India—way back in

November 2005, ten months after the Royal takeover brought the pro-republic Maoists and the pro-constitutional monarchy forces like the Nepali Congress and the UML together. "We decided to give up monarchy in lieu of Maoists agreeing to join peace and democracy", K P Situala, a prominent Congress leader and key negotiator in the process said publicly. The agreement subsequently led to the removal of the monarchy and Nepal being declared a federal and secular state. However, political compromise took precedence over the constitution and due process of changes. Political accountability was rarely enforced in the post April 2006 period. The United Nations Mission to Nepal (UNMIN) was invited for a limited role in the peace process. With UNMIN's arrival in June 2006, Nepal army was forced to confine itself in the barracks and this may continue until the Maoist combatants are integrated and rehabilitated. There is discomfiture in the army which feels humiliated in being 'equated with rebels'. UNMIN's initial one year term is being extended continuously after for an additional six months and quite often it is branded as carrying a "pro-Maoist bias" by the Non-Maoist parties as well as the Nepal Army. In March, Army Chief Chhatraman Singh Gurung told Lynn B Pascoe, Assistant Secretary General of the United Nations as well as its political head that Nepal Army is not going to be confined to the barracks indefinitely. He also said that Maoist combatants cannot be admitted to the army as a group, but he was willing to consider their entry on individual basis provided they fulfill other qualifications. The issue of integrating the Maoist combatants in the security agencies is the single most significant issue that has the potential to spoil the ongoing peace process. The fact that two rivals who fought for almost half a decade do not trust each other yet is understandable.

There is little that the political parties have done to bring them together to convince them that peace cannot be achieved and consolidated in a durable way without their cooperation. While the Maoist combatants enjoy firm patronage in the form of its parent party, the UCPN-M, the Nepal Army has only now begun getting the backing of non-Maoist parties and that too after Maoists began threatening repeatedly that they would capture the state power. Soon after the hand-over of the power by the King, the UCPN-M, the only party that had pro-republic, federal and secular agenda, obviously was seen as the face and key agent of the desired change. Nepali Congress and the UML blindly followed their agenda for the sake of their interest in power-sharing. The Maoists tactfully put the army, the King and his unpopularity on the same platform. The two other parties did not adopt such an aggressive stand against the Nepal Army. The Maoists insisted right from the beginning that the Nepal army must be downsized. "Why would we need this army that is full of rapists and corrupted officers", Prachanda asked during his maiden press conference that marked the end of his underground politics at the official residence of the Prime Minister (G P Koirala then) on June 2, 2006. Nepal Army continued to be his target after he became the Prime Minister in July 2008. He stopped recruitment in the army against regular vacancies, and sacked Gen Rookmangud Katawal, as Army Chief on May 3, 2009 only to be vetoed by President Rambaran Yadav under pressure from 18 major political parties. These political parties were of the opinion that Prachanda wanted to divide and destroy the Nepal Army and spread a psychological message that once the army was weak "the state can be captured'. The competition for security between rival parties made it difficult for cooperation. The Comprehensive Peace Agreement (CPA) signed on November 21, 2006—that forms the basis of the peace process—talks about democratizing the Nepal Army, but does not quite mention the model of Disarmament, Demobilization and Reintegration (DDR) and Security Sector Reform (SSR) to be followed. The European Union, mainly the United Kingdom is in favor of SSR, a model that Maoists have lent their weight behind. The EU is heavily involved, for the first time, in the two crucial areas of formulating Nepal's defense policy and restructuring its Army. It is openly asserting that the secular Nepal must guarantee in its future Constitution the right to (religious) conversion. The issue has far serious connotation and is now being objected to by huge groups of Hindus—both moderate and hardliners—who together constitute more than 80 per cent of the total population. Hence, the issue of security and faith are getting linked closely and this development may lead to serious consequences.

The Hindus in Terai are seething with discontent and demanding the restoration of Hindu identity of Nepal. The EU is also against arms supply being resumed as it feels it goes against the spirit of the peace process while India is keen to lift the embargo it had placed during the Royal takeover. This some say is in violation of the 1950 treaty of Peace and Friendship and subsequent exchange of letters (1965) on arms supply. It is not only India and the EU that are being debated and more visible in Nepal, China— Nepal's northern neighbor which rarely spoke on issues beyond Tibet—is showing diverse and magnified interest. With the monarchy gone, an institution that it worked in trust for more than four decades, China is looking for a trusted ally with whom it can work on short-term and long-term basis. As political parties and political process seem in disarray, it is also simultaneously trying to have a peace and friendship treaty signed with Nepal so that its role in future—especially when there is chaos and uncertainty—could be defined and legitimized. In a way, it is competing and cooperating with India vis a vis Nepal on an issue by issue basis. China's increased interest in Nepal can be gauged by the increasing number of high level official visits. The conflict and post-conflict scenario have also witnessed other crises, mainly related with climate change and food scarcity. Around 3.5 million people are officially declared as hit by food scarcity. Around 35 glaciers, out of 2000 in the country, are listed as being close to danger point of bursting. This could have disastrous consequences with its effect spilled beyond the border of the country. All these without clearly defined consensus based politics, threatened by breach of peace process and resumption of violence, do not augur well for a country known in the past for its social and religious amity as well as land of peace. "Security agenda should respond to real requirements and needs. National interest must also be considered, as when domestic crises are ignored, disastrous consequences are seen".[8] Moreover, both giant neighbors—India and China –see or perceive Nepal's territory as potential foot-hold or swelling ground for forces hostile to their national and security interest.

Conclusion

An internal conflict, if allowed to linger, leaves impact that does not

---

[8] Daniel Rotfeld, "Democracy in the New Concept of Security," *Democracy Forum*, (Sweden:International IDEA,1996), 60

necessarily remain internal as transnational forces blur the boundaries between national sovereignty and international security. The soft power of ideas and communication has fused the national horizon and workers are integrating themselves with the international system. Out of 400,000 workers who enter into the labor market 300,000 migrate abroad in search of jobs and their remittance has contributed more than anything else to the nation's survival and well being. De-linking from the international system is not a realistic option but, there is a need to minimize the negative effects of harmful linkages between politics and policies. The possible nexus between the Maoists in Nepal and India and the consolidation of ultra left groups from across South Asia into the Coordinating Committee of Maoist Parties and Organisations of South Asia (CCOMPOSA) has made militancy based politics a core regional concern. The Bhutan Maoist Party has already given notice to the Druk Government that it is going to launch a movement for Republican Bhutan in the near future. The obvious role model is Nepal's Maoist Party, the strength it gathered as an insurgent group, and the legitimacy it secured through election.

As a result of the conflict, the Nepal police was extensively armed and expanded, a paramilitary force named Armed Police Force was created to combat 'terrorism', and Nepal Army grew in strength from 55,000 in 1996 to 90,000 in 2002. The number of Maoist combatants also grew at an alarming rate. According to reports from the Home Ministry, 109 armed outfits operate in parts of the country, mainly in Terai. Other political parties and ethnic groups are also creating militant wings and militarizing the society. This means that the country would spend more on defense and internal security at the cost of basic needs like food, education, health, jobs and social mobility. Such a situation can also invite the involvement of international actors as is evident in the case of Nepal. It is however, important to note in conclusion that what legitimizes the militants is ultimately the people's mandate and they can be discredited if they chose to use the democratic process as a tactic rather than a legitimate political means. Democratic ends require democratic means and this is the reason for the creation of civilization and security with the minimization of the instruments of violence and insecurity in society.

NEPAL'S COUNTER INSURGENCY CAMPAIGN: IMPACTS AND AFTERMATH

Chiran Jung Thapa

Nepal endured a violent Maoist insurgency for ten years. This insurgency, that raged throughout Nepal and claimed about 14,000 lives, came to a halt after the Comprehensive Peace Accord (CPA) was signed in 2006. Although Nepal brandished a multifaceted counter insurgency campaign, it was predominantly military in nature. It is still debatable as to whether it was the counter insurgency campaign envisaged and executed by the State or the insurgents' strategic victory through alternative means that ended the insurgency. This debate continues because the Nepal Army (formerly Royal Nepalese Army) – that served as the vanguard of the counter insurgency operations asserts that it succeeded in preventing the insurgents from militarily defeating the State. According to the Nepal Army (NA), it was only when the insurgents realized that they could not militarily defeat the State that they changed their strategic gears and opted for political maneuvers to join the political mainstream.[1] By contrast, the insurgents claim strategic victory for having attained their main strategic objectives - the abolition of the monarchy, elections for a constituent assembly (they emerged victorious as the largest party in the election and held power for about nine months) and establishment of a Republic. Certainly these divergent arguments have their own merit. But, regardless of how the outcome is interpreted, the radical and adverse transformation of Nepal that is underway can be directly attributed to Nepal's counter insurgency proceedings.

---

[1] This is the official line of the Nepal Army (NA). This line of argument has been widely disseminated through the media.

This chapter is divided into three segments. First, a narrative of the evolution of the insurgency is presented. Second, the manner in which the State mounted a counter insurgency campaign is discussed. Third, an independent analysis of the impacts of counter insurgency proceedings is presented. In this segment, the status-quo of the institutions – the Monarchy, Nepal Army, Police, Armed Police – that were directly associated with the formulation and implementation of the counter insurgency campaign is discussed alongside the impacts on the State, political system, society and civil-military relations. Since the intent of this chapter is to narrate the counter insurgency campaign and then analyze its impacts and aftermath, it will not dwell on diagnosing the root causes of the insurgency.

Evolution of the Insurgency

The history of ideological Maoist movement can be traced back to the foundation of Communist party of Nepal in Calcutta in 1949.[2] In 1960, the Monarch – King Mahendra, usurped State power by dissolving the elected parliament, arrested the cabinet and banned all political parties. Following this takeover, two divergent factions emerged within the communist party of Nepal; one that preferred to collaboratively work with the King and the other that demanded the restoration of the parliament.[3] Because of the ban on political parties, the communist groupings opposed the King's hostile acquisition of power and continually sought to overturn the status-quo.

In this situation, two radical communist leaders, Mohan Bikram Singh and Nirmal Lama decided to create a new party apparatus slightly different from the main communist party. Unlike other communist leaders who sought to maintain cordial ties with other parties and work collaboratively to restore the parliament, these two and their acolytes began designing a strategy to begin a people's movement through an armed revolt at an opportune moment. Most of the present day Maoist leadership emerged from this school of thought.

---

[2] "The Origins of the Nepali Maoist Insurgency", http://raonline.ch/pages/story/np_mao14.html (Accessed on May16, 2010).

[3] Ibid

In 1983, there was a rupture in the Communist party of Nepal when Mohan Bikram Singh disengaged himself from the main stream Communists and formed the Communist Party of Nepal (Masal). In 1984, CPN (Masal) became one of the founding members of the Revolutionary International Movement (RIM), a grouping of Maoist parties worldwide.[4] However, this party was short-lived due to another schism within the newly formed party. In only two years following the genesis of CPN (Masal), Masal split further into two groups. The present Maoist chieftain - Pushpa Kamal Dahal, who goes by the nom de guerre of Prachanda, was a part of CPN (Masal) leadership. Another prominent founder of the present Maoist movement – Baburam Bhattarai, remained with Mohan Bikram Singh's Masal faction.

In 1990, following a popular movement launched by a coalition of various political parties, democracy and multiparty parliamentary system was restored. Following this, Nepal witnessed the emergence of numerous political parties. Among them, there were four different communist groups with similar ideologies, and they opposed the foremost communist party of Nepal: United Marxist Leninist (UML). These four parties later coalesced under the chairmanship of Pushpa Kamal Dahal "Prachanda" to form a united front known as the "Unity-Center." This group participated in the general election of 1991 and managed to attain nine seats in the House of Representatives. However, before the mid-term elections in 1994, the Unity Centre witnessed a split. Nirmal Lama led one faction, and Pushpa Kamal Dahal led the other faction. The Nepali Election Commission only recognised the faction led by Nirmal Lama as the United Front. Irate with this decision, Dahal's faction boycotted the election.

That same year Dahal's faction espoused a different ideology and labeled their movement as "Maoism". Later that year, his faction became the member of Revolutionary International Movement (RIM). Disgruntled with the political scenario, they decided to launch the "People's War." From their point of view, their movement was a revolutionary movement that sought to institute a fundamental change by uprooting the existing government to end feudalism, rewriting Nepal's constitution, abolishing constitutional

---

[4] Ibid

monarchy and the establishing Nepal as a republic.

The Communist Party of Nepal (Maoists) formally launched their so-called "People's War" on February 13, 1996. Prior to launch, on 4 February 1996, Dr. Baburam Bhattarai – one of the main progenitors of the insurgency, submitted a list of forty demands (see Annex-A) to Prime Minister Sher Bahadur Deuba, and demanded it be fulfilled by 17 February. However, the Maoists launched their offensive by attacking isolated police posts in Rolpa, Rukum, Jajarkot, Gorkha and an eastern district of Sindhuli four days prior to the ultimatum date[5].

Nepal's Counter Insurgency Campaign

During the initial years of the insurgency, the government's response was marked by ambivalence and apathy. Instead of attempting to diagnose the insurgency and initiate befitting measures to mitigate the problem, the government chose to ignore the problem. The Prime Minister at the time – Mr. Sher Bahadur Deuba was totally engrossed in safeguarding his position in the government and showed very little interest in tackling the issue. Hence, no coherent counter insurgency strategy was contrived to neutralize the insurgents.

The governing political forces merely viewed the Maoist insurgents as a bunch of miscreants and malcontents and regarded the insurgency as a law and order problem. Therefore, the initial action against the insurgents was the mobilization of the Police force against them. But, even prior to the inception of the insurgency, however, the government had initiated preemptive actions against the Maoists. In November 1995, the government conducted a police operation known as "Operation Romeo" to crack down on Maoist activities. Later, other similar police operations such as "Kilo Sierra Two," "Jungle Search Operation," and "Search and Destroy", were conducted to quell the insurgency."[6]

---

[5] Deepak Thapa and Bandita Sijapati, *A Kingdom Under Siege: Nepals Maoists Insurgence, 1996 to 2004*, (Kathmandu: The Printhouse, 2006), 85.

[6] Chitra K. Tiwari, "Maoist Insurgency in Nepal: Internal Dimension", *South Asia Analysis Group* Paper No. 187, Januaury 20, 2001, http://www.saag.org/common/uploaded_files/paper187.html (Accessed on May16,2010).

Instead of dousing the flames of the insurgency, these police operations inflamed it. The police force was ill-equipped and had no prior experience or training in combating insurgency. The police operations involved targeting of suspected Maoists. For many, the police action was equivalent to State terror because the Police operated indiscriminately with impunity. There were numerous reports of human rights abuses including predation, torture, rape, unauthorized detention and murder. As a result, many innocent civilians became victims of Police atrocities. Although the government emphatically tried to justify these actions in the name of suppressing the insurgency, the brutal police actions only exacerbated the festering grievances and alienated certain segments of the society; leading to the victims of Police brutality and their kith and kin voluntarily joining the Maoists, simply to take revenge against the Police.

The increasing number of attacks on the Police and government infrastructures, extortion, and forceful recruitment by the insurgents led to a modulation of the government's strategy. The government recognized the Police's dwindling capability to quell the insurgency and also the constitutional constraints that barred the mobilization of a more capable and better equipped Royal Nepalese Army (RNA). As a solution, the beleaguered government erected a separate better equipped 15,000 strong paramilitary unit named Armed Police Force (APF) from scratch with the sole objective of tackling the insurgency.[7]

It was only after the insurgents mounted a daring attack on a RNA base at Ghorahi of Dang district in November 2001 that the RNA sprung into action. Operationally, throughout the period following its deployment, the RNA took the lead role in the counter insurgency campaign. This was mainly because it was largest security agency and also with the most advanced weaponry and firepower. Its conjugal relationship with the King also provided RNA with more leverage. The RNA, however, not only employed force against the insurgents but also employed intellect to engender other socio-economic counter insurgency strategies. For example the "ISDP" and even the "CMCNP" plans that are discussed later in this segment

---

[7] Bhagirath Yogi. "Will the Mediation Work?" *National Spotlight* 20, no. 42, (May 2001).

were tabled by the RNA.

Besides employing brute force, the counter insurgency campaign also comprised of negotiating with the insurgents through dialogue. After receiving an all-party mandate for peace talks, Prime Minister Sher Bahadur Deuba, had called upon the insurgents to cease violent activities, and invited their leadership for a dialogue. On Aug 30th, 2001, both sides met and held three separate rounds of talks. But, no settlement was reached. The talks proved inconclusive after the insurgents unilaterally walked out the peace talks on November 21st, 2001. During another Prime Minister – Lokendra Bahadur Chand's tenure in 2003 also, another of round of dialogue was initiated. Like before, the insurgents unilaterally pulled out from peace talks and resumed their violent attacks. It is believed that behind the scenes dialogue with the insurgents continued throughout the entire conflict.

The counter insurgency campaign employed various pressure tactics as well. Following the attack on the RNA base, the government imposed a state of emergency curtailing all fundamental rights. An anti terrorist ordinance that branded the Maoists insurgents as terrorists was promulgated.[8] The Maoist Party along with its fraternal organizations was banned. The government also issued Interpol red corner notices calling for the arrest of top insurgent leaders. Bounties were also announced for dead or captured senior insurgent leaders.

The Government had also made some strides by formulating policies to ameliorate the socio-economic conditions of the marginally deprived. The objectives of the initiatives were to redress the underlying grievances that were fuelling the insurgency, win popular support and dissuade people from joining the insurgents. As part of the initiative, the government came out with a legislation- the Kamaiya liberation act on July 2000. This act abolished the system of bonded labor and freed an estimated of 17,500 families from virtual slavery and allocated land and provided rehabilitation assistance.[9] The government also passed an act on women's rights and

---

[8] Thapa and Sijapati, *A Kingdom Under Siege,* 2006,123.

[9] Gopal Dahal, "Trapped in a System of Debts", *LWF Nepal.* September 2000.

established the national women's commission. Four anti-corruption bills were passed and a commission was formed to curb corruption in government agencies[10].

Another response was the initiation of the Integrated Security and Development Program (ISDP). This plan was conceived by the RNA prior to being engaged in combat. The objective was to launch developmental projects under the security umbrella of the RNA to win the hearts and minds of the public. However, due to the escalating demand for fighting forces, this program was later abandoned.

The government also garnered the support of the International community. For the most part, the immediate neighbors - India and China and other western countries supported the government's counter insurgency campaign. Nepal received various kinds of international support to combat the insurgency. India assisted the RNA with training, military equipment and intelligence. China also supported the government's effort and called upon the Maoists to give up arms and join the political circle. Nepal received twenty million dollars from the U.S. government for the anti-terror campaign. UK conferred Nepal with a comprehensive package of developmental and military assistance totaling thirty million Pounds.[11]

In early 2003, a more holistic counter insurgency strategy encompassing all the national elements of power was conceived. Until then, the government operated on an ad hoc basis and response to the insurgency was only reactive. This strategy came in the form of Civil-Military National Campaign Plan (CMNCP). The desired result of the CMNCP was the establishment of enduring peace and security under a multi party democracy and constitutional Monarchy. At the operational level, the CMNCP aimed at applying constant and intense pressure in order to compel the insurgents to seek for a peaceful alternative and abort all violent methods.

---

[10] "Countering Money Laundering in the Asian and the Pacific Region", Asian Development Bank http://www.adb.org/Governance/good_gov_anti.asp (Accessed on May16, 2010).

[11] "DFID Statement", http://www.dfid.gov.uk/News/PressReleases/files/pr21jun02.htm (Accessed on May16, 2010).

The strategic objectives of the campaign were:

a. To protect constitutional monarchy & multi party democracy.

b. To rehabilitate the insurgents into the national mainstream.

c. To establish lasting Peace and stability, and by doing so, create a sense of security among the Nepalese people.

d. To implement policies and measures for effective governance.

e. To utilize the political, economic, diplomatic, communication and military resources in an effective and coordinated manner.

The Military objectives of the campaign were:

a. To disarm the Maoists and render them ineffective.

b. To assist the government in establishing peace, security and well being of the people.

c. To create a favorable environment for the government to identify a solution for establishing a lasting peace through meaningful negotiations and dialogue.

d. To assist the government in launching and conducting developmental activities.

e. To Gain support for the Military campaign.

f. To assist the government in demobilizing and reintegrating those Maoists who are willing to assimilate into the national mainstream.

The CMNCP had four distinct phases:

• Offensive Operations.

• Disarmament, Demobilization and Rehabilitation of the Maoist combatants.

• Conduct of National Elections to the Parliament.

• Reconstruction.

To achieve operational efficiency through better co-ordination and control between various security agencies, the concept of "unified command" was formulated and implemented under command of RNA. Under the unified command concept, the strength of the RNA was bolstered by 10,000 Police and 17,000 APF. Even the National Investigation Department (NID) was pooled into the unified command. The government also formed the secretariat of National Security Council (NSC) – which consisted of RNA, Nepal Police, Armed Police Force (APF), and a Secretary from civil service nominated by the Ministry of Defense. NSC was also founded with the intent of bringing together all the security elements under one roof for better coordination to combat the insurgency.[12]

The concept of Unified Command was intended to:

a. Optimize and synchronize use of capabilities and resources.

b. Function in alignment with the Civilian Administrations' Chain of Command.

c. Delegate operational control to RNA in order to establish centralized command and decentralized execution.

d. Conduct joint planning effort under a single chain of command to ensure a sense of responsibility, lawful use of authority and absolute accountability while using coercive force.

e. Avoid duplication of effort.

f. Promote unity of effort in the acquisition of accurate intelligence, minimum but adequate use of force and establishment of a responsive civil administration.

Despite the enumerated policies and strategies envisaged and brandished by the successive governments, in practice, the only effective response was the use of brute force – i.e. a military response. Other responses were effete and most were never even implemented. Even prior to RNA's deployment, the government's response was still the use brute

---

[12] Yogi, "Will the Mediation Work?"May 2001.

force by deploying the Police and Armed Police Force. After the RNA was unleashed, the counter insurgency campaign automatically became its domain because of the wide held perception that it had become the RNA's battle and that it would quash the insurgents in no time. In truth, RNA had carte blanche to execute the counter insurgency campaign. The introduction of Unified Command only reinforced that realm. With the RNA at the helm, the operations naturally became more military in nature. Also, when the King dismissed the political parties and took command, he only had the RNA at his disposal. All other political, diplomatic, economic and social counter measures either ceased or became unavailing. And it was solely the military counter measures that gave continuity to the campaign.

Another crucial aspect of Nepal's counter insurgency campaign that needs to be highlighted is the fact that it was viewed as a battle between democratic forces and anti-democratic forces. The parliamentary parties along with the King represented the democratic forces. Hence, initially, the international community provided full-throttled support to the campaign. But, the equation changed drastically when the King sidelined the parties and took command. This significantly altered the dynamics of the campaign because the entire international community along with the national parties abandoned their support for the campaign. Instead, the Monarchy-RNA couplet became the anti-democratic force. As a result, all went and joined forces with the insurgents to oust the King. And ultimately, they were successful in toppling the King's regime.

Impacts and aftermath

The State, its institutions and the society were naturally affected by the counter insurgency proceedings. As a result of the counter insurgency campaign, there were both positive and negative impacts. Amongst the institutions, those affected most were the security institutions and the Monarchy.

A.   Monarchy

Citing the political parties' inability to conjure up a coherent and holistic counter insurgency strategy and establish a stable political order, the

Monarch gambled big by taking charge in 2005. He sidelined the political parties alleging that they were unable to conduct elections and curb Maoist activities and violence. Then, he spearheaded his own counter insurgency campaign. The Monarch asserted that he had a road map that demanded three years time to neutralize the insurgency, restore peace and stability and functionalize democracy.[13] This move, however, backfired. Both the internal and external forces colluded against the Monarch's initiative. Subsequently, the institution of Monarchy paid a very heavy price for this brazen endeavor.

Abolition of Monarchy was one of the prime demands of the insurgents. Initially, when the insurgency was launched, other political forces were opposed to the idea of abolition. However, as a part of his counter insurgency campaign, when the Monarch shunted the political parties and took direct executive power in 2005, it totally alienated and antagonized the political parties. These disenfranchised political forces later went on to join forces with the insurgents and signed the 12 point agreement brokered by India. Then, emboldened by the synergy and international support, this joint coalition launched a street revolt/uprising against the Royal regime and compelled the Monarch to capitulate.

Following this, a new coalition civilian government was formed and the idea of abolition gained more currency. Buoyed by the success of their uprising, the political parties made the Monarchy their punching bag as they conveniently heaped all the blame on the institution for the nation's woes. Through a carefully orchestrated campaign, the Monarchy was propagated as a taboo and the Monarchists were depicted as outcasts. The Monarch was essentially muzzled and gradually sidelined through the systematic clipping of his powers and prerogatives that had been accorded to him by the previous constitution. And after the constitution assembly was held, without any discussion or debate, the Monarchy was declared abolished by constituent assembly members during the first meet of the assembly.

---

[13] The Monarch had gone on national television to announce his take over. During which he had outlined these as primary objectives of his take over.

B. Nepal Army (NA)

For the NA, it was a mixed bag of results. Certainly, the organization bore a heavy brunt due to its direct engagement in counter insurgency campaign. But, it also gained significantly on other fronts.

As a direct result of the counter insurgency campaign, the ties between the Monarchy and the NA were severed. The NA and the monarchy had maintained a cordial and symbiotic relationship throughout history. However, the abolition of Monarchy signified a coerced divorce of a conjugal relationship that had persisted since the country's naissance.

Regardless of how the NA has propounded its official position, ranks and files in the army privately admit that the abolition of Monarchy was an irreparable loss to the institution. There could be several reasons why they think the loss is detrimental. Most likely, it is because it blaringly demonstrates NA's failure to protect the Monarchy. The King, as the supreme commander, was ensconced at the apex of the NA hierarchy. The primary tenet clearly outlined in the counter insurgency campaign was the protection of Constitutional Monarchy. The abolition of Monarchy has been interpreted by many as NA's inability to protect and safeguard it supreme commander. From what has transpired, it is clearly evident that it was only the supreme commander who was guillotined for a failed counter insurgency campaign. NA's hierarchy and organization have remained totally unscathed. [14]

As a result of the abolition of Monarchy, NA incurred other losses as well. With the Royal title erased, it lost the regality that was pegged to the institution. The pervious glamour and charm attached to the NA uniform also vanished. A lot of historical traditions and ceremonies ceased including the conferral of medals to the ranks. It lost the reassurance and the safety net that had shielded the organization from public glare and scrutiny. The Monarch had served as a guiding patron and also as a moat against external encroachment and political onslaught. But with the Monarchy gone, it has

---

[14] The Rayamajhi Commission was formed to investigate the involvement of those in suppressing the people's movement. Although, it named a few NA officials as being involved, no actions were taken against any NA official.

instilled a visceral sense of vulnerability amongst the top brass of the NA. When the Monarch was the supreme commander, the NA had to pledge their allegiance only to the crown. Now, however, with the emergence of numerous political power centers, there is fear that the diversified political patronage system could debilitate the NA.

Due to its leading role and high handed approach during the counter insurgency campaign, it dealt a severe blow to its institutional image. The previously glorified institutional image of NA has been eroded. Particularly, NA's relationship with other entities suffered. The political parties, civil society, media, and human rights entities were very antagonized with the NA for its role during the King's reign. For having to operate under the RNA as an integral part of the unified command, the Police and the APF hold a grudge against the NA.

Regardless, however, NA also gained a significant amount in other fronts. As a result of government's counter insurgency campaign, the size of the force almost doubled between 2001 and 2006. Prior to the counter insurgency campaign, the NA has remained a ceremonial force without any battle experience. By engaging in counter insurgency operations, it gained vital experience and expertise in asymmetric warfare. Consequently, the NA has emerged as a more battle hardened and professional organization. NA also acquired modern gear and weaponry for the counter insurgency operations. Another vital gain was the formation of elite Mahabir battalion (Rangers). The Rangers comprise of highly trained units optimized for counter insurgency, strike and other special operations.[15]

Another significant gain was the increase in number of women in their ranks. In 2003, a number of other services including Military Police, signalers, office staff, Army band, Military drivers, Military clerks, aircraft technicians, combat and combat support arms opened up for women.[16] Prior to the counter insurgency campaign, women only served as doctors, nurses, legal service providers and parachute folders.

---

[15] *"Ranger - The Warrior."* A hand book published by the Mahabir Battalion.

[16] Nepal Army, *The Nepalese Army a Force with History, Ready for Tomorrow* (Kathmandu: NA Directorate of Public Relations, 2008), 76.

In the current context, NA has emerged as significant power center in national politics. The void that has been left behind by the Monarchy is slowly being filled by the NA. Except for the Maoists and some of their smaller allies, other political forces regard the NA as their sword and shield against the Maoist dominance. The NA was able to out muscle the Maoist government in several tussles. It eventually caused the collapse of the Maoist led government. This has not only bolstered its leverage and standing but also given the impression that there are only two powerful national forces – the NA and the Maoists.

C.   Nepal Police

The Nepal Police on the other hand, was not as fortunate as the NA because it was the security agency that bore the heaviest brunt. Nepal Police suffered the most both in casualties and in other aspects. During the insurgency, they were the prime targets of the Maoists. Later, their indiscriminate operations alienated the general public too. The government did not show much interest in providing the organization with the needed support and resources. While they were at the receiving end, neither did the public show any sympathy nor did the RNA come to its rescue. It was even abandoned by the government they were fighting to safeguard.

After the APF was erected, the organization suffered even further. First, its standing in the security hierarchy was down-graded to third-tier. Second, it divested the funds that would have come to its organizational coffers. Third, many from the Police joined the APF for better perks and position. Ultimately, the APF took the money, manpower and certain mandates away from the Police.

Today, the scars from the counter insurgency experience run deep in the Police. The Police force emerged utterly demoralized and toothless. It has very little capacity to enforce the government's writ because its authority is being severely encroached upon by militias affiliated to political parties. Public confidence in the organization is low. And naturally, the morale has sapped which has greatly affected its professionalism.

D.   Armed Police Force (APF)

One of most significant outgrowths of the counter insurgency campaign was the creation of a new security outfit – i.e. Armed Police Force (APF). It was started from scratch by a senior Police officer – Krishna Mohan Shrestha and founded as a force in October 24 2001.[17] Initially, most of the officer ranks in this newly established institution were filled by those from the RNA and Police; the rest were newly recruited. The incentive of better perks, privileges and positions enticed the officials from the other security wings to join this newly established agency. Although this force was erected because the government could not mobilize the RNA due constitutional constraints, the RNA was mobilized only a month after APF's foundation. Hence, APF could not play the primary role in the counter insurgency campaign as envisaged. It remained under the RNA's lead role in the unified command structure.

Today, to the great consternation of the other two security agencies, APF has emerged as a shrewd security force. Its upper ranks operate in an aggressively competitive manner. Their political lobbying is relentless. They seem to have cultivated cordial ties with the bureaucracy and political leaders of all colors. Their institutional demands are met with little or no resistance. And they are very keen on proving that they are the best security agency in the country. The top brass in APF feel they can take on both the regular policing role as well as NA's role. This is illustrated by their persistent attempt to engage in anything that has security written on it. From the deposed Monarch to the deposed Maoist prime minister, the APF has taken over the responsibility of providing security to almost all VIPs, a number of installations and practically all foreign missions.

E.   State and Political System

In the aftermath of the counter insurgency campaign, the political landscape of Nepal has altered radically. First, the Hindu identity of the country has been discarded. Second, the Monarchy – that had reined Nepal throughout

---

[17] Armed Police Force official webpage. Available at - http://www.apf.gov.np/introduction/introduction.php (accessed on May 14, 2010).

history, has been abolished. Third, a new political setup has been declared. Nepal is now a Federal Democratic Republic. However, since the constitution still has not been promulgated, the future structures of the political system and the State along with the type of federalism that will be adopted is still unclear.

Regardless, the authority of the Nepali State has weakened tremendously. It can certainly be argued that Nepal has never been as weak as it is today. Both the internal domestic sovereignty and external sovereignty have severely eroded. Lawlessness is rife. Destructive and disruptive activities such as agitations, coercive shutdowns and strikes have become a norm. And the government has very little capacity to prevent such untoward activities and enforce its writ. Instead, each time, it is seen bowing to the demands of those organizing such activities. In terms of local governance, village development committees are mostly defunct and there are no mayors in municipalities. More alarmingly, Nepali territory has been blatantly and brazenly encroached upon. But the subsequent governments have proven woefully impotent in thwarting such transgressions.

Furthermore, it is apparent that foreigners are having a larger role in the internal matters of the State. The frequency with which the national leaders flock to neighboring countries to acquire consent and the torrent of foreign delegations pouring in on the pretext of friendly visits, demonstrate the increase in foreign preponderance and meddlesomeness. Not only that, foreign emissaries in Nepal have been behaving like viceroys and foisting diktats upon the government and other political forces. To cite a recent example of such high handed behavior – the French Ambassador, on behalf of the European Union recently urged the government to allow full freedom to proselytize while drafting the new constitution.[18]

F.   Society

The societal fabric too has seen some drastic changes. In the aftermath of the counter insurgency campaign, the positive results have been dwarfed

---

[18] Anil Giri, "EU urges Govt to Allow Freedom to Proselytize", *eKantipur,* April 28, 2010 http://www.ekantipur.com/2010/04/28/top-story/eu-urges-govt-to-allow-freedom-to-proselytise/313242/ (Accessed on May 15, 2010).

by an array of unnerving trends. Amongst many, three ominous trends reflect where the society is headed. First, political polarization is becoming more palpable. Second a culture of violence is taking root. And third, the society seems to be splintering along various lines.

After the counter insurgency campaign ended, the peace process in Nepal got underway. The peace process was expected to harmonize and normalize the relationship between the protagonists. However, that has not happened. The consensus between the signatories of the Peace accord has not only frayed but the protagonists have been acutely polarized.

The fallout between the Maoists and the other political parties is obvious as they gravitate towards the opposite ends of the spectrum. On one side there are the Maoists and a few other parties. The rest of the political parties have ganged up on the other side against the Maoists. The same political forces that zealously colluded to topple the Monarch are now at each other's necks. Both sides continue to hurl incendiary rhetoric against each other and the gulf of distrust is only widening. While the Maoists want to get back into power, the other parties are in no mood to share power with the former insurgents. Both sides have obstinately clung to their positions and neither side is budging. This was clearly evident during the indefinite strike coercively imposed by the Maoists demanding the resignation of the current prime minister and the formation of a new government with the Maoists at the helm. Both sides were recalcitrant and the country suffered as a result. But more importantly, there is no inkling of cooperation over the issue of promulgating the constitution.

Although the counter insurgency campaign is over, the NA and the former insurgents also still appear to be engaged in a battle. It can literally be termed as a cold war because both sides still view each other with utmost distrust and disdain and regard each other as their mortal enemy.[19] And they have been doing their best to outmaneuver each other. The bitter tussles that ensued between the Maoists while in the government and the

---

[19] Hisila Yami, a senior Maoist leader, recently declared that Nepal Army was the biggest enemy of the Maoists.

NA over recruitment, retirement and removal episodes manifested the divergence between these former warring adversaries. And, there is no indication that the two sides will relinquish their distaste for each other any time soon.

As political forces continue to lock horns and squabble, a culture of violence is spreading like wildfire. Previously, the Maoist insurgents were the only significant armed group. Today, however, the number of armed groups has surged exponentially. According to a recent government report, there are now more than a hundred known armed groups operating in Nepal.[20] The surge of violent groups can be directly attributed to acceptance and the ascendancy of the Maoists employing the instrument of violence. These groups mainly derive their inspiration from the Maoist insurgents. Since the counter insurgency campaign was unable to completely quash the insurgency with brute force, these new groups regard the Maoists as victors. Hence, the new groups have taken a lesson from their rise and follow suit hoping to replicate their success story. The fact that the Maoists have not completely eschewed violence even after coming to power has only worsened the trend. Also, to a great extent, the proliferation of small arms in the last three years has only exacerbated the situation.

On top of that, instead of dissuading the formation of armed and violent groups, the parliamentary parties themselves are encouraging such activities by erecting militant youth wings. After the creation of YCL by the Maoists, other parliamentary parties are toeing the same line. Nepali Congress, UML, MJF and many other parties have already created such outfits. This is not only undermining the authority of the State but also instigating more violence as the deadly clashes between these outfits are becoming routine.

Today, the most unnerving trend underway in Nepal is the splintering of society along various lines. Following the end of the counter insurgency campaign, the ideas of federalism, ethnic nationalism and autonomy gushed into the political discourse. But these issues are taking a divisive trajectory.

---

[19] "109 Armed Groups Operating in the Country", *Nepalnews.com*, July 31, 2009, Available at – http://www.nepalnews.com/main/index.php/news-archive/2-political/700-109-armed-groups-operating-in-the-country.html (Accessed on 15th May 2010).

They are accelerating the fragmentation of society even further and breeding more intractable conflicts as people congregate along ethnic lines and make those identities more distinct. And in the name of uplifting one's ethnic identity and status, the clamor for ethnic emancipation is becoming shriller and belligerent. More worrisome is the fact that these ethnic congregations are becoming more organized and forming their own militias. And some are even threatening to take up arms if their grievances and demands are not appropriately addressed.

In truth, due to the absence of a centripetal force or a commonality to serve as linchpin, the Nepali society is disintegrating. Previously, for better or worse, the Monarchy had served as a symbol of national unity and harmony. After the Monarchy was abolished, however, no replacement for the linchpin was present or later presented. In absence of such a uniting factor, a sense of national identity is eroding rapidly and national unity is being shredded by ethnic, racial and religious assertiveness.

G.   Civil Military Relations

The uniqueness and complexity of Nepal's Civil Military Relations (CMR) is due to its Monarchical past and its conjugal ties with the military - i.e. the RNA. This practice of the King remaining at the apex as the Supreme commander continued throughout history until the Monarchy was sidelined and abolished. Due to this dynamic, Nepal's military was always viewed and branded as the King's private Army. The establishment of multiparty democracy and the promulgation of the new constitution in 1990 opened had ushered a new era in Nepalese CMR. The Monarch's full control over the army was somewhat tempered under the new constitutional framework. Despite these constitutional provisions, however, the RNA still remained insular, detached from the civilian sector and still regarded the King as its patron. During the counter insurgency campaign too this dynamic persisted. After the King took executive control with the help of the RNA, the civilian sector became even more distanced.

Today, following the abolition of Monarchy, CMR in Nepal is at its infancy and still an evolving process. The NA is emerging from years of isolation and detachment from the civilian sector. Therefore, there is still an enormous gulf of mistrust between the NA and the civilian sector but an army coup-d'état is highly improbable because Nepal has no history of army coup- d'états. Although the constitutional provisions clearly outline the civilian control of the NA, the civilian sector still has not demonstrated the ability to exercise effective control. There is quite of bit of hesitation as well and "leave the army alone" mentality still persists on the civilian side. Partly, the NA's wary and insular nature is to blame for this. Although the NA has time and again reiterated its full commitment to accept civilian control, it will take time for this commitment to translate into reality. But most importantly, both sides recognize that for enduring and effective civilian control of the NA, there is an exigent need to bridge the gulf of mistrust and misunderstanding, and that both sides need to be more sensitized on the concept and practices of CMR

Conclusion

The outcome of the counter-insurgency campaign was complex. From NA's viewpoint, the campaign was successful in denying the insurgent group the opportunity to overwhelm the State through brute force. There is certainly merit in the argument that the military component of the campaign compelled the insurgents to seek alternative political measures to come to power. Conversely, the State miserably failed to thwart the insurgents from overwhelming the State through alternative means. The way the insurgents ascended to power illustrates failure of the campaign. The campaign seems to have been conducted solely by relying on the military component. But from an overall perspective, the primary reason the insurgents were successful is because of lack of cohesiveness of the other internal political forces (mainly the King and the parliamentary parties) and the intervention by the external forces. In summation, regardless of these varying interpretations, Nepal has been adversely impacted by proceedings of the counter-insurgency campaign.

40-POINT DEMAND

(Submitted by Baburam Bhattarai of CPN (Maoist) to then Prime Minister Sher Bahadur Deuba (Nepali Congress) on February 2, 1996)

Demands Related to Nationalism

1. Regarding the 1950 Treaty between India and Nepal, all unequal stipulations and agreements should be removed.

2. HMG [His Majesty's Government] should admit that the anti-nationalist Tanakpur agreement was wrong, and the Mahakali Treaty, incorporating same, should be nullified.

3. The entire Nepal-Indian border should be controlled and systematized. Cars with Indian number plates, which are plying the roads of Nepal, should not be allowed.

4. Gorkha recruiting centers should be closed and decent jobs should be arranged for the recruits.

5. In several areas of Nepal, where foreign technicians are given precedence over Nepali technicians for certain local jobs, a system of work permits should be instituted for the foreigners.

6. The monopoly of foreign capital in Nepal's industry, trade and economic sector should be stopped.

7. Sufficient income should be generated from customs duties for the country's economic development.

8. The cultural pollution of imperialists and expansionists should be

stopped. Hindi video, cinema, and all kinds of such newspapers and magazines should be completely stopped. Inside Nepal, import and distribution of vulgar Hindi films, video cassettes and magazines should be stopped.

9. Regarding NGOs and INGOs: Bribing by imperialists and expansionists in the name of NGOs and INGOs should be stopped.

Demands Related to the Public and Its Well-Being

10. A new Constitution has to be drafted by the people's elected representatives.

11. All the special rights and privileges of the King and his family should be ended.

12. Army, police and administration should be under the people's control.

13. The Security Act and all other repressive acts should be abolished.

14. All the false charges against the people of Rukum, Rolpa, Jajarkot, Gorkha, Kavre, Sindhupalchok, Sindhuli, Dhanusha and Ramechhap should be withdrawn and all the people falsely charged should be released.

15. Armed police operations in the different districts should immediately be stopped.

16. Regarding Dilip Chaudhary, Bhuvan Thapa Magar, Prabhakar Subedi and other people who disappeared from police custody at different times, the government should constitute a special investigating committee to look into these crimes and the culprits should be punished and appropriate compensation given to their families.

17. People who died during the time of the movement should be declared as martyrs and their families and those who have been wounded and disabled should be given proper compensation. Strong action should be taken against the killers.

18. Nepal should be declared a secular state.

19. Girls should be given equal property rights to those of their brothers.

20. All kinds of exploitation and prejudice based on caste should be ended. In areas having a majority of one ethnic group, that group should have autonomy over that area.

21. The status of "dalits" as untouchables should be ended and the system of untouchability should be ended once and for all.

22. All languages should be given equal status. Up until middle-high school level (uccha-madyamic) arrangements should be made for education to be given in the children's mother tongue.

23. There should be guarantee of free speech and free press. The communications media should be completely autonomous.

24. Intellectuals, historians, artists and academicians engaged in other cultural activities should be guaranteed intellectual freedom.

25. In both the Terai and hilly regions there is prejudice and misunderstanding in backward areas. This should be ended and the backward areas should be assisted. Good relations should be established between the villages and the city.

26. Decentralization in real terms should be applied to local areas, which should have local rights, autonomy and control over their own resources.

Demands Related to the People's Lives

27. Those who cultivate the land should own it. (The tiller should have right to the soil he/she tills.) The land of rich landlords should be confiscated and distributed to the homeless and others who have no land.

28. Brokers and commission agents should have their property confiscated and that money should be invested in industry.

29. All should be guaranteed work and should be given a stipend until

jobs are found for them.

30. HMG [His Majesty's Government] should pass strong laws ensuring that people involved in industry and agriculture should receive minimum wages.

31. The homeless should be given suitable accommodation. Until HMG [His Majesty's Government] can provide such accommodation they should not be removed from where they are squatting.

32. Poor farmers should be completely freed from debt. Loans from the Agricultural Development Bank by poor farmers should be completely written off. Small industries should be given loans.

33. Fertilizer and seeds should be easily and cheaply available, and the farmers should be given a proper market price for their production.

34. Flood and drought victims should be given all necessary help

35. All should be given free and scientific medical service and education and education for profit should be completely stopped.

36. Inflation should be controlled and laborers salaries should be raised in direct ratio with the rise in prices. Daily essential goods should be made cheap and easily available.

37. Arrangements should be made for drinking water, good roads, and electricity in the villages.

38. Cottage and other small industries should be granted special facilities and protection.

39. Corruption, black marketing, smuggling, bribing, the taking of commissions, etc. should all be stopped.

40. Orphans, the disabled, the elderly and children should be given help and protection.

INTERNAL CONFLICT IN NEPAL AFTER THE COMPREHENSIVE PEACE AGREEMENT

Indra Adhikari and Uddhab Pyakurel

Conflict has always been a part of human life and is as ancient as human history itself. It can be seen as an essential aspect of the social and political life of human beings, as it occurs within human relationships. In fact, conflict is ingrained in many aspects of society, from marriage to interstate war. Since society, as a concept, is dynamic and has been transforming from a simple to a much more complex direction, the nature of conflict also has been following the similar pattern of being more complex and complicated day-by-day. Everybody is aware of the fast moving global situation today in which the whole world system is in structural crisis and confronted by an age of transition.[1] In this situation, traditional states, which were formed on the basis of legitimate political forces, have been struggling to maintain their status quo. Contrary to this, the various deprived sections of the society, are struggling not only for their access to power and control over resources, but also their right to live with dignity and respect. Indeed, such traditional states mark a democratic deficit[2]. That is why, conflict is defined as "a struggle over values and claims to scarce status, power and resources in which the aims of the opponents are to neutralize, injure or eliminate their rivals"[3].

---

[1] Immanuel Wallerstein. "New Revolts against the Systems," *New Left Review*, 18 (November-December 2002): 37

[2] David E. Apter. "Democracy, Violence and Emancipatory Movements: Notes for a Theory of Inversionary Discourse", *Political Violence and Social Movements,* Discussion Paper, No. 44 (May 1999): 38, http://www.unrisd.org/unrisd/website/document.nsf/(httpPublications)/EB6E36BD54C41 FF980256B65004872E7? OpenDocument (Accessed on August 30, 2010)

[3] Lewis A. Coser, *The Functions of Social Conflict: An Examination of the Concept of Social Conflict and Its Use in Empirical Sociological Research,* (New York: The Free Press, 1964), 7.

Conflict, as a part of human life, always brings about a change—either positive or negative-in society. It is always neither undesirable nor destructive; rather it brings both the constructive and destructive results. Nepal's Maoist insurgency, which was almost a decade long conflict in the country, can be taken as an example that has brought positive and negative changes in the Nepali society. While the positives include an awareness of their rights as citizens of a state, the negatives involve it has expanding the culture of intimidation and popularizing the violent means of struggle in the country. It has also more effectively promoted the anti-systemic ways rather than the systemic one using peaceful means, while opposing the existing socio-political, economic and legal system of the state or demanding for change.

Several studies show that the main contributors boosting the growth of conflicts are structural, political, socio-economic, and cultural-perpetual factors[4]. Within the structural factor, there are three major components; weak states, inter-state security concerns and ethnic geography. According to Brown, a weak state is one which lacks political legitimacy, politically sensible borders, and strong political institutions capable of exercising control over its territory, faces a vicious circle of crises to not only tackle but also resolve the conflict. The trend of weakening of the state structure often leads to the eruption of violent political conflicts. A weak state lacks the capacity to collect adequate tax revenue that helped undertake a self-sufficient state building project with required and justified distribution. Thus, social groups develop pre-national political solidarity and tend to be more able to assert themselves politically by claiming more power and autonomy to a higher extent like rights to self-determination. In addition, some powerful business and political groups develop an interest in the economy of violence through arms deals, perpetuation of illegitimate power circles or other strategies that fend off efforts towards reconciliation and peace process. A weak state may hardly deal with them. It can neither ensure the security of individuals nor groups. But all these groups affected and benefited from the conflict must then seek their own security[5]. The situation helps in further

---

[4] Michael E. Brown, *The International Dimensions of Internal Conflict.*,(Cambridge: The MIT Press, 1996)

[5] Ibid.

weakening the already weak state in the public eyes that leads to hopelessness, insecurity and terror in the society. Encounters between political groups, while trying to be defensive, is characteristic of conflict. The problem is that the political group within the system always counters the rival group by using the security agencies. Such a situation obviously creates a threat to the security of others[6], resulting in widespread violence in the society, unless and until the elites in government do not try to manage it responsibly and amicably in time.

CPA

The Comprehensive Peace Accord (CPA) is the agreement signed on January 6, 2007 by the Interim Government formed by the Seven Party Alliance (SPA) and the then CPN (Maoist) which has now been renamed and become the United Communist Party of Nepal-Maoist (UCPN-Maoist). It not only declared the "End of conflict"[7] for "giving permanency to the ongoing ceasefire between both the parties—Government of Nepal and the UCPN-Maoist"[8]— but directed senior leaders of the parties to be sincere in "the main policy for long-term peace"[9] as decided in the earlier meetings. It is an output of several other important efforts made by the SPA and the UCPN-Maoist in different periods of time and contexts, since its preamble acknowledges many of the previous agreements: 12-Point understanding signed on 22 November 2005; 25-Point Code of Conduct agreed on 25 May 2006; 8-Point agreement signed on 16 June 2006; others formal-informal consensuses reached between the SPA led Interim Government of Nepal and the UCPN-Maoist; and the letter sent to the United Nations by both the sides with the similar viewpoints after the successful Mass Movement in 2006[10]. The CPA along with the ongoing peace process of

---

[6] Andreas Wimmer and Conrad Schetter. "Putting state-formation first: some recommendations for reconstruction and peace-making in Afghanistan",*Journal of International Development*, 15, no. 5 (2003): 525-539.

[7] Comprehensive Peace Accord, Article 6, 22 November 2006 quoted in Uddhab P. Pyakurel, *Maoists Movement in Nepal: A Sociological Perspective*, (New Delhi: Adroit Publishers, 2007) 184.

[8] Ibid., Article 6.1

[9] Ibid. Article 6.2

[10] Ibid, Preamble of CPA, 175.

Nepal is an indigenous accord and is, as mentioned before, an output of the several confidence building measures that became the gate pass the UCPN-Maoist needed to enter into mainstream politics. The process of mainstreaming the UCPN-Maoist was initiated and formalized by allowing its members in the reinstated Parliament in 2006 and Interim Government in 2007. The treatment of the state and society to the UCPN-Maoist as to other parliamentarian political parties helped them assimilate with and adopt the culture of multiparty democracy. It created a well-matured ground for making the interim constitution as per the spirit of the historical *Jana Andolan* 2006.

"Declaring the beginning of the new chapter of peaceful collaboration between the parties" the CPA initiates for "forward-looking political resolution", and commands both the parties to go through the spirit of earlier consensuses by internalizing and respecting the respective issues of either side. It orders the UCPN-Maoist to reiterate their commitment "towards democratic value accepting competitive multiparty democratic system of governance, civil liberty, fundamental rights, human rights, full press freedom and concept of rule of law"[11]. It also obliges the SPA "to ensure the sovereignty of people through the election of a Constituent Assembly (CA), restructuring the state and socio-economic and cultural transformations"[12]. That is why the CPA is a document that initiates the radicalizing of the mainstream political parties, and mainstreaming the UCPN-Maoist by bringing it in the competitive party politics through a peaceful manner. In fact, the spirit of 12-point understanding between the UCPN-Maoist and the SPA followed by other agreements was for establishing "absolute democracy"[13] in the country. Full-fledged democracy was possible only

---

[11] Ibid, and Point 4 of the 12-Point Understanding between the SPA and the Maoists, 22 November 2005.

[12] Preamble of CPA in Uddhab P. Pyakurel, *Maoists Movement in Nepal: A Sociological Perspective*,184; Point 3 of 12 Points Understanding between the SPA and the Maoists, 22 November 2005

[13] However, the phrase was defined on the basis of their (the SPA and the Maoist) respective understandings and policies. On the one hand, it was defined by SPA as the end of the autocratic nature of monarchy bringing it under the constitution along with the establishment of other universal principles of democracy, and on the other, the Maoist defined it as removal of the institution of monarchy and establishment of republic country, Nepal.

after "ending autocratic monarchy"[14] and also assuring equality and justice to the people. Thus, the concept of the federal structure of the state was assured by amending the Interim Constitution and the notion of inclusive and participatory democracy was accepted as a major requirement for leading socio-political transformation to a greater extent.

Hence, the peaceful abolition of the 240-year old institution of monarchy and establishment of the Democratic Federal Republic has been seen as the biggest achievement of the Jana Andolan-II. Also, the representation of marginalized communities such as Dalits, Adivasis, Madhesis, women and other minorities in the elected Constituent Assembly (CA) has given a remarkable positive message to the world. The strength distributed in the CA is more than 33% by women, 38% by Janajatis, 33% by Madhesis, and 8% by Dalits, etc. The three major marginalized groups, irrespective of their party position, have deserved the required critical masses in the CA now. Without their consent, no major decision, while writing the constitution, is possible[15].

Task Initiated by CPA

The CPA talks about the process of democratization of Nepal Army (NA) defining it so as to bring the NA under the civilian control and begin the process of professionalization of the Maoist combatants. The restructure of the state is another issue that makes the system more inclusive (by allowing more opportunities to the people from the marginalized groups based on caste, ethnicity, gender, region, religion, etc.). The main focus of the CPA is to transform the UCPN-Maoist from an insurgent group into a 'civilian political party'. Thus, it orders the UCPN-Maoist to follow a couple of the measures i.e., to return the property confiscated during the insurgency to the owner; to allow other political parties for political campaign in the country in general, and in the UCPN-Maoist controlled villages in particular. Similarly, the High Level Special Committee for Army Integration, Truth and Reconciliation Commission, Commission for the Investigation of

---

[14] Point 1 of 12-Point Understanding between the SPA and the Maoists, 22 November 2005.

[15] The constitution says that every decision should be taken either by consensus or by two-third majority of the Assembly.

Disappeared People, State Restructuring Commission, etc., for making federal structure were other important tasks opened up by the CPA. Furthermore, the election of CA for the making of a new constitution was the major task as at that particular time, the state was moving from a divided past to a shared future and required the capability and feasibility not only to create a just order, but to perform its basic state functions also. This can be seen in the provisioning of the State Reconciliation Commission in the Interim Constitution of Nepal 2007, though it is yet to be materialized by the governments.

The Agreement on Monitoring of Management of Arms and Armies reached between the Government of Nepal and the UCPN-Maoist on 28 November 2006 was one of the major provisions under the CPA, since the management of Maoist combatants and their arms is a most important and difficult issue. To facilitate the work of the arms and army management, the United Nations Mission in Nepal (UNMIN) was established on January 23, 2007 on the request of the Interim Government and the UCPN Maoist in accordance with the guidance of the CPA. The UNMIN started working in Nepal as per the United Nations Security Council Resolution 1740[16] having a limited role, i.e., "monitoring and supervising the peace process".[17] The role basically being to monitor whether the respective parties confine their activities in accordance with the agreements reached between the parties. In fact, the UNMIN has no right of taking a decisive role for the peace process but it can facilitate the respective parties to follow and implement the agreements in letter and spirit. The management process of the combatants of the UCPN-Maoist began on 8 January after a Joint Monitoring Coordination Committee (JMCC) was formed[18] and the UNMIN

---

[16] For more on the UNMIN, see www.unmin.org.np

[17] Letter to the UN by the Government of Nepal, Agreement of the UN with Government of Nepal and the Maoists.

[18] Accordingly, the UNMIN recruited a total of 126 monitors including 15 UN monitors, 111 Gurkha ex-servicemen who had served in the Indian and British Armies for the management and verification of the Maoist cantonments and weapons. The monitors were kept under the Joint Monitoring and Coordinating Committee (JMCC) of the Agreement on Management and the Monitoring of Arms and Armies that was constituted by three members representing UNMIN, ex-PLA and NA.

announced the first result of the verification of Maoist combatants on 27 December 2007[19].

The structure, role and responsibilities of the Army Integration Special Committee, which has been formed "in order to inspect, integrate and rehabilitate the Maoist combatants",[20] are neither effective nor authorized to independently work as required. It was formed for technical purposes and has no power to do anything unless there is a political consensus among the major political parties in the CA. The issue of management of Maoist combatants was politicized to that extent that stopped the whole peace and the constitution writing process. The advocacy and counter-advocacy on the issue of the Maoist combatant's management has made the process more complicated. The UCPN-Maoist's demand to make a "national army" by integrating all its combatants in NA, and the position of some politicians along with few in-service and ex-service Nepal Army personnel being the exact opposite have not only helped get the peace process derailed but also helped in politicizing the Nepal Army. It has been reported that both the Nepal army and the Maoist combatants could not resolve their past antagonism after the CPA was signed. But doubt and distrust between the old rebellion groups continued against each other even after the UCPN-Maoist became part and parcel of the government. Ram Bahadur Thapa, the then Defense Minister after the CA election mentioned, referring the Maoist party's intelligence report, that the topmost officers of the NA have been mobilized by foreign power[21]. Prime Minister Pushpa Kamal Dahal took an oath for the post in the security arrangement of the Maoist combatants, as it was not recognized as a state security force. The expression of the Minister of Defense and attitudes of PM on NA proved that the Maoist party and its government could rely on neither the information

---

[19] The type of weapons registered so far are 91 mortars (of which 55 were locally made), 61 machine guns, 2,403 rifles, 61 automatic weapons, 9 sub-automatic guns, 114 side arms, 212 shot guns, 253 miscellaneous and 244 home-made weapons.

[20] Article 4.4, *Comprehensive Peace Accord* between the Government of Nepal and CPN (Maoists), 22 November 2006.

[21] Indra Adhikari, *Chisido Sena-Sarkar Sambandha*(Cooling Civil-MilitaryRelations), *Kantipur,* February 1, 2009.

nor security guarding of the NA. The attitude of Maoist leaders in government to promote their own combatants and party intelligence in guarding and spying not only undermine psychologically the institutional role and responsibility of NA, but also humiliate its personnel at individual level. Also, the UNMIN failed to give a right track to the peace process; it was neither able to stop new recruitment of the NA personnel nor could it detach the Maoist combatants from its party rank and file. The mistrust and controversy began while 7,000-8,000 original Maoist combatants[22] reached 30,852 during the entry into the cantonments, and the numbers of Maoist combatants and their register of weapons did not match[23]. The JMCC of the UNMIN also declared ineligible some thousands of them as "new recruits" that reduced the strength of the Maoist combatants in cantonments up to 19,603—15,757 men and 3,846 women. The situation further weakened the peace process while a debate was initiated about how to manage the Maoist combatants, how many are genuine combatants and "eligible for possible integration in the security agencies fulfilling standard norm,"[24] and how the rest should be rehabilitated in the society.

The UCPN-Maoist had not been ready to manage its combatants even after the latter were kept in the cantonments. If one follows the Kharipati decision of the UCPN-Maoist which came just after the party led the government, there were mainly two strategies of the UCPN-Maoist regarding the management of its combatants; the first one was to try to integrate all verified combatants into the NA, along with the senior combatants into the higher rank of NA so that the NA as an institution would be either influenced or weakened through infiltration and division; the second being that if the UCPN-Maoist could not successfully integrate

---

[22] A highly controversial tape record of Prachanda's indoctrination programme in the Shaktikhor Cantonment, Chitwan.

[23] 31, 152 PLA members registered at the seven main cantonment sites and 21 satellite cantonment sites. The total number of weapons registered by the UNMIN was 3,475 including 522 weapons for perimeter security and 96 weapons registered outside of cantonments., Sanjaya Dhakal, "Arms Discrepancy", *Nepalnews.com*, March 16, 2007, http://www.nepalnews.com/contents/2007/englishweekly/spotlight/mar/mar16/national1.php

[24] Agreement on Management and the Monitoring of Arms and Armies reached between the Government of Nepal and the UCPN (Maoist), 28 November 2006.

them all into the NA, to keep them in the cantonment for a longer period. By prolonging the life of the temporary cantonment with its combatants, the UCPN-Maoist wanted to benefit financially and politically, as it had been receiving a huge amount of money from the cantonments,[25] and it had been used as a camp for training the people and hiding criminals[26]. The Central Committee of the UCPN-Maoist decided on July 2, 2010 that even if total integration into NA is not possible, its combatants would be under an institution or in a group. It seems that the ultimate motto of the UCPN-Maoist is to keep its combatants under its command forever, if not at least till the next election, so that the psychological strength of its leadership and bargaining capacity of the party remain high.

Prohibited Actions According to the CPA

The agreement prohibits mainly: (1) to hold, carry and display arms, use of violence and armies for creating terror and fear; (2) to intimidate and use any type of violence against people—kidnap, murder, and torture to hurt or render mental pressure against any individual; (3) to recruit additional armed personnel or conduct military activities; (4) to collect cash or goods and services or levy against one's wishes and against the existing law; (5) to restrict free movement of people and goods; (6) to spy on military activities of either sides; (7) to publicize for or against any side and support or protest against any side, (8) damaging and seizing public/private/governmental and non-governmental property, etc. As the CPA was a detailed and comprehensive agreement, it was categorical even in each and every small issue such as leave of the Maoist combatants put inside the cantonment. It has a provision that no more than 12 per cent of the total retained force of the Maoist combatants can be on leave under the deferent cause-medical referrals, visiting families—of a given cantonment.

But in practice, nothing was implemented in a serious manner. In fact, only five out of the nine restricted activities under the CPA, and only

---

[25] Uddhab Pyakurel (2008) "Sociology of the Maoists' Cantonment," *Kantipur*, 23, January 2008.

[26] Sambidhan Sabha Sambadh, Interview of Subodh Pyakurel broadcast on Kantipur TV on June 26, 2010 at 9.00pm.

seven out of 19 clauses under the Agreement on Monitoring of Management of Arms and Armies reached between the Government and the UCPN-Maoist on 28 November 2006 were implemented by the latter; it was the UCPN-Maoist which started recruiting youths to increase the number of the Maoist combatants in cantonments just after it signed the CPA. The UCPN-Maoist called the youth openly by establishing a "recruiting center", cantoned the 'new recruits'. Such recruitment camps were launched by hanging banners at many of the district headquarters, with the assurance of a good salary (a promise of Rs. 7,000 salary per month) and job guarantee in the Nepal Army.[27] This led to young students not only running away from the houses and schools catching the golden opportunity to join the Maoist combatants, but also led to many of the youths from villages being abducted by the UCPN-Maoist for this purpose.[28] Children-including some as young as 12 years-were taken away from their families to take part in the Maoist combatants and militia activities with some of them have received military training with weapons since the ceasefire was declared. Even if internationally recognized organizations such as the Office of the High Commissioner for Human Rights (OHCHR) and UNMIN[29] raised questions by reporting, neither the then government nor the UCPN-Maoist initiated any measure to stop the process. Rather, the UCPN-Maoists' supremo Prachanda, with pride boasted how he and his party fooled domestic counterparts as well as international community saying that his party successfully increased the number of its combatants from 7-8,000 to 32,250

---

[27] INSEC Online report, "Maoists Running Recruitment Camps," www.inseconline.org [Accessed on September 3, 2006]

[28] It has been proved that the seven children of Bhaludhunga Secondary School of Bishnu Paduka School were, in fact, abducted on September 6, 2006 and they were given military training in Motipur VDC of Morang after conscripting them in Ratna Sakunta Brigade Second Battalion. For details, see "Maoists Recruiting Children against Code of Conduct", www.inseconline.org, September 19, 2006. It is reported that some recruitments are voluntary where those who were not physically fit to get jobs in Nepal army and police force, join the PLA with the hope of the merger of the PLA and Nepal Army soon.

[29] United Mission in Nepal Press Conference on April 8, 2008, Kathmandu , http://www.unmin.org.np/?d=media&p=press (Accessed on July 6, 2010); see also UNMIN Election Report No. 3, April 6, 2008 available at http://www.unmin.org.np/downloads/publications/2008-04-06-UNMIN.Election.Report.3.ENG.pdf (Accessed on July 6, 2010)

through new recruitment.[30] Also, the UCPN-Maoist continued its activities of extortion, intimidation, abductions, ill-treatment, violation of rights of internally displaced people[31] and even killings after the CPA, though the numbers of such activities are considerably low. They continued their so-called parallel governments till the completion of CA election, and try to stop political activities of other political parties till today. According to the OHCHR report[32], the rebels were responsible for the death of at least 16 civilian, mostly innocent villagers and for abduction of at least 184 individuals since the ceasefire declaration of April 26. Though UCPN-Maoist leadership also issued a directive to end human rights abuses in September 2, 2006, no evidence has been found which assures the earlier commitment by the UCPN-Maoist leadership. Here, the question of accountability can be raised before the UCPN-Maoist leadership.

---

[30] As mentioned in his video taped speech which was his one and a half hour long address to the Maoist combatants at Shaktikhor Cantonment. In the address he urged his cadres to remain calm till they capture power and establish "People's Republic" as envisaged by Mao and Lenin. Some excerpts of the video is available athttp:// www.google.comh?q=Prachanda+Shaktikhor+ Video&hl=en&client= gmail &sa=X&rls=gm&prmd=v&source=univ&tbs=vid:1&tbo=u&ei=0f8xT PGrG4SY r AfEvrDHBA &oi=video_result_group&ct=title&resnum=1&ved=0CB0 QqwQwAA, (Accessed on July 5, 2010)

[31] Of these, most of the deaths in the Maoists custody were because of "extreme beatings and torture" by them after abduction (See Prem Nepali Pokhar, "Maoists Abduct, Kill Teenager", *The Kathmandu Post*, September 16, 2006. The Maoists issued a statement claiming that the boy died after 'accidentally' falling off a cliff). Cases of abduction, intimidation, beating of people and extortion are increasing by the day- Ameet Dhakal, "Life beyond Communism", *The Kathmandu Post*, September 1, 2006. It was reported that many industries were closed due to Maoist intimidation and "the majority of Nepali entrepreneurs were on the verge of being displaced due to the Maoists' extortions". See "FNCCI Warns of Protests if Maoist Extortion Continues," www.ekantipur.com September 17, 2006. Hotels in Nepal faced the threat of closure due to extortion drives and "illogical demands" by the Maoists. See "Nepal: Maoist Threats Forcing Closure of Hotels," *The Indian Express*, September 5, 2006. Maoists abducted youth as young as 13 years and have not spared even students studying in grade seven. For details see,"Maoists Continue Abductions, Intimidation, Extortions", *The Kathmandu post*, August 2, 2006. They detained a 15-year-old young man to 60-year-old man in their "labor detention camp" (see http:// www.kantipuronline.com/kolnews.php?&nid=83978). Accessed on April 3, 2008.

[32] The OHCHR released the previous report on June 27, 2006 which also stated that the rebels were responsible for at least nine deaths since the ceasefire declaration where the UCPN-Maoist leadership expressed the commitment to end such atrocities.

On the other hand, neither the Truth and Reconciliation Commission[33], nor the Commission for Investigating the Displaced People was formed to manage the peace process and address the victims during the conflict. So, interest of conflict between the rival forces resumed again while the UCPN-Maoist succeeded in making total combatants up to 32,250 without any disturbance of the then government. Later, Nepal Army also initiated the new recruitment[34] process of soldiers advertising on a government owned national daily—Gorkhapatra on November 2, 2008.

Major Movements after the CPA

In fact, the CPA becomes a turning point for various political/social movements in Nepal. The restoration of democratic system after the successful Jana Andolan-II was the context which provided a background for enhancing their movements. The nationwide Janajati Movement had the demands of secular state status and ethnicity based autonomous federal structures. Dalit groups were launching a movement to end caste-based discrimination. Madhes Movement of August 2007 led by the MJF had the demand to declare Nepal as a federal democratic republic and a full

---

[33] Nepali democracy faced ups and downs in the past because the guilty were spared in the name of "reconciliation" after each and every successful movement. The regressive forces had made a comeback and hatched a conspiracy against the democratic system due to failure of the then government to punish the guilty proved in the Mallik Commission Report in 1990. Again, it got repeated in the country as the recommendation of Raymajhi Commission report 2006 got ignored and was not implemented. That was one of the causes of creating mistrust and dissatisfaction over the new government formed right after the successful Jana Andolan II. Unnecessary delay in implementing the declaration of the House of Representatives which made very radical announcements as per the mandate of the movement was another shortcoming of the government. Any excellent declaration having no implementation has no meaning and does not support in the process strengthening and deepening democracy. The Maoists, who played a major role on their part in derailing the democratization process in Nepal from the very beginning, have continued killings, extortion, abductions and recruitment activities after they declared truce and signed various agreements, including the 25-Point Code of Conduct.

[34] According to the provision of CPA, the Maoists combatant would be managed within six months of CA. When it became impossible, the then government was convinced that the professionalism of the NA should not be captive because of the delay of the management of the Maoist combatants. Then, the process of new recruitment on the vacant posts in technical area of the NA was initiated to fulfill the posts. The recruitment was not additional but fulfillment of the vacancy within the existing strength.

proportional representation system for the election of CA. The Chure Bhawar movement (August-October, 2007) was known as anti-Madhes, because it had opposed the demand of Madhes Movement II led by United Democratic Madhesi Front from December 2007 to February 2008 to declare autonomous 'One Madhes, One Pradesh' and to amend the Election Commission Act in increasing the relaxation for inclusive candidacy (from 20 per cent to 30 per cent). Similarly, the Tharu Movement from March 2-14, 2009 demanded the government to withdraw its ordinance, which had defined the identity of all communities residing in the flat-land as Madhesi. It had also demanded to replace the terminology "Madhes" by "Tarai-Madhes," and recognize the Tharu as a separate ethnic identity in Madhes and form a federal state for Tharus with their prior-rights on the local natural resources: water resource, jungle and land (*Jal, Jangle ra Jamin*) available in their particular territory. Federal Limbuwan Movement is also an ethnic movement, especially launched in nine districts of the Eastern hills with their main demand being to form an Autonomous Limbuwan State. These were the major social/political movements witnessed after the CPA was signed and most of these movements have demanded proportional share in each and every government body. The government of Nepal tried to be engaged with these movement groups and signed the following agreements to address the problem of respective groups. The major Agreements signed by the Government after CPA are given below:

- With Janajatis (August 7, 2007)

- With Madhesi Janadhikar Forum (August 30, 2007)

- With Chure Bhawar Pradesh Ekta Samaj (September 13, 2007)

- With National Badi (a hill Dalits group) Rights Struggle Committee (October 15, 2007)

- With United Democratic Madhesi Front (February 28, 2008)

- With Federal Republican National Front (March 2, 2008)

- With Federal Limbuwan State Council (March 19, 2008)

Internal Conflict in Nepal Today

Nepal faces multiple conflicts today. However, focus of this section is on conflicts which are violent in nature. It is reported that some 69 semi-armed groups are active in Nepal (till March 2009) and most of these have mushroomed particularly after the CPA. However, the government of Nepal has recorded that there are 109 armed, semi-armed, and criminal groups intensifying their activities in Nepal and most of these are active in Tarai-Madhes. The number has been increasing day-by-day. Samyukta Jatiya Morcha is the newest organization which was identified for the first time on June 1, 2010 after it took responsibility in planting a bomb in Sindhupal chowk district. It had been creating terror in the hilly districts, especially in Kathmandu Valley and its neighboring places and now it is broadening its area of influence and nature of work. Apart from the Samyukta Jatiya Morcha, the following is the list of some of the major armed and criminal groups which are active in Nepal. It is said that most of the groups have their own military wing and their strength varies from 150 to 2000 in number.

Table 1: Armed/Semi-Armed Forces Established After Peace Accord

(November 22, 2006 – June 30, 2009)

1 Akhil Tarai Mukti Morcha	9 Janabadi Ganatantrik Tarai Mukti Morcha
2 Bahun Chhetri Newar Saamuha	10 Jana Samrakshan Sena
3 CPN [Maoist (United Bidrohi Morcha)	11 Janabadi Kirant Workers Party
4 Chure Bhawar Shanti Sena	12 Janatantrik Tarai Mukti Morcha (Goit)
5 Deshbhakta Army Nepal	13 Janatantrik Tarai Mukti Morcha (Himmat Singh)
6 Gorkha Mukti Morcha	14 Janatantrik Tarai Mukti Morcha (Jwala Singh)
7 Gorkhaland Mukti Sena (Tista Kangada)	15 Janatantrik Tarai Mukti Morcha (Prithvi Samuha)
8 Gorkha-Line Mukti Sena Samaj	16 Janatantrik Tarai Mukti Morcha (Visfot Singh)

17 Karebian Dog	40 PalloKirat Limbuwan Rastriya Monch
18 Khambuwan Rastriya Morch	41 Paribartan Nepal
19 Janatantrik Party Nepal	42 Rajan Mukti Samuha
20 Kirant Janabadi Workers' Party	43 Rajdhani Army
21 Liberation Tigers of Tarai Elam	44 Ranabir Sena
22 Limbuwan Democratic Volunteers Force	45 Rastriya Army
23 Limbuwan Mukti Morcha	46 Rastriya Army Nepal
24 Madhesi Mukti Force	47 Rastriya Samanantar Jwala Mukhi
25 Madhes Raksha Bahin	48 Revolutionary Left Wing (National Red Guard)
26 Madhesi Special Force	49 Samyukta Janatantrik Tarai Mukti Morcha
27 Madhes Sena	50 Samyukta Mukti Morcha (Ulfa)
28 Madhesi Bises Dasta	51 Saghia Limbuwan Rajya Parishad (Lawoti)
29 Madhesi Commando	52 Sanghia Limbuwan Rajya Parishad (Palung)
30 Madhesi Janaadhikar Forum	53 Sanghia Limbuwan Rajya Parishad (Lingen)
31 Madhesi Mukti Tigers (Raman Singh)	54 Sanghia Lontantric Rastriya Morcha
32 Madhesi Tigers	55 Save the National Army Nepal
33 Madhesi Virus Cleaners Party	56 Shahi Mukti Morcha
34 Mangolian Revenge Group	57 Shantikalagi Tarai Kranti
35 National Terrorist Encounter	58 Shiva Sena
36 Nepal Ajinger X Samuha	59 Sudur Parswim Krantikari Party
37 Nepal Mukti Morcha	60 Sup Kranti Dal
38 OBC Regiment	61 Tarai Army
39 Nepal Rakshya Dal	62 Tarai Bagi

63 Tarai Camando Lig	68 Tarai Uthan Sangathan
64 Tarai Cobra (Naagraja)	69 Taraibadi Madhesi Mukti Force
65 Jarai Janakrantikari Bal	70 Tharuhat Swatta Rajya Parishad
66 Tarai Ganatantric Mukti Morcha	71 Trishul Sena Nepal
67 Tarai Parishad	72 Samyukta Jatiya Morcha

Source: Bishnu Pathak and Devendra Uprety, "Tarai-Madhes: Searching for Identity Based Security", *CS Center*, Situation Update No. 88, October 14, 2009

Talking about the objectives of different armed and semi-armed groups, some of them are working for the reinstatement of Hindu state; some for the reinstatement of the institution of monarchy, but mostly the groups claim to have a political intention based on ethnic identity. Tarai-Madhes and eastern hill areas are the most affected regions today by the armed and semi-armed groups.

It is also said that there are groups working against other established groups and identities. Almost 60 militant groups in Tarai are working against the Pahadis (living in Taria from hill origin). Out of them, very few are seriously working with the political motto. Others want to intensify their criminal activities under the political cap. Similarly, Limbuwan Volunteers are working against those who oppose Limbuwan as a federal state comprising 27 per cent Limbu population that constitutes 1.6 per cent of the national population. They have a slogan, "Opponents of the Limbuwan cannot be alive in this region," and "No Limbuwan, no Entry." Their claim is that they have already organized 100 fulltime militant cadres in each of the eastern hill districts out of nine. Even Tharuhat Liberation Army is formed to "revolt against the states", "Khas Chauvinism". Other ethnic communities, i.e., Tamang, Gurung, Magar, etc., have a strong possibility to form their military wings, since they have already formed political fronts to fight against the High Caste Hilly Hindu domination.

Causes behind the Mushrooming Militant Conflicts after the CPA

While dealing with the main causes of the mushrooming violent conflict in specific countries even after introducing the peace process to resolve a conflict, the state power and government policy are the major components dealing with whether to intensify more violence or resolve it. Ungar et.al.[35] explains the following as key points:

- Political regime change, including recent transitions to democracy, commonly inflames violence among groups;

- Persistent patterns of violence, along with state rights abuses, exist in every country;

- Large scale economic changes, including programs for economic reform, are associated with rising level of violence, particularly among distinct groups and classes;

- Violent scape-goating of racial, religious, ethnic and sexual minorities persists in many countries; and

- Violence remains a component of many groups' responses to the state, from spontaneous protests to armed rebellion.

Analyzing and contextualizing the cause of mushrooming conflict in Nepal, Kumar mentions the following indicators[36].

- Low level of socio-political cohesion;

- High level of political violence occasioned with state repression;

- Political conflict over organizing ideology of the state;

---

[35] Mark Ungar, Sally Avery Bermanzohn and Kentor Worcestor. "Violence and Politics" in Kentor Worcestor, Sally Avery Bermanzohn and Mark Ungar eds, *Violence and Politics: Globalizations' Paradox* (New York: Routledge, 2002), 2.

[36] Dhruba Kumar. "Nepali State and Politics: Inevitable Crisis and Harrowing Transition" , Center for Nepal and Asian Studies, December 12, 1997, 20 cited in Dhruba Kumar. "Proximate Causes of Conflict in Nepal " *Contribution to Nepalese Studies,* 31 no. 1(January, 2005): 60.

- Major recent change in the structure of political system;

- Existence of proportionally small urban middle class;

- Rampant corruption and government unaccountability;

- Low absorbing capacity of foreign aid and its utilization; and

- High level external penetration.

The existence of any one mentioned above would be sufficient to mark the state as being weak, instable and conflict prone[37]. Several research works suggest that there are several overlapping problems that are directly-indirectly responsible for increasing the numbers of armed and semi-armed groups inside Nepal after the CPA[38]. It can be seen that all these problems came mainly 'due to low regulative capacity[39]' of the Nepali state and due to a very limited "presence of the state" that badly affected government-run development and other activities[40]. In fact, the SPA government lost its cohesive power before the UCPN-Maoist entered the political arena. Even if it tried to implement most of the commitment for making a suitable atmosphere for the peace process such as freeing all the UCPN-Maoist cadres from prison, withdrawing all the cases filed in the courts, lifting the terrorist tags on the UCPN-Maoist, etc., it was a little too late. The situation encouraged the UCPN-Maoist to get more than their expectations and they started bargaining further. The tough times were not only for the UCPN-Maoist but also when the whole process began, when people started counter-action[41]against the UCPN-Maoist activities by taking law and order on their hands. When the UCPN-Maoist led the government after the CA election in 2008, the situation worsened.

---

[37] Dhruba Kumar. "Proximate Causes of Conflict in Nepal " *Contribution to Nepalese Studies,*31 no. 1(January, 2005): 60.

[38] Ibid.

[39] Ram Kumar Dahal. "Nepal's Neighborhood: Ties During the Interim Government" in *POLSAN Annual Journal on Nepalese Foreign Policy*, Vol. 6 & 7 (1998): 99-115.

[40] "Presence of State and its Effect", *The Kathmandu Post*, September 16, 2006.

[41] Maoists were beaten and even killed by the villagers when people found the Maoists guilty of killings and beating up innocents. The transport entrepreneurs and hoteliers protested against the Maoists and Federation of Nepalese Chamber of Commerce and Industries

Awareness and expectation were increased by the catchy slogan of the UCPN-Maoist during the insurgency that radicalized the entire society. But these raising expectations remained unfulfilled after the political change. Even if they came in the peace process, participated in the government and parliament, became the single largest party in CA election, and then formed the government under their leadership, the UCPN-Maoist could not make any policy change towards peaceful and democratic ways[42]. In fact, their modus operandi to run the country proved to be more corrupt, irresponsible, unaccountable, incompetent to provide the good governance and less honest to the expressed commitment. As a result, hopelessness and frustration was increasing among the various deprived communities who had no expectation from other parties, and had been helping the UCPN-Maoist with high hopes for change. Here, we want to put those main circumstances into different categories of the causes to ease the analysis.

(FNCCI), on September 17, 2006, they warned to launch a nationwide protest if the Maoists continued extortion and intimidation. Getting excited by such counter attacks in the village and in city, US Ambassador James A. Moriarty expressed skepticism toward the possibility of holding constituent assembly elections in a free and fair manner. He said, "You can't have peace and violence at the same time contradictorily". He mentioned, "Everybody realizes that the Maoists are engaged in lot of violence right now even here in Kathmandu. There is a lot of extortion, beating, intimidation of people going on, that sort of activities will obviously threaten the peace process. See, *The Kathmandu Post*, 16 September 2006 and also "Sorry if I offended anyone: Moriarty," *The Kathmandu Post*, 16 September 2006. Donors working in the development sector in Nepal have started rolling back their programs from the districts due to strong pressure from the Maoists Department for International Development (DFID) of the United Kingdom working for poverty reduction and development in poor countries, including Nepal. See, *The Kathmandu Post*, September 1, 2006. Concerns shown by United Nations Resident Representative and Humanitarian Coordinator in Nepal, Matthew Kahane acknowledged on September 16, 2006 about the rapidly increasing Maoist influence in the countryside.

[42] Indeed, the SPA and the Maoists reached an agreement several times to "reinstate the displaced civilians in their homes and to return all land, houses and property seized unjustly". But till the date, they have neither returned the property nor allowed people to stay in their homes in the village. The Maoist party has played a dual role while talking to implement agreements—the Maoist leadership welcome "displaced people" in the villages by words and circulates secret order to their local cadres not to implement, whatever the leadership said, in action. Then the Maoists' behavior in the village has not changed at all, except the armed activities (For details see http://www.kantipuronline.com/kolnews.php?&nid=83973).

- The first is about the unfulfilled hope of people[43] in general, and ethnic community on the issue of ethnicity based autonomous state in particular. It was the Maoist party which distributed the hopes to the ethnic groups by proposing ethnicity based autonomous states to them even if they comprise less than 30 per cent population in the particular regions. They proposed for a Limbuwan state for those Limbu (with 1.6 per cent national population) which occupy 27 per cent population in the area. Kochila state was proposed for less than 24 per cent population of such groups. Gurung state was proposed for less than 22 per cent population of Gurungs in the particular region. And Magar state was proposed for 28 per cent Magars in the regions. When the UCPN-Maoist signed the CPA, the communities and their leadership saw less hope of having a state based on the UCPN Maoists' proposal. Later on, when the leaders of these communities came to know that the UCPN-Maoist leadership is not serious about the federal set up as declared during the insurgency, a large numbers of UCPN-Maoist cadres and supporters belonging to Madhesis, Tharu, Newar, Limbu and other communities started going away from the UCPN-Maoist Party to start their own movements. More people from indigenous groups, including Madhesi left[44] the UCPN-Maoist party when they first signed the CPA and agreed to promulgate the Interim Constitution 2007 without mentioning Nepal as a federal democratic republic. Interestingly, they continued replicating the UCPN-Maoists' strategy of selling the emotions of indigenous/ethnic communities and adopting their mobilization tactics as well even after they left the UCPN-Maoist. Indeed, they have become smarter and more intelligent through the knowledge gained by their involvement with the UCPN-Maoist during the insurgency. The cadres indoctrinated

---

[43] Uddhab Pyakurel, "Sambidhan Sabha Ka Lagi Purba Sarta"(Preconditions for the Constituent Assembly), *Nepal Samacharpatha,*27 March, 2007.

[44] The series of deserting the Maoist party was started just after 5 years when Bharat Dahal left the party. Then Jaykrishna Goit along with more than 100 Maoists from Madhes had left the party just before the royal coup followed by Laxman Tharu, Matrika Yaduv and others.

by the armed tactics of the UCPN-Maoist have mostly led the armed groups and they are active in attacking and weakening the state again for pressure.

• Secondly, the violent conflict has increased due to the weak and personalized peace process. Conflict management is a process of concluding a dispute or conflict in which the adversary parties, with or without the assistance of mediators, negotiate or otherwise strive toward a mutually acceptable agreement or understanding, taking into account each other's concerns.[45] Any conflict resolution can be defined as a new formation that is acceptable to all actors and can be made sustainable by them only. The trends of emergence of conflict suggest that mostly the sources of conflict are indigenous in nature and means and methods of resolution of such conflict also should be searched at local level where the formation of conflict is rooted. The logic is that the indigenous method can be only a sustainable solution. If some outside parties, as a mediator is called, use the carrot and stick policy to pressure the parties either to accept its measures or to be ready to bear the punishment, then there can be no acceptability or sustainability, unless one assumes that the 'mediator' is a part of the conflict formation.[46] It is neither the outsider nor certainly the above conflicting parties. Most importantly, the sustainability of violence depends on whether the indigenous resolution method has managed adequate provision for the post-conflict arrangement and addressed maturely the transition and questions of reconciliation[47] or not. If we go through each and every agreement along with the CPA, we can find many good and

---

[45] Louis Kriesberg. "Conflict: Social" in Adam Kuper and Jessica Kuper eds. *The Social Science Encyclopedia.*(London: Rutledge, 1999), 413.

[46] Johan Galtung. *Peace by Peaceful Means*, (Oslo: PRIO, 1996), 89 cited by Dev Raj Dahal. "Conflict Resolution: A Note on Some Contending Approach" in Ananda P.Shrestha and Hari Uprety eds., *Conflict Resolution & Governance in Nepal*. (Kathmandu: NEFAS, 2003), 20.

[47] Dev Raj Dahal. "Conflict Resolution: A Note on Some Contending Approach" in Ananda P. Shrestha and Hari Uprety eds., *Conflict Resolution & Governance in Nepal*, (Kathmandu: NEFAS, 2003). pp20-21

catchy terminologies put there to move forward the peace process into a logical conclusion. But Nepali transition and peace process could not go smoothly because of lack of effort to institutionalize it. In fact, it was like the personalized issue especially between the two actors—the then PM Koirala and the UCPN-Maoists' Supremo Pushpa Kamal Dahal. Many important decisions taken between them were not documented; people could have any basis to interpret/ analyze it. The second rank person neither in the UCPN-Maoist nor in the NC was fully aware of any consensus between them. To make other leaders of SPA aware of the mutual understanding between them was beyond imagination. As a result, if there was crisis of confidence between two leaders, the concerned parties were polarized as per the ideology rather than as per the spirit of several formal agreements. Why was the whole peace process not documented after the CPA? The simple answer is that the motive of both was to secure their importance permanently in the power and polity of the nation, so that they could change and play the rules of the game in accordance with their respective interests. For them, to establish a stable system, which was expected for fulfillment of people's aspirations—civil liberty, freedom, basic needs and identity, was second priority.

- Thirdly, use of vague, ambiguous and ambivalent terms in each and every agreement led to allowing the signatories to define the agreements as per their interest.

- Fourthly, the government's modus operandi to deal with the movement groups helped increase the armed and semi-armed groups in the making. When the government had no culture to recognize the opposition and was left listening to the voices raised through peaceful means or protests, many peaceful movements were compelled to harden their movements by adopting violent means. In other words, when the government established a precedent by showing that it gives attention to the peoples' demand only if the people opt for violent means, the increase in such groups and for them to follow anti-systemic and extra-constitutional modes of struggle was the ultimate result. Similarly, unnecessary excuse and political protection given by the government to the UCPN-Maoist cadre's criminal activities even after they signed the CPA helped weaken the state security mechanism and cohesive capacity. It also ultimately demoralized policy action and gave high hope to the militant groups.

- The fifth cause of the increment of such groups, is also the UCPN-Maoist and the government which left their prior agendas-peace, progress and democracy, but started playing double roles with multiple tones. For example, in the case of abolition of Monarchy, the Maoist leadership started saying that they have no problem in accepting the monarchy if the people want, and the SPA leader, then PM Koirala, started talking about a baby king. Both positions seemed to be expressed against the people's aspiration during Jana Andolan-II. Similarly, they both had changed their position about the federal issues after they faced a big threat by Madhes assertion. That is why both the SPA and the UCPN-Maoist were reluctant to frame the provision on federal structure in the Interim Constitution, which was promulgated in the consensus of both the forces. It seems that both the forces tried to engage with regressive and traditional forces for balancing them also, after they won their respective battles.

- Sixth, the reluctant role played by civil society and media after the UCPN-Maoist and the then government signed the peace agreement is another cause that led to promoting and provoking the armed groups. Neither the media nor the civil society groups, which had played a vital role during the Jana Andolan-II, engaged in the role of the critic to the new regime after the movement was successfully ended and the UCPN-Maoist declared a truce. As a result, no critics came for the non-implementation of clauses agreed/signed by the parties, and non-adherence to the code of conduct signed/agreed by the UCPN-Maoist and the interim government.

The so-called civil-society was divided as per the party ideologies when parties decided to allocate some seats for the civil society members in the restored parliament. Its division on Maoist and non-Maoist lines erased the actual role of civil society as a watchdog, and issues raised by the members of civil-society were also taken subjectively. Both the parties became free to follow respective paths that automatically encouraged violating the code of conduct and interpreting it in favor of one's own interest. Ultimately, it helped make a more anarchical situation that was never before. Then the situation shifted politics of consensus among the parties to the politics of confrontation.

- Seventh, the UCPN-Maoists' deliberate attempt to create anarchy and instability became instrumental in increasing the number of armed and semi-armed groups in Nepal. The UCPN Maoists' leadership responded to them provocatively, so that an opportunity could come to vitalize the role of their combatants kept in cantonment, and to catch the fish of the power in the turmoil water. They on the one hand said that "Anarchy and instability help the UCPN-Maoist to consolidate power for the further revolution— people's republic" and blamed some genuine movement groups as criminal outfits, imperialist's outfit, etc.,[48] for defaming them. It is proved by the proposal and action of the UCPN-Maoist while the Madhes was uprising. The UCPN-Maoist first provoked the peaceful movement by gunning down a man who participated in the peaceful movement organized by Madhesi groups, proposed for the mobilization of its combatants to control the situation in Madhes, and suggested to the then government not to be engaged with the movement groups through dialogue. Neither the government nor the UCPN-Maoist leaders realized the fact about no military solution was possible to control people's peaceful

---

[48] Dr. Baburam Bhattarai said "The naike (derogatory word for leader) of the criminal group [read that as Madhesi People's Rights Forum] must be arrested and the outfit must be outlawed". Speech of Dr. Bhattarai at Tundikhel's Khulla Manch in Kathmandu on March 23, 2007.

assertion. Again, the Tharu community was also provoked by the UCPN-Maoist when it was leading the government. When the government came up with an ordinance to define the identity of all communities residing in the flat-land as Madhesi, the Tharu Movement was witnessed from March 2-14, 2009.

The seven points mentioned above can be considered as general causes which helped in increasing the culture of violence and intimidation all over the country after the CPA was signed. Along with those, there are some specific causes which helped Madhes in becoming the heartland of the armed conflict after the UCPN-Maoist 'renounced' the violence. These are:

1. The Madhes were not influenced by the UCPN-Maoist during the insurgency, and the SPA, especially the NC and UML, also lost their base after the Madhes Uprising 2007. As a result, there was a vacuum due to lack of existence of the state and the mainstream political parties.

2. Secondly, the strategic geographical area of Tarai. While there was Maoist insurgency, the hilly region became a strategic geographic location for their shelter as the state had less access to the region, and systemic parties were quite strong. But later on, the situation was reversed in Tarai after the Madhes movement when the NC and UML also exited from the region.

3. Madhes used to be a more violent place in comparison to the hilly region with records of killing, kidnapping etc. in the past, especially during the time of elections. When Nepal had a better law and order situation, some of the criminal groups used to take shelter in India especially in different parts of the states of Uttar Pradesh (UP) and Bihar. And now it is said that the situation has reversed; the law and order situation in Bihar and UP states is under control, but has weakened in Nepal. Now many criminals in the border area take shelter in Nepal and commit criminal activities.[49] They

[49] Uddhab P. Pyakurel. *Maoist Movement in Nepal: A Sociological Perspective.* (New Delhi: Adroit Publishers, 2007)

even managed to wear the political cap by capitalizing on the transitional situation of Nepal and expanding their activities in Tarai.

4. Foreign role; when Madhes became vulnerable, all the international players including China,[50] USA and EU[51] tried to engage with it, considering it as one of the strategic locations to influence Nepali politics as well as to weaken Indian influence in internal politics of Nepal.

5. The role of Terai elites. The elite from political parties and civil-society of a particular country and society engaged in leading the conflicting sections, dealing with them, and leading the conflict towards the resolution are the vital actors while talking about the conflict management or resolution. That is why, recreating the conflict, resuming the conflict and sustainability of the conflict resolution is dependent on the capacity, responsibility, honesty, accountability and transparency of the respective elites or leadership engaged in the peace process. But misunderstanding and threat to the peace process can be created, while "elite conflict occurs...[and] an elite attempts to undermine another elite's capacity to extract

---

[50] Today China, which used to support establishments, had no access to the people and leaders of any political party, seems to be interested to be engaged in Nepal's internal matter especially after abolition of Monarchy. It wants an assurance from the Nepali state that Tibetan refugees living in Nepal and their agitation for establishing Tibet as an autonomous state would be in control in Nepal.

[51] The EU which used to be active in establishing and strengthening democracy now not only started giving suggestion (rather insisting) to the government, but also invested a huge amount of money in helping ethnic conflicts. For example: (1) EU compelled the government to expel the then Education Minister Ram Chandra Kuswaha charging him of being 'corrupt', (2) A 10-member team of the European Parliament, which arrived in Nepal for a week-long visit in June 2010, had visited the Tibetan Camp on 24th May secretly without taking permission of the Nepal Government. (3) They even had a schedule on 28th May to meet the extra-systemic organization called Limbuwan Rajya Parisad and Khumbuwan. These meets were cancelled after the Nepal Government's strong objection. (4) After the Maoist called off its last month indefinite strike, they kept suggesting to the Prime Minister to resign for reciprocating the Maoist's move and it was good to form a consensus government ruling out the option of majoritarian Government in democracy if there is no consensus.

revenue from non-elites"[52]. It is purely implacable to the Madhes in Nepal where Madhes has mainly become the battlefield of the new Madhesi elites and the old elites scattered all over Nepal. When one watches the marathon of Madhesi leadership selling their popular strength, the level of compromise they can reach for the Madhesi sentiment for the opportunity of being a Member of Cabinet under different governments formed after 2006; how easily they can sideline their agenda raised during the struggle; and how they can be more divided and competed for their petty interest rather than be united for the interest of the region. The demands[53] put forward by Madhes-based parties before taking part in the election of the CA help substantiate the argument. They are neither able to show their commitment in the local issue of Madhes nor do they have faith in the participatory and inclusive. All causes together help Madhes to be the heartland of violent conflict.

In brief, it can be said that organizational transformation from armed rebels to peaceful politicians depends on three preconditions—faction, followers and friends; (1)The rebel group's degree of internal cohesion during the peace process, (2) its level of popular support among the population at large at the time of the transition, and (3) the amount of legitimacy that the international community is willing to grant to the rebels through the transition period helps in examining how the rebellion groups are being transferred.[54] But when the UCPN-Maoist opts for playing with their two-line struggle, it seems that they have lost their internal cohesion over the party cadres. In fact, this weakness of the Maoist party ultimately provided a clue not only for its cadres to continue criminal activities along with extortion, intimidation, killing, abduction, etc., but also for other groups who were waiting for a favorable situation to initiate the armed movements to

---

[52] Richard Lachmann, "Class Formation Without Class Struggle: An Elite Conflict Theory of the Transition to Capitalism" , *American Sociological Review*. 55 no.3 (1990): 403.

[53] As per the demand, Madhesi parties were exempted by the provision of inclusive candidacy in the CA. The amendment was not made mandatory for those political parties which fill up less than 30 per cent candidates in the election.

[54] Mimmi S. Kovacs, *From Rebellion to Politics*. (Sweden: Uppsala University, 2007), 8.

influence the state. That is why we find some commonality in most of the groups today if we follow their movement and demands seriously. In every negotiation talk between the government and the armed groups, they commonly demand eventual integration of their combatants into security forces including the Nepal Army. Militant's integration into security forces has become one of the major hopes of most armed groups. In other words, possible integration in security agencies and rehabilitation in society with handsome amounts of money from the national treasury becomes precedence. The violent armed activities become the guiding principle to the unemployed youth. Thus, the agreement between the government and the UCPN-Maoist for the management of the latter's combatants encouraged others to take to arms who are also interested in entering into the security agencies through back-channel negotiations. The trend is likely to be viable for years to come due to the high rate of unemployment of the youth. Today, youth of Nepal can easily join any of such armed group with the motto of just entering into the security forces, which previously used to be very difficult unless one had a political influence. Another cause of possible sustainability of such armed groups in Nepal is due to social respect if one joins in the security forces, especially in Nepal Army.

Internal Conflict and External Consequences

Generally, it is very difficult to term a conflict as an internal problem and its risk spilling over neighboring areas. Indeed, the regional dimension has become "increasingly important in South Asia, if for no other region, having an 'exclusive security complex' and 'security interdependence' "[55] among the countries. That is why regionalism and conflict are related in many different ways and the multiple "aspects of regionalism, security and development are complementary and mutually supportive ways."[56] As Lt. Gen. (Retd.) V.R. Raghavan[57] rightly pointed out, even an internal conflict

---

[55] Bjorn Hettne, "Conflict Dynamics and Conflict Management" in John P. Neelsen and Dipak Malik (eds.) *Crisis of State and Nation: South Asian States Between Nation-Building and Fragmentation.*, (New Delhi: Manohar, 2007), 47.

[56] Ibid., 48-49.

[57] V.R. Raghavan, "Valedictory Address", seminar on "Internal Conflict in Nepal: Transnational Consequences", Banaras Hindu University, Varanasi, June 3-5, 2010.

will have external consequences. It is very much applicable to the Nepali context. The reality is that Nepal's internal conflict will have a heavy consequence on India; due to various factors such as socio-cultural proximity between the two countries (Nepal-India), geographical location through which Nepal is situated in the heart of India and surrounded by it from three sides, India cannot remain unaffected by any kind of internal problem in Nepal. That is why it is called "indo-closed" and "indo-opened" with the sharing of not only open border, but also security problems which emerged in either country. The dual characters-open border[58] and socio-cultural proximity lead to "people flow" between the two neighbors and an established people-to-people relation for centuries.[59] At the same time, Nepal's internal conflict will have no consequences, or, at the most, will have a negligible impact on the rest of the countries in the world, including its northern neighbor-China. It is not only due to the open border but also "other natural and practical considerations"[60] wherein it cannot be put on equal footing with India and the rest.

However, the responses of the majority of the people, including the government officials, of both the countries (Nepal and India) on the issue of mushrooming internal conflict are disappointing. They neglect other factors and blame the open border for woes. As Madhes of Nepal has become the most unstable and deeply troubled region due to today's armed and semi-armed conflicts, many Nepalese perceive that the Indo-Nepal open border helped create such a situation in the bordering area-the Terai. On the other hand, many Indians especially the bureaucrats also believe in false arguments

---

[58] In fact, Indo/Nepal border, which is open, is 1580 kilometers long with 940 KM land boundary and 640 KM river boundary.

[59] The political and economic implication of such a relation is worth mentioning. Nepalese prefer to go to India which is an emerging economy in South Asia not only for hunting jobs but also for taking shelter or asylum while there is any kind of political crisis in Nepal. It has been witnessed in the past that the migration from Nepal to India used to increase when there was insecurity in the country due to insurgency and state violence. Similarly, the history says that Nepali leaders and students living in India were in jail with their Indian counterparts who were struggling for independence of India. Also, not only the working class but also business classes of Indian people are doing their jobs in Nepal.

[60] Indra Adhikari, "The 'China Card': Perception and Reality", *Global Nepali* (May/June 2009)

that the Indo-Nepal porous border has helped increase influx of criminals as well as terrorist activities in India. It meant that both the Nepali and Indian side see an open border through biased eyes; they looked upon open the border "as a constraint and not as an instrument for developing and enduring and beneficial relationship."[61] In this situation, the long practice of an open border followed by the India-Nepal Peace and Friendship Treaty 1950 seems to be affected in the near future.

In fact, the 'warm' and 'special' relation between both Nepal and India, by tradition, was legitimatized keeping in mind the emerging complexities created by the changing times and circumstances. These relations were formalized by the various provisions including the 1950 treaty. Here, people having anti-Indian sentiment always raise questions against India referring to the 1950 Treaty blaming it as an unequal treaty. Weaknesses identified so far are : (1) position of signatory of the treaty are unequal; (2) it was signed by the oligarchy of Nepal having no popular will and base; and (3) it is a treaty accompanied with letters of exchanges, but the letters were kept secret for several years after signing it. However, both the time and context have changed; the treaty which was signed from the traditional security perspective to secure the borders of either country. In other words, the main thrust of the treaty i.e. defense and security, has become irrelevant today after it has time and again been defied by both the countries. People of both sides of the border, who lack basic amenities and infrastructure, are using the open border for their interests. Any change in the provision of open border will neither help India's security concern nor make Nepal's Terai safe. The border, regulated or porous, hardly matters to both the terrorists and criminals as they do not follow rules and regulations of international boundary treaty. Also, neither could USA save the Pentagon (from an attack) nor could India avert the Mumbai attack from Pakistan based terrorists even if they both are very much concerned about the regulated border.

---

[61] Ram P. Rajbahak. *India-Nepal Border: A Bond of Shared Aspirations.* (New Delhi: Lancer Publishers, 1992)

Finally, of the 268 violent conflicts which occurred between 1968 and 2006, 40% were eliminated by police and intelligent agencies, and 43% reached a peaceful political accommodation with their government; 10% of insurgent groups achieved victory and only 7% of the terrorist groups were eliminated by military action.[62] The data mentioned above helps to draw a conclusion that both thoughts—achieving a victory through violent means; and eliminating the groups by military action are either illusions or well accomplished task. Political accommodation through dialogue is the only way which ensures peace and makes the internal social transformation easy. For a successful dialogue to reach a common ground, the process must be as inclusive, transparent, and institutionalized as possible.

---

[62] Seth G. Jones and Martin C.Libicki. *How Terrorist Groups End: Lesson for Countering Al Qu'ida.* (Santa Monica, CA: RAND Corporation, 2008)

IMPACT OF INTERNAL CONFLICT ON THE NEPAL ARMY

Keshar Bahadur Bhandari

With the beginning of the people's war, launched by the Communist Party of Nepal (Maoist) in February 1996, Nepal faced the most serious internal upheaval since the country was unified in its present form in the late 18th century. There is no sector of the government and section of the society that has not been affected by the uprising. Nepal faced a major economic setback during this conflict and the after effect is no less. According to Zartman, conflict is a universal condition, inevitable, often necessary, and sometimes beneficial.[1] Yet the physical and economic losses due to the conflict could be estimated in billions and billions of rupees which have pushed Nepal many years behind in its development effort. The unprecedented human loss of some fifteen thousand people that Nepal witnessed cannot be compensated at any cost, and no logic whatsoever can justify it. Amongst the security bodies, the Nepal Army (NA) is one institution that has been affected most in many ways because of the conflict and post conflict developments. This paper makes an endeavor to analyze the impact of the internal conflict on the NA.

Nepal Army: A Brief History

Nepal's recorded history dates back to 350 BC and the institution of the army initiated just after 350 AD. In the middle age, the Newar Malla Kings ruled over the Kathmandu Valley and surrounding areas and Khas Malla

---

[1] William Zartman, "Preventive Diplomacy: Setting the Stage" in William Zartman ed., *Preventing Negotiation: Avoiding Conflict Escalation.*(New York: Carnegie Commission on Preventing Deadly Conflict, 2001), 1-18.

Kings who had maintained strong armies ruled over the Karnali region in the far west in Nepal. In the 17th century, Nepal was divided into many different principalities and King Prithvinarayan Shah hailing from one of the principalities called Gorkha, initiated a unification campaign in 1740 AD. King Prithvinarayan Shah captured the Kathmandu Valley (then known as Nepal) after conquering the three key city kingdoms of Kantipur, Patan, and Bhaktapur (September 1768 - November 1769); and made Kathmandu his capital.[2] Subsequently, King Prithvinarayan Shah's Gorkhali Army came to be known as NA.[3]

Prime Minister Bhimsen Thapa, in his 31 years of powerful rule (1806-1837),[4] had modified the structure of the army and its modus operandi, and generated a rank structure, equal attire, modern training and barrack system. He also established new industry of arms and ammunitions. The NA has a glorious history of meritoriously fighting and defeating the British and Chinese/Tibetan armies.

The tradition of making the prime minster as the commander-in-chief of the army during the Rana rule changed with the political transformation of 1950, but the army remained under the control of the King, who had the executive authority of the state. The constitution of 1990, which transformed Nepal into a constitutional monarchy, did not bring about adequate changes to the role of the King vis-à-vis the army. Therefore, the NA from the days of its establishment has always worked under the executive authority. Similarly, the name of the Army has been changed over time from 'Tilanga' to the 'Gorkhali Army' under King Prithvinarayan Shah, to 'Nepal Army' under Prime Minister Chandra Shamsher to 'Royal Army' under King Mahendra, and 'Royal Nepal Army' under King Birendra and now finally the parliament of the day named it 'Nepal Army' again after the political changes in 2006.[5]

---

[2] Sriram Upadhya, *Nepal Ko Samikshyatmak Itihas*[*Critical History of Nepal*] (Kathmandu : Sajha Prakasan, 1999.),154-155.

[3] Directorate of Public Relations, *The Nepalese Army a Force with History Ready for Tomorrow.* (Kathmandu: Nepal Army, 2008), 3.

[4] Upadhya, *Nepal Ko Samikshyatmak Itihas,* 202.

[5] Narhari Acharya, "The Nepalese army" in Bishnu Sapkota ed, *The Nepali Security Sector: An Almanac.* (Hungary: Brambauer Publishers,2005), 127-142.

The gallantry and sincerity of the "Army of Gorkha" or "Gorkhali" had impressed the British East-India Company; and because of this when they started recruiting Nepalis into their forces, they gave the name "Gurkhas"[6] to their new soldiers of Nepali origin. Britain and India still keep 'Gurkha Rifles' in their armed forces. Some time it is misunderstood that the Nepal Army is also a part of the British and Indian Army; and even all Nepalis as 'Gurkhas'. In simple terms it could be said that "all Gurkhas are Nepalis (by origin), but not all Nepalis are Gurkhas."[7]

Maoist Movement - A brief background

The history of communist movement in Nepal began with the formation of the Communist Party of Nepal (CPN) in 1949. The Maoist movement can be traced back to the late 1960s, when a group of young communists inspired by the Cultural Revolution in China and the Naxalite movement in West Bengal (India), ventured into an armed uprising in Jhapa District, eastern Nepal bordering India's West Bengal. The journey of the Maoist movement began with the formation of CPN's Fourth Convention in 1974, and over a decade the party grew substantially.

The internal dynamics of rifts within the communist party led to various splits and alignments amongst the parties and the Communist Party of Nepal (Maoist) [CPN (Maoist)] came into being in March 1995. The CPN (Maoist) led by Pushpa Kamal Dahal famously known as 'Prachanda' along with Dr. Baburam Bhattarai formally adopted the doctrine of armed struggle. A political orientation program began in Rukum and Rolpa in October, which also targeted those considered 'class enemy'. The western district of Rukum and Rolpa has a long history of communist uprising.[8]

---

[6] Ibid, 4.

[7] C. K. Lal,'Nepal's Maobaadi' in Deepak Thapa (ed). *Understanding the Maoist Movement of Nepal*. Kathmandu: Martin Chautari, 2003) p.135; Also see Pathak, op cit.The government trashed the demand submitted by Dr Bhattarai Baburam, CPN (Maoist) leader and the Maoist started people's war by attacking three police post in three districts four days before the deadline expired.

[8] Bishnu Pathak, *Politics of People's War and Human Rights in Nepal*, (Kathamndu: BIMIPA Publication, 2005), 94-98.

The 40-point demand submitted by Baburam Bhattarai to then Prime Minister Sher Bahadur Deuba (Nepali Congress) on February 2, 1996 called for the election to constitutional assembly and cutting down all the royal prerogatives and power, drafting of a new republic constitution and revolutionary redistribution of land and property etc. These demands seemed to be more like a wish list as the deadline to complete them was a mere 15 days.

The latest struggle for ideological and political control began with the launch of the 'People's War', as it is locally known or considered as a 'war of liberation' in Maoist terms, on 13 February 1996. The Maoist attacked three police posts in Rolpa, Rukum and Sindhuli four days before the deadline expired.[9] The government tried to quash the Maoist activities with police force by launching Operation Romeo. The wrong handling of Operation Romeo alienated a large number of people, many of whom were virtually forced to side with the Maoists or at least sympathize with them. This set the stage for the beginning of the people's war[10].

Conflict and Post Conflict Effect on the Nepal Army: Critical Analysis

The dynamics of conflict in Nepal have been described as an amplified manifestation of mistakes in every sphere of the Nepali society. Yet politics in Nepal has always been a game between the center and periphery. The center, whether elected or appointed, assumes a core position while the people are pushed to the periphery. The inner sphere, or the nucleus of the nation, is composed of decision-making elite in control of state power and resources. The subsequent rings of society emanate from the periphery, representing the group which is farther most from the center. Clearly, conflicts do not occur in a vacuum. The emergence of conflicts varies with many different criteria. Yet structural conflict theory sees conflict as a

---

[9] C. K. Lal, "Nepal's Maobaadi" in Deepak Thapa ed, *Understanding the Maoist Movement of Nepal,* (Kathmandu: Martin Chautari, 2003), 135; Also see Pathak, *Politics of People's War,* 2005

[10] Deepak Thapa, *Understanding the Maoist Movement of Nepal,* (Kathmandu: Martin Chautari, 2003), ix-xii.

direct result of the socioeconomic structure with the society divided into spheres of power. Since the 1970s, Edward E Azar, along with John Burton, has been researching the phenomenon known as protracted social conflict (PSC)[11]. The people's war in Nepal may be classified as a PSC with a prolonged and often violent struggle by communal groups for very basic needs such as security, recognition, and acceptance, fair access to political institutions and economic participation. The preconditions for PSC include communal content, human needs, role of governance and the state, and international linkages. All these preconditions are present in the Nepali conflict.

Parties in Conflict

The key conflicting parties in Nepal were the institution of monarchy, the government of the day, security bodies and the CPN (Maoist) that took to the armed revolution against the institution of monarchy and the system of the government. The other parties in the conflict were major political parties namely the Nepali Congress and CPN (UML) which sided with the monarchy during different periods of conflict while in office. The Panchayat time leaders and their parties were supporting the King whereas most of the left parties supported the CPN (Maoist). External influence with their own interest had played a major role in giving an impetus to the conflict and the parties in conflict. The United States supported the government of the day and the army in particular and the Nordic countries were soft on the CPN (Maoist), which significantly affected some dimensions of the conflict. The influence of the neighboring countries had two dimensions; they were supporting the government of the day and at the same time at least one neighbor provided support and protection to the rebels giving them a safe haven to operate from. The other stakeholders of the conflict like business communities and the elites, though sided with the monarchy, were forced to pay heavy donations to the Maoist. The main victims of the conflict indeed were the common people, especially the deprived sections of the society.

---

[11] Edward E. Azar, *The Management of Protracted Social Conflict: Theory and Causes*, (Gower: Brookfield, VT, 1990)

The 10 years old armed conflict between the Maoist rebels and the government of Nepal took a different turn with the signing of the 12-point understanding on November 22, 2005 between seven political parties and Maoists. This understanding forged an alliance to fight the government formed after a disastrous 2005 royal takeover. The people's movement of April 2006, popularly known as the Jana Andolan – II, forced the King to re-instate the dissolved House of Representatives through a royal address on April 24, 2006. This paved the way for Maoist rebels to come to mainstream politics; and the Comprehensive Peace Accord (CPA) was signed on November 21, 2006. A new interim constitution was drafted, which was adopted on January 15, 2007.[12] The election of the Constituent Assembly (CA) was successfully conducted in 2008, and the results made the CPN (Maoist) the largest party with 220 elected votes out of 601 seats in the CA. The CPN (Maoist) led the coalition government but the second largest party the Nepali Congress opted to remain in opposition.

The Effect on NA

The people's war waged by the Maoists against the government of Nepal and the state system has affected the NA in various ways both during the conflict and post conflict environment. The effects have been obvious mostly in areas such as Army organization, replenishment of arms and ammunition, recruitment, training, and civil-military relations. Other areas that have affected the army significantly are the logistics, accommodation, health and medication, and morale, discipline, and Human Rights issues.

After the CA election, the first sitting of the CA declared the Kingdom of Nepal the Federal Democratic Republic of Nepal on May 28, 2008 and with the amendments to the interim constitution of 2007, the president of Republic of Nepal is designated the supreme Commander in Chief of NA.

---

[12] The Interim Constitution drafting Committee was formed in June 2006, chaired by retired Supreme Court Justice Laxman Aryal. After the signing of Comprehensive Peace Agreement (CPA) in November 21, 2006, the Constitution came into being with several refinement/amendment over the original draft including the inclusion of new provisions about Human Rights Commission and about the army and its democratization.

A provision of National Defence Council (NDC)[13] was made for mobilization, operation and use of NA.

A. *Organizational Changes*

From the initial days of the Maoist uprising, Nepal Police was fighting the Maoists with its strength of around 42,000 but was facing major setbacks with heavy human losses. The Armed Police Force was raised on the behest of political parties with its initial strength of 15,000 to fight the Maoists. The biased psychology of the political parties towards the army and its loyalty was the motive behind raising the Armed Police Force which will be loyal to them. The army institutions remained neglected for nearly a decade after the restoration of democracy in 1990 because of the politically biased attitude of the government. This was more acute specifically during the period of conflict when the police were fighting the Maoists. The Maoists had only about 2,000 fighting cadres in 2001. Though no significant increase in strength took place, the Maoist disclosed that they had three brigades when they attacked the military barrack at Dang on November 23, 2001. This attack dragged the army in the war against the Maoists, and this affected the NA in several ways.

B. *Changes in Structure and Strength*

The NA witnessed major changes and developments in the organizational structure during the conflict period. Its initial strength of 46,000 was increased to around 92,000[14] during the conflict period. After the army got involved into the war against the Maoist; three more infantry divisions – the Central Division (Hetaunda), the Mid-Western Division (Pokhara) and the Far-Western Division (Dipayal) – were added to the existing three divisions –

---

[13] The provision of National Defence Council (NDC) consisting of Prime Minister (PM) as Chairperson, Defence Minister and Home Minister and three other Ministers designated by the PM representing three different parties as members was made under the clause 145 of the Interim Constitution of Nepal 2007. NDC was made to recommend the Council of Ministers on mobilization, operation and use of NA; and the President in turn would operate and mobilize the army on the final recommendation of the Council of Minister.

[14] DGMO Department. *A Brief Introduction of Nepalese Army* (Kathmandu: Nepal Army, 2006), 65.

the Eastern Division (Itahari), Valley Division (Kathmandu) and Western Division (Nepalgunj) – thus making six combat divisions, one each in the five development regions and one in Kathmandu valley (See Annexure 1). The strength of NA dramatically increased after the emergency of November 2001, and especially during the active rule of the King since October 4, 2002 and after the royal takeover of February 1, 2005. As per the Adjutant General's Department (Record Office), the strength of NA was 90,226 as of July 2008[15] that was increased to around 92,000 in April 2009.[16] The number of officers' corps including senior level General ranks also increased significantly. First ever women infantry officer cadets and soldiers were enrolled in the history of Nepal Army.

The post-conflict development drew a lot of attention regarding the rationality of the present strength of the army and the issue of its right size. In the absence of the National Security Policy (NSP) of Nepal, the government has not been able to come out with the new role definition of NA which will have a direct bearing on the size and strength of the army. In the absence of NSP, no contemporary defence policy and defence strategy in the post conflict environment has been formulated, besides the one prepared by the Army HQ. In the absence of the above mentioned documents the discussion on the subject regarding the right size of the army will be premature and speculative. In addition, the issue of integration of Maoist combatants in the security bodies is likely to add new dimension to it.

C. *Issue of Integration*

With the increased number of the NA, the Maoists also claimed increased number of combatants in several divisions and brigades. After the CPA, 19,602 Maoist combatants were verified by the United Nations Political Mission in Nepal (UNMIN) and cantoned in 28 cantonments. The integration of Maoist army combatants has been a major issue and bone of contention affecting the ongoing peace process. The supervision, integration and

---

[15] Ibid, 70.

[16] Ibid, 65.

rehabilitation of combatants of the Maoist army have been mentioned in the Interim Constitution, CPA and Agreement on Monitoring of the Management of Arms and Armies (AMMAA)[17] but in a little vague manner, giving room for divergent interpretations by different parties to suit their interest. The peace process is not likely to conclude without resolving the issue of the integration of Maoist combatants. The number of the Maoist combatants to be integrated in the security bodies and especially in NA has been the main issue of disagreement between the Maoist and other political parties.

The Maoists want to integrate a maximum number, if not all of its combatants in the security bodies and preferably in the NA. On the other hand the political parties want to integrate a reasonable number of Maoist combatants in the security bodies with least number in the Army fearing that the NA may be influenced by the Maoist party. The NA as one of the main stakeholder though not in favor of integration has also shown some flexibility regarding the number that could be integrated in the army and other security bodies. As the peace process is getting prolonged its adverse effect in the functioning of the NA in various sectors is becoming more and more obvious.

D. *Recruitment Issue*

The post-conflict environment has affected the NA in its recruitment program as well. The NA has faced a lot of controversy and resistance from the CPN (Maoist) in its effort to fulfill the vacant positions. The Ministry of Defence (MoD) during CPN (Maoist) led Government claimed that the NA had violated the CPA and AMMAA[18] and issued an order to stop the

---

[17] Interim Constitution 2007, Clause 146. Interim Provision for the Combatants: The Council of Minister shall form a special committee to supervise, integrate and rehabilitate the combatants of the Maoist Army; CPA, November 21, 2006, Clause 4.4. The Interim Cabinet shall work to supervise, integrate and rehabilitate the Maoist Combatants; i.e. constitute a Special Committee to carry out monitoring, adjustment and rehabilitation of the Maoist combatants; AMMAA, December 8, 2006, Clause 4.1.3. Registration of Maoist army combatants at cantonment sites: Only those Maoist Combatants who have been properly registered at cantonment site will be eligible for possible integration into the security bodies fulfilling the standard norms. Those who are eligible for integration into the security forces will be determined by a special committee.

army's ongoing recruitment that had already reached half way through the process. UNMIN had also shown its support over the claim made by the CPN (Maoist) regarding the violation of CPA and AMMAA on the recruitment issue further adding fuel to the controversy. The Supreme Court had issued a stay order in 2009 for the future recruitment but the final decision on stay order has not come as yet. The NA tried to justify its stands for not recruiting additional troops but an effort to fill those vacant positions that have been created by natural attrition. Presently Nepal army has more than 10 thousand vacant positions that need to be filled. Again this year the NA with the permission of MoD has started a fresh recruitment for some technical positions and the Supreme Court has overruled the writ lodged against it for the reason of the importance of those positions. The dispute arising from the interpretation of the CPA clause related to recruitment should have been resolved by a joint mechanism comprising CPN (Maoist) and Political Parties.[19] This uncertainty has affected the army's daily functioning and especially the medical corps, technical branch and the training institutions.

E. *Psychological Dimensions*

After the restoration of Democracy in 1990 the government of the day neither took the army into confidence nor provided it the guardianship in real term. The army, looking for guardianship and patronage, remained

---

[18] Interim Constitution of Nepal, 2007, Schedule 4, UNDP Nepal, Kathmandu, 2009. In keeping with the letters to the United Nations (UN) Secretary General of 9 August and Comprehensive Peace Accord of 21 November 2006; Agreement on Monitoring of the Management of Arms and Armies (AMMAA) was signed on 8 December 2006. Under the clause 5.1.2 Ceasefire of CPA, it is mentioned that 'Both sides shall not recruit additional military forces, and shall not transport arms, ammunitions and explosives or conduct military activities against each other". Similarly, under the AMMAA - Clause 5: Compliance with the Agreement, sub-clause 5.1 Prohibited activities: Recruiting additional armed forces or conducting military activities against each other, including transporting weapons, ammunitions and explosives (unless mutually agreed by the parties and notified in advanced according to the terms of this agreement.) has been mentioned.

[19] CPA, Clause 10.4. If any dispute arises in the interpretation of this agreement, a joint mechanism comprising both sides shall make the interpretation as per the spirit of the preamble and the documents annexed to this agreement, and such interpretation shall be final.

close to the King - the Supreme Commander in Chief provisioned by the Constitution of Nepal 1990.[20] In the beginning of Maoist insurgency the Royal Nepalese Army (RNA) was in the frame of mind that the problem will be settled politically and it might not be involved in direct conflict. The RNA was mobilized by the government in April 1998 for six years under the scheme of Integrated Security and Development Plan (ISDP), but not with a motive to fight the Maoist directly. The campaign was an effort to win the hearts and minds of the people through development work and by ensuring security; thus by restricting the movement of Maoists and causing least collateral damage. The sole aim was to exert pressure on Maoists and bring them to negotiations for political settlement. The ISDP was slowly becoming popular and it had affected Maoists by restricting their movement in several districts of Nepal. It is believed that the Maoists wanted to stall/ halt or avert the ISDP at any cost and in whatever way possible. Hence, the Maoists seem to have taken a decision to launch an attack on the army barrack; and the first ever attack took place at the army barrack in Dang district on November 23, 2001. The Maoist had taken a lot of chance, even risking their future, but the attack was successful given the army's much delayed decision to retaliate. The Maoists looted a good number of military weapons which changed the balance of power and the incident dragged the RNA into the war against the Maoists.

Fighting insurgency on the ground was new, though not unfamiliar, to the RNA. Due to the lack of government will to use the army against the Maoist insurgents, the RNA had not prepared itself for direct involvement in the war against the Maoists. Moreover, for various political reasons and for no convincing real cause to fight, the army was not mentally prepared to take on the Maoists directly. When the army was dragged into the war after November 2001, it was fighting more for self defence and its own institutional interest rather than for any political cause or for the King. Moreover, after the February 2005 royal takeover the army had to fight the war against the Maoists all by itself and in isolation without support from any political parties and cooperation from any quarter. This was the case

---

[20] Cause 119 of the Constitution of the Kingdom of Nepal, 1990, made the King - the Supreme Commander in Chief of the Royal Nepalese army.

although right from the beginning there was an untold and unofficial understanding that the army was fighting to compel and force the Maoists to negotiate a political settlement. In this effort the army lost 1,014 of its men leaving a scar which may not be easily forgotten by the NA and this psychology may pose difficulties in the integration effort.

During the conflict the army had to live in a very poor physical state in terms of accommodation and other amenities for long in the field, besides the persistent threat to their families at home. No family accommodation could be provided even to those facing highest degree of physical threat. Still the moral of the troops was good and they fought well in all fronts with a few exceptions. The cumulative stress of being on the field for a very long reflected in Human Rights violation charges against the army personnel.

Several things turned around after Jana Andolan II of April 2006 that brought a paradigm shift in political culture and setup. The parliament was reinstated through the royal address on April 24, 2006 and the first session of the house declared Nepal as a Secular Democratic Federal Republic and suspended Monarchy. All the heads of security forces were suspended except for the Army Chief, and change of guard in Army took place after 90 days. An Interim constitution was drafted and Constituent Assembly (CA) elections were successfully conducted; the 240 year old institution of monarchy was abolished; and the CPN (Maoist) emerged as the largest party in the CA.

The paradigm shift in Nepali politics brought in an element of confusion in the army regarding its role, allegiance and direction. The army was placed in a very difficult position then and its effect is very obvious even at present with the post conflict developments.

Loyalty, Political Awareness, Discipline and Morale

Loyalty

The institution had always been guided and directed by centralized power under unitary system with a long culture of serving under the Monarchy. Their unquestionable loyalty towards the King is not true as the army, quite often than not, had changed their loyalty. The Ranas with the support of the army confined the King if not imprisoned him inside the palace and ruled Nepal for 104 years. The last example is the Jana Andolan II that toppled the 240 years old institution of Monarchy, and the RNA did not or could not come to the King's rescue.

Discipline and Political Awareness

Even against all odds the discipline of the army during conflict period was quite up to the mark. The post conflict development has witnessed a shift in the standard of awareness and culture of the traditionally established discipline. The increased education level, speedy changes in the political environment and influence of the fast changing society have affected the army as well. The political awareness in the ranks and file has remarkably increased and the army is more aware about their rights. The rapid expansion in its organization has compromised quality training and in turn the quality of officers and soldiers; a few disciplinary cases are a reflection of this. An example of increased political awareness in the army can be seen with an example of the pattern of vote casted at the Army Headquarter during the CA elections as shown in the table below.

Table 1: Pattern of Votes Casted at the Army Headquarters

Total votes casted	1900
United Marxist-Leninist Party	1400
Nepali Congress party	400
Communist Party Nepal (Maoist)	100

Source: Personal conversations with army personnel

Morale

The following issues have affected the morale of the army:-

a. NA lost 1,014 personnel including a Brigadier General and a Colonel during the conflict. The whereabouts of nine army personnel abducted by the Maoist are still unknown. Some 228 army personnel are disabled and children of 529 army personnel are orphaned.[21]

Medical support that the casualties should be receiving and the education that the orphaned children are entitled to does not seem to be satisfactory due to inadequate budget. For security reasons the families of the army personnel are mostly concentrated in the district administrative headquarters and capital Kathmandu. The limited welfare fund[22] of the army is insufficient to either support the education or treatment of families of the army personnel as with their numbers have increased substantially with the increase in number of troops during the conflict period.

b. During the conflict most of the troops were living on the field and did not require permanent accommodation. Since, the war is over and the peace process is in progress the soldiers need permanent barrack accommodations. As this was not planned earlier and the current locations have limited permanent barracks, the army is facing severe constraints in accommodating the troops.

c. Due to the inconsistency in the fiscal policy of the government the army personnel suffered several curtailments in their allowances and privileges which should have been otherwise during the conflict. Every fiscal year some kind of uncertainty has prevailed in the existing system of retirement financial guarantee scheme. In addition the issue of downsizing in the name of maintaining the right size of the army has raised fears of losing jobs across the ranks and files.

---

[21] Directorate of Human Rights (DoHR), *Human Rights Journal*.(Kathmandu: DoHR, Army Headquarters, 2008),   90-197.

[22] Directorate of Army Welfare Programme,*Kalyankari Darpan*.(Kathmandu: Nepal Army, 2008)

Operational Readiness

a. ***Logistics:*** Due to the conditional clauses of AMMAA, the replenishment of arms and ammunition for the army has become another major issue[23] in keeping the army professionally ready. The army has not been able to import arms, ammunitions, spares and raw material required to manufacture the ammunitions in its factory. This constraint is posing a major problem in the maintenance of the army and even in the conduct of training. The procurement of military hardware needed for UN peacekeeping missions also has faced difficulty (AMMAA Clause 4.2.4).

b. ***Training:*** The training sector of the army has been severely affected as a result of the post conflict development. Controversies over the conditional clauses of CPA and AMMAA have hampered the regular recruitment of the army. The Military Academy is lying vacant in absence of Officer's Cadets after the last batch passed out about a year ago. Similarly the Recruitment Training School is lying vacant for more than a year without a job for the lack of fresh recruits. The situation in other Division Recruitment Training Centres is no different.[24]

Due to the restriction on movement, outdoor training exercises and annual collective exercise are confined to the barrack areas. The field firings have been severely affected both due to restricted area and shortage of ammunitions. The restrictions are imposed

---

[23] Under the AMMAA Clause 4.2.4. Deployment and Concentration of Forces - NA permitted activities includes: Regular training in barracks and camps; Limited live firing activities at designated live firing ranges with 48 hours advance notification to The Joint Monitoring Coordination Committee (JMCC); Regular maintenance and replacement of non-lethal equipment including transport. It further mentions that the Maintenance and replacement of lethal weapons will take place only with the determination of the interim government or agreement by both parties.

[24] Clause 5.1.2 Ceasefire of CPA, 'Both sides shall not recruit additional military forces/ troops, and shall not transport arms, ammunitions and explosives or conduct military activities against each other." Similarly, under the AMMAA - Sub-clause 5.1 Prohibited activities: include recruiting additional armed forces.

both by the CPN (Maoist) and the Joint Monitoring Coordination Committee (JMCC) of UNMIN.[25]

***Defense Budget*:** The post conflict defence budget of the last two years is found to be a little over 5 percent of the total budget. Out of the total budget it is estimated that some 92-95 percent is expended on its regular tasks like rations, salary and allowances, and other routine expenditures. Only 5-7 percent is allotted for skill enhancement and to buy equipment and spares. The table below gives shows the comparative budget allocation in some sectors.

Table 2: Comparative Budget Allocation across Various Ministries of the Government of Nepal

Ministry or Body	FY 2008/09 (in percentages)	FY 2009-2010 in (in percentages)
Ministry of Education	16.56	16.30
Ministry of Health and Population	6.33	6.23
Home Ministry	5.28	5.74
Defence Ministry	5.20	5.45
Ministry of Water Resource	2.52	2.94
Ministry of Agriculture & Cooperatives	2.44	2.75

Source: Report of the Finance Ministry on Estimated Expenditures, 2008/09, www.mof.gov.np

---

[25] The Security Council resolution 1740 (2007) of January 23, 2007, establishing the United Nations Mission in Nepal (UNMIN). Under the Clause 6.1. The Joint Monitoring Coordination Committee (JMCC) of AMMAA: The nine members JMCC will have a chairman appointed by the UN mission, United Nations Mission in Nepal (UNMIN). There will be two vice -Chairmen, one each from the Maoist Army and Nepal Army. The remaining six members will be two UN, two NA and two from Maoist army, all as selected by the parties respectively. The three main functions of JMCC are - central coordinating body for monitoring arms and armies; dispute resolution mechanism; and assist in confidence building.

Civil-Military Relations

The fundamental premise of democratic civil-military relations is that civilian control of the military is clearly possible without democracy, but democracy is not possible without civilian control of the military. However Civil-Military Relations (CMR) is a very new subject in Nepal. Nepal's armed force is comprised of only a land force which is the Nepal army. Although it is considered as an important element of national power it has been looked upon as expensive and defense budget cuts have been advocated.

In recent days enormous political and social changes have come about and the army has continued to be at the forefront as the subject of concern for the polity and civil society. With the socio-political changes the relationship between the army, political parties and the society as a whole is also going through a transition in various dimensions and stages. CMR in recent days has become a dynamic element of governance and also a key component for the stability of the government.

CMR in Nepal has to be looked into and understood within the backdrop of different time periods as the dimensions have changed over time. The army under the patronage of the King remained untouched by civilian authority. After the restoration of multi-party democracy in 1990, the Constitution of the Kingdom of Nepal had ensured civilian control over the army. However, democratic malpractice and misgovernance led to the neglect of army and its needs for over a decade (1991-2003). The party and the government failed to take the Army into confidence even while the Maoist insurgency was growing strongly. The government rather humiliated and deprived the army of its very basic needs (clothing, shelter, training, allowances and facilities) and tried to reduce even their morale. This period is sometime mentioned as the 'decade of the deprived army'. This forced the Army to come close to the King - the Supreme Commander in Chief by Constitution[26], and made the King more powerful.

The paradigm shift in Nepal's politics brought about by the Jan Andolan of 2006 led to the strong existence of communism and the CPN (Maoist)

---

[26] Ibid.

tried to define CMR in terms of civilian supremacy and civilian control, but on their own terms. The concept of "civilian control" as such has never been satisfactorily defined. Samuel P. Huntington in his book *The Soldier and the State: the Theory and Politics of Civil-Military Relations* has described the varieties of civilian control and advanced the theory of objective civilian control in contrast to subjective control.[27]

The legal and institutional restrictions on the military's autonomy had been in practice for a very long time in Nepal, and this kind of subjective civilian control remained strong even after the restoration of democracy in 1990. The process has usually maximized the power of some particular group or groups - like the King and his circle or the political party in government. At the same time the power of military has been minimized through objective civilian control i.e. by professionalizing the Nepal army, rendering the army politically sterile and neutral and preserving the essential elements of power necessary for the existence of the military. In a nutshell it could be said that there existed a kind of mix of both the subjective and the objective civilian control over the army in Nepal.

The CPN (Maoist) led government tried to reduce the power of the military by establishing their party's army, like in totalitarian regime, or at least tried to influence the national army, but lacked the capacity to bring about a shift in the overall power balance with the state force.

In the post conflict phase, there are difficulties in developing a cooperative relationship among three partners in Nepal - the military, the political elites - especially the CPN (Maoist) elites and the citizenry and this needs to be addressed pragmatically.

Democratization of the Nepal army

Democratization of the NA is one of the most talked about and debated issue in the post conflict phase. It is one of the provisions enshrined in the

---

[27] Samuel P. Huntington, *The Soldier and the State: The Theory and Politics of Civil Military Relations,* (Dehradun; Natraj Publishers, 1985)

Interim Constitution of Nepal as well as mentioned in CPA[28] and Army Act 2006. In the post conflict scenario the issue of democratic restructuring reflecting the national and inclusive character has drawn a lot of attention, but the government has not been able to formulate an extensive work plan. If one examines the provision made by the constitution, the Defense Ministry, National Security Council (NSC), Council of Ministers and the Parliamentary Committee are directly involved in the operation and control of the Army. The existing constitutional provisions show that the army is under control of the democratic bodies and hence is democratized.[29]

Here, it will be worthwhile to examine the definition of DCAF (Democratic Control of Armed Forces) DCAF refers to the norms and standards governing the relationship between the armed forces and society, whereby the armed forces are subordinated to democratically-elected authorities and subject to the oversight of the judiciary as well as the media and civil society organizations."[30]

---

[28] 1. Interim Constitution of Nepal 2006 - Part 20 Provisions Regarding the Army; Clause 144. Formation of the Nepal Army: The Council of Ministers shall appoint the Commander-in-Chief of the Nepal Army; The Council of Ministers shall control, mobilize and manage the Nepal Army in accordance with the law; The Council of Ministers shall, with the consent of the political parties and by seeking the advice of the concerned committee of the Legislature-Parliament, formulate an extensive work plan for the democratization of the Nepal Army and implement it; In the case of formulating and implementing the action plan - determination of the appropriate number of the NA, its democratic structure and national and inclusive character shall be developed, and training shall be imparted to the army in accordance with the norms and values of democracy and human rights. 2. CPA, Clause 4-Management of Army and Arms: Mentions about democratization and restructuring of the Army; confinement of Maoist army in temporary cantonments and verification and monitoring by United Nations. Clause 4.7: The Council of Ministers shall control, mobilize and manage the Nepali Army in accordance with the new Military Act; and prepare and implement the detailed action plan for the democratization of the Nepali Army, under this, among other things, right-sizing, democratic restructuring reflecting the national and inclusive character and imparting training to the Nepali Army on the values of democracy and human rights.

[29] Bishnu Sapkota ed, *The Nepali Security Sector: An Almanac.* (Hungary: Brambauer Publishers,2005), 134.

[30] The Geneva Centre for the Democratic Control of Armed Forces (DCAF) was established by the Swiss government in October 2000. The Centre's mission is to promote good governance and security sector reform in accordance with democratic standards. The Centre conducts research on best practices, encourages the development of appropriate norms at the national and international levels, makes policy recommendations and provides in-country advice and assistance programs.

The existing practices in the Army are very much oriented towards the process of democratic governance, and most of the democratic provisions made by the constitution, Nepal Army Act 2063 (2006)[31] and CPA are followed. However, it still has a long way to go to reach to the stage of democratic control according to DCAF.

Inclusiveness

An inclusive character is one of the important parameters in democratizing the Army. The government has passed a new law regarding representation, which envisioned the equal participation of communities and regions that are weak and marginalized. In practice there is no real discrimination in recruitment for any cast, creed, race or ethnic group in the Army. There exists a practice of equal opportunity employment for all Nepali citizens, and ample transparency has been ensured through the representation of the Public Service Commission as a Chairperson or member of the Selection Board. However it is true that there is no proportional representation of all ethnic groups, geographical regions and gender. This has been case due to the ethnic group's preferential choice of service, lack of awareness campaigns and encouragement from the government. The present state of inclusiveness amongst the 92,000 Army personnel is as follows:-

---

[31] The Army Act 2063 (2006) replaced the Army Act 2059 (2002)

Table 3: Ethnic and other Representation in the Nepal Army

Chhetris	42.24%
Janajati (Magars, Newars, Tamangs, Gurungs in majority)	34.85%
Brahmin	11.44%
Dalit (Biswokarma, Damain, Sarki in majority)	6.65%
Thakuri	4.1%
Others	1.39%.
The Terai groups (Madhesi, Tharu, Muslim etc)	6.0%

Note: The representation of female both officer and other ranks is 1,100 which otherwise should be 8,000 as per the new inclusive norms.

Source: Military Record Office, April, 2009

Nevertheless the Nepal army has realized and internalized the sentiment of the people and the policy of the government and has started making its recruitment process more inclusive.

Civilian Supremacy and the Civilian Control

Civilian supremacy and civilian control over the army were the most debated issues during the conflict as well as the post conflict period.

One of the gravest strains on CMR in Nepal was witnessed in July 2002 when the Prime Minister passed an order to mobilize the army against the Maoists following the abduction of police personnel by the insurgents. This did not comply with the provision in the Constitution and the Army neither denied nor obeyed the order. The Prime Minister took it as an offence and as a case of military disobedience to civilian order. According to the Constitution of the Kingdom of Nepal, 1990[32] the army could be mobilized

---

[32] The Constitution of the Kingdom of Nepal 1990, in its clause 118 (2) has spelt that His Majesty shall operate and use the Royal Nepal Army on the recommendation of the National Defence Council. The Interim Constitution of Nepal 2003 has suspended the Constitution of the Kingdom of Nepal 1990.

only by the King based on the recommendation made by the National Defense Council headed by the Prime Minister. The case could be debated.

As a post conflict development, CMR during the CPN (Maoist) led government further deteriorated in 2008, and reached the stage of an institutional confrontation between the government and the army. Even the nation seems divided over the issue of the dismissal of the Army Chief by the government and his subsequent reinstatement by the President's decree on the same day.[33] This case raised the row to its apex and culminated with the fall of Maoist led government over the issue of civilian supremacy. In the post conflict development and especially the nine months period of CPN (Maoist) led government, Nepal experienced the worst ever civil-military relations in its history. The rational of government action and the justification of President's step could be debated.

Human Rights Issue and the Nepal Army

The army has been blamed by the Nepal based Office of the United Nations High Commissioner for Human Rights (OUNHCR), National Human Rights Commission (NHRC), ICRC and other human rights activists for violating Human Rights (HR) during the period of conflict. The alleged high profile HR incidents that have drawn national and international attention are the case of extra judicial killing of a teenaged girl Maina Sunuwar and the case of disappearance of 49 Maoist activists from custody. The Army is facing a lot of pressure at home and from the international community and is finding difficulties in clearing itself from the stigma of HR violations.

The officers and men found guilty of HR violations have been punished as per the Military Act that includes 14 personnel from UN missions and 67 personnel alleged during the conflict. The army has forwarded justifications for 2,688 cases out of the 4,381 allegations; and this clarification amounts to 58.6% of the entire allegations made.

---

[33] General Rookmangad Katwal, the Chief of the Army Staff of the Staff of NA, a commoner by background but protected by royal palace became most controversial chief the NA ever had. He did not save the king and the institution of centuries old monarchy of Nepal. He survived the difficult days of Maoist led government and retired on September 2009 after completing his term in office.

These cases definitely have some adverse effect on the morale of the army personnel. Nevertheless, the army learned the lessons in a hard way and has taken precautionary as well as awareness building measures through training and education on HR, enforcement of Rule of Engagement (ROE) and proper documentation. The establishment of a Directorate of Human Rights as a separate body simply proves the seriousness the Nepal army has shown towards HR issues.

Conclusion

The changing social structure, philosophy of life, cultural norms and values and the psyche of the society brought about by post conflict development and political changes have also affected the army's various sectors.

Keeping the army is definitely not a cost-effective venture but when one makes a cost-benefit analysis, the benefit a nation gets far outweighs the cost. The Nepal army remained apolitical during the conflict and continues to remain so firmly. There are examples in our region of the army has undermining civilian control and acquiring great political power, but the NA has never shown such ambition in the past and is not likely to do so even in future.

Culturally, NA is conservative by nature. It remained isolated from foreigners and politics. Hence it is reluctant to come in contact with the public. In the post conflict phase NA needs to convey its opinion on issues of national importance as well as raise awareness about its activities.

During the conflict when the NA operated under the provision of Unified Command with the police forces, HR cases had been drastically reduced due to proper record keeping. NA wishes not to be singled out on the HR issue and believes that both the warring parties the Maoist and NA have to be brought to the book. Hence, the formation of a High-level Truth and Reconciliation Commission may do the needful and is also favored by NA.[34]

---

[34] Article 33 (f) of Interim Constitution has set the provision of Truth and Reconciliation Commission; Clause 5.2.5. of CPA - Management of Army and Arms:Both sides agree to set up with mutual consent a High-level Truth and Reconciliation Commission in order to probe into those involved in serious violation of human rights and crime against humanity in course of the armed conflict for creating an atmosphere for reconciliation in the society.

NA has always shown its willingness towards democratic control of their affairs and prefers to constitutional control over the practice of civilian control. NA must obey/oblige to all orders/duties coming from the Government of Nepal authority that complies with the provision made under the Constitution. This is even more important in the transitional period. NA wishes to preserve its institutional interest and is concerned about being politicized in the name of democratization.

As the issue of integration of the Maoist army combatants cannot be avoided, it needs to be addressed and managed professionally. The effort should be to integrate a minimum number in security bodies. The government must develop a strategy of counseling and encouraging the combatants to reintegrate into the society with various attractive packages and jobs after skill training.

NA is a society within the society but the Nepali society and the NA are mutually inclusive. People have internalized the value of NA as the last resort and thus want this institution to be the best in term of democratic norms, transparency, loyalty, accountability, and apolitical character. This is the reason why even a small incident or issue regarding the army draws the attention of the public. The NA should take it positively and try to understand the positive concern and sentiment shown by the people.

The proper definition of the democratization and role definition of NA, its size, structure, and military rules have not materialized yet causing delay in the democratic reform of NA. this underlines the importance of drawing out extensive work plans and their implementation. An enhancement of CMR need not be emphasized more in the changed context of Nepal. Civilian supremacy will prevail only when the new constitution of Nepal is drafted in time, and law and order and stability prevail.

The objective should be to develop a competent professional army that is able to contribute to policymaking in national security but not dominate it; stand as a formidable force in time of need; be a savior of the citizens and work hand-in-hand with the people of Nepal for a peaceful future.

Annexure 1

Source: Directorate of Public Relations. 2008. *The Nepalese Army a Force with History Ready for Tomorrow.* Kathmandu: Nepal Army Headquarters.

CONFLICT IN NEPAL: IMPACT ON ENVIRONMENT AND ITS CROSS-BORDER IMPLICATIONS

B.C. Upreti

Plural societies, authoritarian and dictatorial political systems and discriminatory and underdeveloped economies which are faced with several complex situations are prone to various types of horizontal and vertical conflicts. In countries where all these factors are combined together conflicts become more vibrant and intensive in nature. In such cases the settlement of conflicts and building peace on a sustained basis becomes a vital aspect of the process of nation-building. Social inequalities and social discriminations, authoritarianism, exclusive nature of the democratic political systems, failure of the governments in delivering goods and realizing basic needs of the people, inequalities, economic disparities and discriminatory development, *etc.* have been the major causes of conflicts in most of the cases. It is thus clear that conflict is the manifestation of differing situations, perceptions, attitudes and approaches of groups/communities within a society. It occurs due to different views, ideologies and beliefs about a particular situation.

It is not surprising that the south Asian states have faced many violent conflicts. In some instances these conflicts have led to the eventual disintegration of the state. Social complexities and backwardness, economic disparities and underdevelopment and absence of inclusive democratic governance have given rise to various conflicts in the region. However, what is important is that, due to geographical compactness and continuity and socio-cultural linkages, these conflicts have cross-country implications.

Although Nepal has faced several conflicts over time, they were contained by the authoritarian rulers through the use of coercive powers. The socio-economic and political discriminations and disparities were for long being pushed under the carpet of authoritarian rule.[1]. After the 1990 democratic change it was expected that an inclusive political system and equitable and just socio-economic order would help realizing needs and aspirations of the people. Unfortunately, the democratic governments of the day neither succeeded in giving way to an inclusive democracy and the transformation of the feudal-hierarchal socio-economic order nor in realizing the rising aspirations of the people. It was not merely the question of failure of the democratic governments in the post-1990 phase in delivering goods, but the continuation of the political dominance of the monarchy and the perpetuation of the feudal social order that had become a source of discontent. It annoyed the leftist forces particularly the hardcore communists who were against the continuation of the monarchic and feudal state.[2] It may be noted here that in the 1990 nationwide democratic movement, all the political forces including the communists had extended their full support to the movement but the hardcore communists were soon disillusioned by the nature and dynamics of democratic governance. They, however, utilized the democratic space for raising a war against the state that ultimately culminated into the Maoist insurgency beginning in early 1996.

The Maoist insurgency that continued for almost a decade proved to be a phase of deep structural crisis in Nepal affecting every dimension of the Nepalese society.[3] In the post 2006 period considerable efforts have been made towards creating conditions for peace, stability and democracy in the country. One has to take note of the fact that the restructuring of a post-conflict society requires a well founded strategy of peace building. To what extent the post-conflict Nepalese state has been able to do that is a

---

[1] B.C. Upreti, "State and Society in Nepal: the Emerging Issues of their Restructuring and Transformation", *Indian Journal of Nepalese Studies*, XIII (2007): 33- 40.

[2] B.C.Upreti, *Nepal: Democracy at the Cross Roads: Post 1990 Dynamics, Issues and Challenges*, (New Delhi: Kanishka, 2007), 15- 45.

[3] For a detailed discussion see, Deepak Thapa and Bandita Sijapati, *A Kingdom Under Siege, Nepal's Maoists Insurgency, 1996- 2003,*(Kathmandu: Printhouse, 2003).

different issue. However, a broad based strategy needs proper understanding of the implications of the conflict and the ways and means to overcome the damages done by the conflict.

Any conflict of the nature of a protracted war is bound to have wide ranging implications for the society, economy and polity. One vital aspect of the implications of a conflict in modern times is the impact on the environment. In fact, it is now being realized that the conflicts have highly devastating impacts on the environment. There is a closer nexus between conflict and environment and peace building needs to incorporate the diverse aspects of environmental regeneration. The shared nature of the eco-system and some of the natural resources in particular in a compact geographical region, result in cross border implications of a conflict within a state. This chapter outlines the impact of the Maoist conflict on the environment in Nepal.

Maoist Conflict in Nepal: An Overview

Nepal suffered the worst kind of conflict in the form of the Maoist insurgency that has no parallels in the recent political history of the country. The 'people's war,' an armed uprising by the Maoist extremists began in February 1996 in four districts of western Nepal but by the end of 2001 it had expanded to most parts of the country thereby posing a major challenge to security and stability of the country. The Maoist insurgency was a reflection upon the complex nature of the Nepalese state and society and the deep rooted contradictions that it was faced with.[4] Several factors are behind the rise of the Maoist conflict in Nepal. These factors include a long list starting from variations in infra-structural development; poverty; un-employment; lack of fulfillment of basic needs; class, caste and region based disparities and discriminations; highly centralized power structure; exclusive political representation; development mismatch and failure to denial of access to and control over production resources; Nepal's failed development; false impression of a monolithic society; social divides and political mishandlings; radical ideological orientation; operational contradictions within democratic

---

[4] B. C. Upreti, "Dealing with Maoists: Nepal's Experience with Peace Negotiations" in Manas Chatterji and B.M.Jain eds. *Conflict and Peace in South Asia*, (Bingley, UK: Emerald, 2008), 213- 215

political parties and power politics and opportunism.[5] The Maoist insurgency was basically targeted against the state and the institutions, parties, groups and individuals having an alliance with the feudalistic state in one form or the other. It should be noted that in most of the cases of prolonged insurgencies it is the common people, the youth, and the weaker sections of the society which become victims of the conflict. This has also been the case with Nepal in the last decade.

The Maoist Movement grew over the years in terms of its capabilities, strength, influence, strategies, and violent operations.[6] In fact, one may argue that the Maoist insurgency had reached a critical stage and succeeded in paralyzing the Nepalese economy, society and polity in a big way. The Maoist movement of Nepal took advantage of the prevailing socio-economic and political conditions in the country and grew into a strong movement, sustained itself, and reached a stage of challenging the state apparatus. It is true that the Maoists had linkages with a number of international revolutionary organizations. Nevertheless, it is a fact that the Maoist revolutionaries of Nepal cultivated strong constituencies, took possession of arms and finances by force, raised their army of young and committed revolutionaries, and in ten years time brought nearly one third of the country under their influence.[7] The Maoist movement flared up in Nepal at a time when the international communist movement was experiencing a low profile.

The demands of the Maoists could be understood at two levels: Firstly, the socio-economic agenda, which was related to the issues of socio-economic reforms, equality, and distributive justice. Secondly, the political

---

[5] See, Arjun Karki and David Seddon, *The People's War in Nepal*, (Delhi: Adroit Publishers, 2003); Bishnu Raj Upreti, *Armed Conflict and Peace Process in Nepal*, (Delhi: Adroit Publishers, 2006); Uddhav P. Pyakurel, *Maoists Movement in Nepal: A Sociological Perspective*, (Delhi: Adroit Publishers, 2007); B.C. Upreti, *Maoists in Nepal, From Insurgency to Political Mainstream*, (Delhi: Kalpaz, 2008); B.C. Upreti, *Nepal, Transition to Democratic-Republican State*, (Delhi : Kalpaz, 2010).

[6] See Panch N. Maharjan, "The Maoists Insurgency and Crisis of Governability in Nepal ", in Dhrub Kurmar ed., *Domestic Conflict and Crisis of Governability in Nepal*, (Kathmandu: Centre for Nepal and Asian Studies, 2000).

[7] B.C. Upreti, *Maoists in Nepal, From Insurgency to Political Mainstream*, (Delhi: Kalpaz, 2008).

agenda related to transformation of the Nepalese political system by converting it into a Republican State. It would have been possible for the Nepalese state to deal with the Maoists separately on these two types of agendas. A strong economic package would have diluted the propensity of the movement. It would have also minimized the social bases of the Maoists. It may also be argued here that movement or no movement; socio-economic transformation should have been the primary agenda of any government after the establishment of democracy in Nepal. The absence of good governance in the post 1990 period gave strength and justification to the movement. In fact, the issue of offering an economic package to the Maoists had come up in 2001, but the government did not agree to it. The question of the Constituent Assembly and a republican constitution has not been new to Nepal. These demands have been raised repeatedly since 1950. Why should the ruling elite and political parties feel shy about taking up these issues for a wider consideration? Is it not possible to initiate a public debate on these issues and create a national consensus over their implementation or rejection? It appears that the narrow political interest and divisive politics came in the way of discussing these issues. The Maoists took advantage of this divisiveness and raised a movement on that basis. The Maoists succeeded easily in tapping the discontent among the ethnic groups, Dalits, women, Madhesi's and the youth in general. It was due to the support of these groups that Maoists could easily hit back at the state of Nepal which was considered to be largely responsible for discrimination and the elite who were regarded as exploiters and profiteers.

There was a stage when Maoists had acquired a lot of sympathy and support, mainly in the countryside, particularly due to their stand against social abuses. However, gradually the popularity of the Maoists was at stake. People were fed up with the continuous strikes, violence, threats, forced inclusion of young children in the Maoist army, and economic hardships. They feared being killed either by the army or the Maoists. The people in the countryside realized that even the Maoists had not been able to do anything better. The Maoists gradually lost the earlier earned popularity in the countryside. However, they did not lose control. Despite resentment among the people in rural areas, they continued to control vast areas.

Since the first ceasefire by the Maoists in August 2001 till the end of the last round of talks between the Maoists and the government in November, 2001, there was sufficient scope for a negotiated settlement to the problem. But neither the government, the Maoists, the democratic political parties and nor the civil society of Nepal could take initiative. While the two negotiating groups remained adamant on their respective positions, political parties and the civil society organizations were less concerned or had no solution to the problem. The situation changed drastically with the declaration of state emergency in November, 2001 and the subsequent deployment of the Royal Nepalese Army for the containment of the Maoists. The state of emergency not only resulted in more powers for the army but also resulted in the curtailment of press and political freedom. The conflict became more violent and intensive in the years following the government's emphasis on finding a military solution.

The escalation of the protracted war also gave an opportunity to the monarchy after mid 2001, when a new King took over the thrown, to hit back at the government for its failure and incapability in handling the conflict situation. The elected government of Sher Bahadur Deuba was dismissed by King Gyanendra in October 2002, on the grounds of its failure to hold general elections on time and manage the Maoist conflict. It was clear that the monarchy was trying to consolidate its political powers and position by taking advantage of the conflict situation. The second round of peace talks in 2003 also failed, although the King himself had shown interest in initiating the peace negotiations.

The political ambitions of king Gyanendra became evident when he assumed all powers in early 2005.[8] The authoritarian rule of the monarch, abuse of power and authority, control over civic liberty, freedom and rights, use of state power to control unfavorable civil behavior, *etc.* made political parties realize that the monarchy was the main stumbling block for democracy. It led to the formation of a Seven Party Alliance to fight against authoritarianism and restore democracy. The Maoists developed an understanding with the democratic political parties and agreed to join the

---

[8] B.C. Upreti, "Will the Monarchy Survive?", *Seminar,* 548, (2005): 17- 20.

constitutional and democratic path for the realization of their goals. They declared a ceasefire and lent their support to the democratic parties in raising the second democratic movement in April 2006. The CPN (Maoist) and the Seven Party Alliance (SPA) developed an understanding over the issues of republican state, Constituent Assembly and secular – federal state. The Maoists joined political mainstream in the post 2006 period. The interim constitution of early 2007 and the Maoist entry to the interim government, the emergence of the CPN (M) as the largest party in 2008 Constitutional Assembly elections, the formation of the Maoist government and then the fall of the Maoist government in late 2009 were all dramatic developments and of challenges.[9] Despite political understanding and peace process there was always a lingering fear of a return to the conflict situation. However, one may agree that the Maoist movement gave a new direction to Nepalese politics.

It may also be pointed out here that any conflict is bound to have adverse socio-economic and other implications. While the socio-economic impacts of a conflict can be much more devastating and wide-ranging, the impact of a conflict on the environment is equally important. This chapter outlines the impact of the Maoist conflict on the environment in Nepal.

Conflict and Environment: Some Issues

Human beings are an integral part of the eco-system. The activities of the human beings, constructive or destructive, are bound to affect the environment in either way. The human history is full of evidences of conflicts that have plundered the environment. There are three important aspects of the impact of conflict on environment. Firstly, the nature and intensity of environmental degeneration due to a conflict would depend upon the intensity and longevity of the conflict itself.[10] Secondly, the conflict may have direct as well as indirect implications for the environment. Thirdly, it is not

---

[9] See, B. C. Upreti, "Challenges in the Post Election Scenario in Nepal ", *Economic and Political Weekly*, March 14, 2009: 23- 25.

[10] Mark L. Murphy, Krishna P. Oli & Steve Gorzula, "Conservation in Conflict: the Impact of the Maoist- Government Conflict on Conservation and Biodiversity in Nepal ", IISD Publications, 2005, http://www.iisd.org/pdf/2005/security_conservation_nepal.pdf

necessary that the conflict would have negative consequences only, there can be certain positive impacts as well depending upon the goals and strategies of the conflict. However, it can be said that the positive consequences are minimal in comparison to the negative consequences of a violent conflicts.

Most of the theoretical propositions regarding the interlinkages between the conflict and the environment are concerned with the environment related conflicts.[11] In fact environment related conflicts have increased in our times and have acquired a place in the development agenda of nation states. Land grabbing or green conflict, illegal settlements, occupation of forest areas, dependence on forest based resources, resettlement and displacement, sharing and utilization of renewable natural resources, exploitation and control of mineral resources etc. are major issues in environmental conflicts.

Environmental conflicts may be caused due to a number of factors[12] such as:-

1. Scarcity of natural resources caused largely due to population pressure.

2. Uneven distribution of resources.

3. Control over natural resources.

4. Exploitation and sharing of natural resources.

5. Abundance of resources leading to their misuse.

Environmental hazards caused by a violent conflict provide an entirely different dimension of the linkages between conflict and environment. The

---

[11] See, Thomas Homer-Dixon, *Environment, Scarcity and Violence,* (Princeton, Princeton University Press:1999)

[12] For detailed explanations see, Bishnu Raj Uprety, *Nepal's Armed Conflict: Security Implications for Development and Resource Governance,* (Kathmandu: Swiss National Center of Competence in Research, 2006), 2-4. Also see, David Seddon & K. Hussein, *The Consequences of Conflict: Livelihood and Development in Nepal, ODI Working Paper* 185 (2002).

impact of the conflict on environment can be multi-dimensional involving the following issues:

1. Destruction of natural resources due to a war like situation.

2. Excessive exploitation of natural resources and bio-diversity by the conflicting groups in order to raise funds.

3. Misuse of conflict situation by vested groups for smuggling and illicit trade in natural resources and bio-diversity.

4. Displacement and resettlement of people from conflict affected areas.

There are several examples where conflict has caused serious environmental hazards. Examples can be traced back to the Vietnam War where the US army had dropped chemicals that devastated vast areas of Vietnam's countryside causing genetic disabilities. In the 1990's, civil strife caused environmental hazards in many countries such as Algeria, Angola, Burundi, Chad, Democratic Republic of Congo, Uganda, Eritrea, Ethiopia, Nigeria, Senegal, Sierra Leone, Liberia, etc.[13] In Afghanistan in 2002, people displaced by the conflict fled to remote areas where they began to over-exploit the natural resources. During the Kosovo conflict, 50 industrial sites were bombed in Serbia causing environmental problems. In South Asia also conflicts of various sorts have been causing environmental degeneration such as in Sri Lanka, India and Pakistan.

Keeping in view the widespread environmental consequences of conflicts, the UN has launched the UN Environment Programme and environmental regeneration is gradually becoming an important aspect of peace processes.

---

[13] For some case studies relating to the fallout of conflict see, Darry D'. Monte, "The Environmental Fallout of Conflict", *Infochange-environment*, March 2010, http://infochangeindia.org/Environment/Eco-logic/The-environmental-fallout-of-conflict.html; Jeff Dorsey & Steven Opeitum, "The Net Economic Cost of the Conflict in the Acholiland Sub Region of Uganda", Civil Society Organisations for Peace in Northern Uganda (CSOPNU), Kampala September 2002, http//www.csopnu.net, accessed on May 13 2010; Amanuel Mehreteab, *Wake Up Hanna! Reintegration and Reconstruction Challenges for Post War Eritrea,* (Asmara, Eritrea: Red Sea Press, 2004).

Impact of the Maoist Conflict on the Environment

Nepal has been an agrarian economy with over 80 percent of the people dependent on agriculture for their livelihood. The land distribution has been inequitable[14] and poor people live on lands that measure less than one hectare which can hardly support a family's needs. There is intense and widespread competition for available natural resources, leading to conflict for space, ownership and control. At the same time fast depletion of resources, the rapidly increasing population, the faulty land distribution system, insecure tenancy rights, etc have caused problems particularly for the tenant farmers and agricultural laborers. It has resulted in increasing pressure on natural resources leading to the environmental conflict.[15]

It is true that the degree of human reliance on the environment differs from place to place. The situation is quite different in the Nepalese hills. The lives of people in the Nepalese hills depend on natural resources to a large extent. However, the region is quite inaccessible, fragile and diverse and their capacity to adapt to changes in the eco-system is poor. As such the environment carrying capacity of the hills is quite low. With repeated and high-intensity use of limited resources the chances of damage to the environment become quite high.[16] The utilization of mountain resources has resulted in deforestation, soil degradation, erosion, flooding, etc. The increased demand for food exerts high pressure on the available land. In the mountains, agriculture is almost non-existent, while the hills that occupy more than 60 percent of Nepal's land area offer only 35 percent cultivated

---

[14] G.R. Aryal and G. Awasthi, "Agrarian Reform and Access to Land Resources in Nepal: Present Status and Future Perspective Action", Philippines, Environment, Culture, Agriculture, Research and Development Society (ECARDS)—Nepal: 2003, http://www.cerai.es/fmra/archivo/nepal.pdf

[15] See, Jugal Bhurtel & Saleem H. Ali, "The Green Roots of Red Rebellion: Environmental Degradation and the Rise of the Maoists Movement in Nepal ",Vermont,University of Vermont: 2003, http://www.uvm.edu/~shali/Maoist.pdf

[16] See, Pitamber Sharma, *Draft Sectoral Reports on Sustainable Development Agenda for Nepal:Mountain Development, Sustainable Community Development Programme*,International Centre for Integrated Mountain Development, ICIMOD Kathmandu, Nepal, 2002

land.[17] This makes it clear that the opportunity for farming is far less in Nepal, except in Terai, due to inadequate precipitation, low temperature in mountains, infertile land and inadequate means of irrigation. The livelihood of rural people depends largely on forests and hence the forests of Nepal are one of the most exploited natural resources. According to one estimate, only 21 percent of the total land area of Nepal is under forest cover. The eco-system of Nepal is very fragile and people depend heavily on natural resources. Therefore, any conflict is bound to have wider consequences for the environment.

It can be said that the Maoist insurgency acquired the characteristics of a protracted war and it had wide ranging consequences for the environment in Nepal. However, in the garb of the conflict a number of vested interests, persons and groups also took advantage of the situation and exploited the environment for their own benefits and interests. Some of the areas where the impact of the Maoist movement was visible are as following:-

1. Impact on the Protected Areas

The development of national parks as protected forest areas and wildlife conservation began in Nepal in 1973. The use of resources from these protected areas is regulated to promote sustainability. Nearly 18.33 percent of the total land area of Nepal is under protected area status.[18] The Royal Nepalese Army was positioned in these areas to prevent poaching and illicit trade of wildlife species. These areas also became target of the Maoist attacks due to the presence of the army. The Maoists also began their assault on the infrastructure of protected areas by destroying and outlying guard posts and forest offices. These were in the remote areas and vulnerable hence the guards and other forest staff were constrained to leave these places. After November 2001 the army was withdrawn from these protected areas. Prior to the Maoist attacks there were 112 guards in

---

[17] Pradyumna P. Karan and Hiroshi Ishii, *Nepal: A Himalayan Kingdom in Transition,* (Tokyo: UNU Press, 1996), 40-66

[18] Ministry of Forests and Soil Conservation, *Nepal Biodiversity Strategy,* Government of Nepal, 2002.

protected forest areas. It was reduced to 34 by 2002.[19] In some of the protected forest areas like Makalu – Barun National Park and Dhorpatan Hunting Reserve, which were not properly guarded, the Maoists established their training camps.

The attacks on infrastructure in the protected forest areas, occupation of these forest areas by the Maoists training their cadres, and the withdrawal of forest guards due to the threat from the Maoists made these protected areas insecure. This resulted in the decline of tourists. Some of the reserve sanctuaries of Nepal have been of famous the world over and have attracted tourists from around the world. Tourism has been a major source of foreign currency earnings. After 2001, there was a decrease of 50 percent in tourism in national parks.

---

[19] Pralad Yonzon, "The Wounds of Neglect", *Habitat Himalayan*, IX, No. 1 (2002)

The Problems in National Parks

Source: DHPWC Annual Report 2003 in Mark L Murphy et.el Conversation in
Conflict, IISD< Manitoba, Canada, October 2005

2. Loss of Bio-diversity

The Maoists conflict also caused loss of biodiversity in the wildlife sanctuaries and other protracted forest areas primarily due to the withdrawal of security forces and officials from there due to the fear of the Maoists. It was reported that a large number of Asian one horned Rhinos were pouched between 2001-2004 in Royal Bardia National Park and Royal Chitwan National Park which are world famous for these species. Wildlife smuggling increased tremendously from 1998-2003.[20] A number of reports appeared during 2001-2005 indicating increase of smuggling of precious wildlife species.

3. Setback to Community Forests

In Nepal community forestry has emerged over the years as a highly successful strategy for the regeneration of the forests.[21] It involves handing over of user rights and management of the forests areas to local people who have been traditionally using the forests for various purposes. It incorporates localized control over forest resources, so that a proper balance is maintained between resource utilization and management. The conflict was a serious setback for this form of forest conservation. The breakdown of law and order threatened community forestry institutions. Some of them even stopped functioning due to the fear of the Maoists. The Maoist conflict adversely affected employment and funding in conservation and development sector and many poverty reduction programmes were affected.

In some areas the Maoists had forced the NGO's working for community forestry and the Community Forestry User's Groups (CFUG) to register with the people's government so that they could keep a track of the flow of funds to these organizations and levy taxes on them. The government of Nepal imposed taxes on revenues earned by the CFUG. As a reaction to this the Maoists took over the Community Forestry Users

---

[20] See, Ek Raj Sigdel, "Poaching- How to Fight It", *The Kathmandu Post*, March 6, 2003; K.C. Shandip , "Nepal Still a Hotspot for Illegal Wildlife Traders", *The Kathmandu Post* , April 27, 2002.

[21] Mark, L. Murphy et.al, Conservation in Conflict, 2005

Groups in some areas by expelling elected members and replacing them with their own men. According to a report, the Maoists had allegedly seized 210 of 255 community forests in Achham district alone.[22] Such incidents had been reported in other areas as well.

The State of Community Forests in Nepal

Year of Community Takeover	Number of User Groups	Hectares of Forest Handed Over	Number of Households Involved
1988	1	27	53
1989	10	567	35
1990	42	1973	1115
1991	87	5012	4492
1992	349	20845	12973
1993	737	52121	36214
1994	1225	88763	80944
1995	1655	120818	142839
1996	1763	156899	178670
1997	1588	133695	196614
1998	1442	135767	177366
1999	1156	100027	168770
2000	1067	90714	135406
2001	841	83600	121746
2002	592	50667	93827
2003	557	40833	62230
2004	430	32449	49109

Source: Department of Forestry, Nepal, 2004.

---

[22] Ibid.

4. Problem of Pollution

There were also problems of pollution in many areas. Dead bodies of the people killed in the attacks in many areas like Pili, Beni, Solukhumbu, Dang, *etc.* were thrown away in rivers and forests and the decomposed bodies led to pollution around the deposed areas. Further, land mines laid by the Maoists also polluted these areas. Security forces would set the forests on fire in areas where the insurgents were suspected to be hiding. Such forest firing not only damaged flora and fauna but also polluted the environment.

5. Impact on Genetic Resources

The conflict had caused severe disruption of the farming system and seed flow mechanisms, besides disturbing forest management, encroaching on forest land and exploiting non timber forest products, rare species of flora and fauna. There was over exploitation of some high value medicinal plants (e.g., Yarsagumba, Kudki, Sugandhawal,etc.) by rebels for the economic benefits. It was reported that the Maoists were engaged in collecting these high value herbs in order to raise funds. It also gave opportunity to the smugglers to over exploit the bio-diversity for illicit trade.

6. Conflict over Land Resources

Land is considered to be a symbol of power, prestige and social status in the rural areas. It is because of this reason that there have always been instances of power brokers and local elites capturing valuable land resources by using their networks and connections in the government and the traditional power structures. In Nepal too land is one of the major means of exploitation and it was obvious that land became the most prominent target of the Maoists. They evicted all local landlords and village elites from their villages and captured their land. In the Maoist controlled areas, they distributed the lands of landlords to poor people but these poor were not able to utilize the situation for the fear of security forces. The local landlords were not able to cultivate their lands which led to the under utilization of the scarce resource. Commercial farming had been either controlled or disturbed by the Maoists and such control had ultimately forced the commercial farmers to leave the areas. Rich and medium commercial farmers were facing continuous pressure to pay to the Maoists huge amounts of money. Such extortion had greatly affected commercial farming such as tea gardens, fruit gardens, livestock farming, cardamom growing, broom grass and ginger growing, *etc.*

Investment in agriculture sector by the Agriculture Development Bank (ADB) and other financial institutions had decreased due to the uncertain conditions created by the Maoist conflict. It became extremely difficult for the ADB staff to visit fields, as the insurgents were against ADB loans and they had damaged several branches of the bank and destroyed their documents. Many farmers could not return bank loans due to loss of their business. Big farmers and entrepreneurs were not ready to take the risk of investing in agriculture due to insecurity.

7. Problem of Safety of Conservation Organizations

The escalation of the Maoist violence after 2001 caused the withdrawal of staff from many NGO's and field organizations to district headquarters. Some organizations stopped their work temporarily. There were incidents of extortion, kidnapping and murders. The organizations that became victims of the conflict were CARE Nepal, German Technical Cooperation (GTZ), DANIDA, SDC, CIDA, Peace Corps Nepal, DFID, etc. The withdrawal of these NGO's or disruption of their activities had an indirect impact on the environment as many of them were involved in programmes supporting environmental protective measures.

Cross-border Implications

Environmental degeneration cannot remain confined within the boundaries of a state and the cross – country impacts are obvious where more countries are part of a compact ecological zone.

The impact of the Maoist conflict on the environment of Nepal also had its implications on Indo – Nepal relations. The two countries share the Himalayan river system. Nepal is rich in river water resources and it is next to Mexico in terms of hydro – power potential. India can cooperate with Nepal for the utilization of river water resources thereby benefiting both the countries in several ways. However, the sharing of the river water resources has been a complex issue between India and Nepal.[23] Maoists made this issue much more complex by strongly reacting against the Indo–Nepal cooperation for water resources development. The Maoists considered India as an imperialist power. They termed all the treaties concluded between India and Nepal unequal and hence demanded that these treaties be scraped. This adversely affected the water resources development cooperation between India and Nepal. Some of the ongoing projects got delayed due to the conflict.

The implementation of water resources development projects such as the Mahakali Treaty had become difficult due to the ongoing conflict in Nepal. Although, it is difficult to say that the Maoists insurgency alone was responsible, the Maoists had taken a strong position against it. The Karnali and Sapt Kosi projects also met the same fate. The floods from Kosi and Gandak rivers have been a perennial problem for the Indian plains in Bihar.[24] It is a fact that the floods in Bihar cause loss of human lives, loss of livestock, livelihood and homelessness. Further agricultural land is submerged and the sand-castings due to floods create problems for further cropping. These rivers also cause devastating floods in Nepal's Tarai as well. India's strategy of building embankments to prevent floods has been questioned by Nepal. It is not only India which has to face the sorrow of Kosi but the Nepal Terai is equally devastated by these floods. The Maoists blamed India for causing floods in Nepal Terai due to constructions of embankments on its side and tried to make it a hot political issue. The Maoists strongly condemned India's flood preventive measures. The problem of floods is a complex issue. It needs proper management and active cooperation between the two countries. But the Maoists created such an atmosphere that nothing could

---

[23] B.C. Upreti, *Politics of Himalayan River Waters*, (Delhi: Nirala, 2003)

[24] See, Rameshwar R. Iyer, "Floods, Himalayan Rivers, Nepal: Some Heresies", *The Economic Political Weekly*, November 15, 2008; Dinesh Kumar Mishra, "The Kosi and the Gandak Story", *Economic & Political Weekly*, November 15, 2008; Rajiv Sinha, "Kosi: Rising Waters, Dynamic Channels and Human Disasters", *Economic & Political Weekly*, November 15, 2008.

be done to prevent floods from Kosi and other rivers. The Maoist continued with these postures over water issues even after 2006. It may also be noted here that India and Nepal share the great Himalayan ranges which are considered to be sensitive and fragile. Any sort of environmental degeneration is bound to adversely affect the ecology of the Indian plains. Hence the implications of a conflict on the environment in Nepal also have its implications for India.

To conclude, one may state that any conflict is bound to have an impact on the environment. The intensity of the environmental fallout of a conflict depends on the nature and dynamics of the conflict. The Maoists conflict in Nepal had wide ranging consequences on the environment as is discussed above. The conflict situation also provides the scope for individuals and groups to exploit natural resources and biodiversity for their benefits thereby causing great harm to flora, fauna and wildlife resources. It is necessary that the environmental linkages of an armed conflict be realized by the stakeholders of peace, stability and democracy.

The environmental fallouts of a violent conflict can have cross-border implications where the natural resources are shared by the concerned countries. It not only results in the loss of resources and adverse impacts due to their mismanagement but also creates rifts in the relations between countries. It is for this reason that the environmental linkages of a conflict become a much more sensitive issue. On the whole it is clear that the Maoist conflict had several direct and indirect implications for the environment in Nepal. These issues become much more important when natural resources, the bio diversity and the flora and fauna are a source of earning for a majority of the people. Hence the management and conservation of the eco-system is an important element in any post-conflict phase and should be considered vital to the search for sustainable peace.

CONFLICT IN NEPAL AND ITS TRANSNATIONAL RAMIFICATIONS

Anjoo Sharan Upadhyaya

Violent conflict and state fragility are major development challenges: conflict causes misery, destroys communities and infrastructure, and can cripple economic prospects.

World Development Report 2011

Nepal has been in throe of political turmoil spanning over six decades, frequently igniting conflicts between people and the state as also between different groups.[1] Mostly waged around the unquenched demand of democracy and development, these conflicts marked an intense jostling for political power by various social and political entities. By the nineties these conflictual impulses proliferated to the common masses across regional and socioeconomic barriers. The depth and breadth of people's involvement came out vividly during the so-called people's war, spearheaded by the Maoists during 1996-2006. This violent transference in people's movement successfully brought on board the hitherto neglected demands of progress, justice and inclusion in the public discourse as also the state policies.[2]The transition from people being treated as 'subjects' thriving on state dispensed

---

[1] Major flashpoints in this continuum were the Jan Andolan-I 1990 and the Jan Andolan –II 2006.

[2] Mahendra Lawoti, "Managing Conflicts between the Society and the State: Explorations into Class and Identity Issues" in Nepal , D.B. Gurung ed., *Nepal Tomorrow Voices & Visions,* (Kathmandu: Koselee Prakashan, 2003), 81.

welfare to the assertion of their legitimate rights as 'citizens' has been quite an achievement in the erstwhile Himalayan Kingdom. This critical shift is often acknowledged by analysts as one of the positive attributes of the conflict in Nepal.

However the decade long armed conflict in Nepal has engendered a range of consequences which are yet to be thrashed out. The detractors for instance highlight the ominous portents of the conflict and how it has crippled the development and governance imperatives. The ambiguities in Maoists agenda and the frustrating pace of the peace process have disillusioned those who had found transformative prospects in the people's war. While the polemical utterances of Maoists leaders continue to spell ominous portents, the sudden spurt of violence and lawlessness in the plains of southern Nepal has raised security anxieties within and across Nepalese borders. Seemingly the culture of violence held high by the Maoist has imbued the way social and political conflicts are to be played out in Nepal's fragile and rudderless polity.

There is a strong felt need to explore the diverse ways in which the conflict in Nepal has impacted the national and transnational security. In this paper we have reckoned with the overall sway of the decade long conflict in Nepal, according special attention to the less traversed conflict in Southern Nepal. The paper proposes to examine the problematic through both traditional and nontraditional referents of security including human security concerns.[3]

Conflict and the Aftermath

Undoubtedly it was the declaration of the people's war by the Communist Party of Nepal-Maoist (CPN-M) in Feb 1996 which transformed the long drawn struggle for democracy in Nepal.[4] The conflict on the one side saw

---

[3] Human security refers to the freedom from fear and freedom from want, which includes safety from chronic threats such as hunger, disease and repressions, and protection from sudden and hurtful disruptions in the patterns of daily life. See United Nations Development Programme, 1994, *Human Development Report 3 (1994)*.

[4] For the history of Maoists and conflict see, Deepak Thapa and Bandita Sijapati, *A Kingdom Under Siege; Nepal's Maoist Insurgency, 1996 to 2004* (London: Zed Books, 2004), 76-79.B.C. Upreti, *Maoists in Nepal*, (Delhi: Kalpaz, 2008), Nischal Nath Pandey, *Nepal's*

a tri-polar jostling for political power between the Palace, Political Parties and Maoists and on the other, it raised structural issues of social exclusion and inequalities related to gender, caste, class, ethnicity, religion and language, regional disparity etc.[5] Fought on the revolutionary grounds of inclusion and justice, the conflict saw an unprecedented counter repression unleashed by the State forces. The bloody decade saw an estimated 13000 people dead[6] and over 1000 missing.[7] It caused enormous misery to teaming millions and immeasurable loss in material resources.

The violence prone civil war ended through a ceasefire in April 2006 followed by a much hyped Comprehensive Peace Agreement (CPA) in November.[8] The accord envisioned a step by step approach to build an all inclusive peace through a democratic constitution. Both G.P. Koirala and Pushpa Kamal Dahal (Prachanda) claimed that the CPA was "a historic document heralding a new era of peace and democracy in Nepal" and a model for other countries of how to resolve internal conflict successfully.[9]

Maoist Movement and Implications for India and China, (New Delhi: Manohar Publication, 2005); Bishnu Pathak, *Politics of People's War and Human Rights in Nepal,* (Kathmandu:BIMIPA Publications, 2006); "Nepal's Maoists: Their Aims, Structure, and Strategy", *Asia Report no.104(2005),*International Crisis Group and "Nepal's Maoists: Purists or Pragmatists?" *Asia Report* no.132 *(2007).* International Crisis Group

[5] Ramesh Kumar Sharma, *Changing Realities and Challenges for the Peace Process of Nepal,* http://peacenetwork.se/documents_general/Ramesh%20Kumar%20Sharma%20-%20Changing%20Realities%20andRamesh_Kumar_Sharma.pdf (accessed on 20 June 2010); Lynn Bennett, "Gender, Caste and Ethnic Exclusion in Nepal: Following the Policy Process from Analysis", Draft Working Paper for World Bank Arusha Conference, *New Frontiers of Social Policy,* December 12-15, 2005 at http://siteresources.worldbank.org/INTRANETSOCIALDEVELOPMENT/Resources/Bennett.rev.pdf (accessed on 13 June 2010)

[6] The task force of the Nepalese Ministry of Peace and Reconstruction in September 2009 places the number of deaths significantly higher, at 16,274.

[7] The International Committee of the Red Cross (ICRC) reported over 1,300 missing as of April 2009. "Families of Missing Persons in Nepal: A Study of Their Needs", *ICRC Report,* April 2009,1, http://www.icrc.org/web/eng/siteeng0.nsf/html/nepal-missing-persons-report-300609 (accessed on 12 July 2010)

[8] The government and the Maoists also signed the 'Agreement on Monitoring of the Management of Arms and Armies', forming a nine-member Joint Monitoring Coordinating Committee (JMCC) comprising three members each from the government, the Maoists and the UN.

[9] David Seddon, "Nepal: The End of the War - But What Next?", *Socialist Review; Third World Report (Asia);* December 2006, http://www.socialistreview.org.uk/article.php?articlenumber=9913 (accessed on 9 July 2010)

The successful election of an extremely inclusive constituent assembly led by the Maoist leader 'Prachanda' as the Prime Minister raised high hopes of post conflict peace building.

However, the post accord euphoria has been withering away. The failure of political parties to evolve a consensus on constitutional framework and their continued bickering dampened the initial optimism. The Maoists and the Seven Party Alliance (SPA) jostled for their greater share in the power pie that was relished almost entirely by the Monarchy previously. The Maoists were accused of being deceptive in their negotiations, and 'concerned less about development policy and post-conflict peacebuilding than about powerful positions in government and rigging elections'.[10] While the negotiations faltered on the key issues of power-sharing and the reintegration of former PLA in Nepal army, the disaffected marginalized groups did not find much at stake in the peace process.[11] The eventual collapse of the Prachanda led coalition in May 2009 and the inability of Madhav Kumar Nepal (UML) to carry on the mantle of Prime Minister eroded the consensus building process so essential to create a new constitution.[12]

The political vacuum and pervasive instability has naturally worsened the law and order situation. While the number of deaths attributed to the Maoists or the State came down sharply after the peace agreement, the killings and other acts of violence by other groups have gone up considerably. In 2009 alone over 473 persons were killed according to the Nepal Human Rights Yearbook 2010.[13] The violent conflict compelled thousands of individuals and families to relocate to the district headquarters and urban

---

[10] Jason Miklian, "Post-Conflict Power Sharing: The Case of Nepal", *PRIO South Asia Briefing Paper no. 2*, (20 July 2008), 7, http://www.prio.no/sptrans/1382171794/Post-Conflict_Power_Sharing_(South_Asia_Briefing_Paper_2).pdf (on 25 August, 2010)

[11] Madhesi Janadhikar Forum (MJF) has often decried the Constituent Assembly for evading the interest of minorities : Madhesis, Dalits and other marginalised communities.

[12] Madhav Kumar Nepal (UML) who became the new Prime Minister, resigned in the last week of June 2010 amid continued stalemate on the issue of Constitution making.

[13] Human Rights Yearbook, *INSEC*, 2010,http://inseconline.org/index.php?type=news&id =6359&lang=en (accessed on 14 July 2010)

areas for livelihood and security. The government estimated the number of displaced people to be 5,656, the UNDP estimated it to be somewhere between 150,000 and 200,000 and Force Nepal estimated it to be 400,000.[14] The increased violence coincided with the eroding legitimacy and capacity of legal institutions and mechanism.

The other platform of the armed militancy is predicated on the poverty, economic inequity, and social exclusion. The exacerbating social decomposition, economic catastrophe and above all the specter of a failed state have diminished people's capacity to meet their basic human needs. This has led to a rising discontent in impoverished and deprived youth in far flung areas of Nepal against the perceived discrimination by the more powerful political groups making them easy prey to the siren song of extremism.

Violence and Militarization

A significant outcome of the Maoist war has been the growing salience of force and violence among other militating groups. The Maoist organizations' legitimization of violence as a political tool has had a demonstrative impact on many disgruntled groups particularly in Southern Nepal. The rise of Youth Communist League (YCL) and their unconstrained public demeanor has provoked many political parties and ethnic groups to create their own militant wings.[15] There are reports that some 109 armed outfits operate in parts of the country, mainly in Terai.

Impunity for past crimes has been one of notable feature of the post conflict Nepal. This has encouraged and emboldened the members of party youth wings and armed groups to resort to extortion and intimidation and also political killings. The much publicized withdrawal of charges against

---

[14] Hari Bansh Jha, "The Economics of Conflict and Peace ,with Focus on Nepal" in Bishnu P. Poudel, Hari Bansh Jha eds. , *The New Dynamics of Conflict in Nepal,* , (Kathmnadu: The National Advisory Council-South Asian Affairs & Center for Economic and Technical Studies, 2009), 25

[15] The YCL is reported to have captured many public buildings schools and property for occupational de-facto barracks and are often involved in threatening, assaulting or obstructing members of other political parties.

Maoist cadres has set up a precedent which other political groups employ routinely to seek impunity for their erring members.[16]

This conflict phase also saw a rise in the militarization of the state and increasing use of armed forces vis-a-vis internal unrests. The conflict era saw Nepal police being reinforced and a new a para-military force (Armed Police Force) being raised to combat 'terrorism'. The police actions against the Maoists were brutal and targeted anyone suspected of being a sympathizer. [17]

The Royal Nepalese Army (RNA) used rarely in the internal crises before the onset of Maoists' insurgency was initially brought in by the government in April 1998 under the scheme of Integrated Security and Development Plan (ISDP) ostensibly to pressure the Maoist to give up their violence. But the increasing domination of Maoists increased army's involvement after the royal takeover in February, 2005. The strength of Royal Army rose from 46 thousand in 1996 to around 92 thousands by the time the conflict came to an end in 2006.[18]

A key issue in the struggle for democracy has been the security sector reform (SSR) which aimed to detangle the army from palace and bring it under civilian control. One of the consequences of post conflict SSR was that the Army was brought under the control of the Parliament and its immunity from prosecution has been revoked. However there are still unresolved issues in terms of identifying roles and responsibilities between the Nepal Police, the Armed Police Force and the Nepal Army, which is now confined to its barracks according to the peace agreement.[19]

---

[16] "Nepal: Peace and Justice"; *Asia Report* N°184, (2010), International Crisis Group, http://www.crisisgroup.org/en/regions/asia/south-asia/nepal.aspx

[17] Operation Romeo (1995) and Operation Kilo Sierra II (1998) are two instances wherein suspected civilians were targeted brutally. See "Nepal: Killing with Impunity", *Amnesty International*, 20 January 2005, 4, http://asiapacific.amnesty.org/library/Index/ENGASA310012005?open&of=ENG-2AS

[18] DGMO Department, Army HQ., *A Brief Introduction of Nepalese Army,* (Kathmandu: Nepal Army Publication, 2006), 65

[19] Karon Cochran-Budhathoki and Colette Rausch, "Nepal in Transition: Developing Security and Rule of Law Strategies", *Peace Brief* , http://www.usip.org/resources/nepal-transition-developing-security-and-rule-law-strategies (accessed on 10 July 2010)

However, the Nepali Army has lately shown greater assertion, particularly in resisting the proposed integration of 3000 PLA combatants.[20] The ambiguous position of Maoists on national army and cease fire has further raised the security anxieties of the army.[21] Unsurprisngly, the army has pressed for new arms import in a complete breach of ceasefire agreement.

Human Rights and Human Security

The decade long conflict in Nepal waged over the issues of justice and inclusion, however countenanced a conspicuous spree of human rights violation. While the royal government unleashed it on the name of law and order and Maoists legitimized it as a part of their revolutionary tactics. The direct and structural violence perpetrated through such acts however brought the human security parameters of common people to an abysmal low.[22]

The Nepalese state, as a result, became less and less insensate towards the human security imperatives in the course of its engagement with the Maoist challenge. Starting with the Operation Romeo and Operation Kilo Sera II in nineties through the promulgation TADO in 2002 and beyond, the Police routinely arrested, maltreated and tortured the suspected Maoists as well as bystanders, especially around strikes and blockades. The state security forces, unrestrained by legal accountability, were accused by civil society for the gross violation of human rights under the directions of palace or party leaders. They were blamed for hundreds of disappearances and unlawful killings, rampant torture and other abuses of the civilian population.[23]

---

[20] Maoists are demanding that all 19,600 combatants merge in the NA.

[21] The contention over the infamous Shaktikhor Video episode is yet to be over which showed the UCPN(M) leader Prachand hatching a plan to use the current democratic phase to politicize the national Army and camouflage the exact numbers of combatants and arms.

[22] See for instance, Narad N Bharadwaj ,Shiva K Dhungana et al., *Nepal at a Crossroads: The Nexus between Human Security and Renewed Conflict in Rural Nepal,* (Kathmandu: Friends for Peace and International Alert Nepal, 2007), http://www.internal-displacement.org/8025708F004CE90B/(httpDocuments)/6931A722625045CBC12573B50034D2E8/$file/Nepal+at+a+crossroads+—The+Nexus+between+Human+Security+and+Renewed+Conflict+in+Rural+ Nepal.pdf (accessed on 10 July 2010)

[23] "Nepal: Peace and Justice"; *Asia Report* N°184, (2010), International Crisis Group

The Maoist too targeted and torture those suspected of being the class enemy (varg-shatru) and government agents. There are also episodes of bombing of public transport as well, most infamous being in Chitwan in 2005. The movement's critics, even among the Nepalese left, have argued that the Maoists have isolated themselves by killing not only class enemies but also innocent civilians. Many of their victims are real or imagined government spies and informers.[24] The long years of chaos and disorder threatened the physical and human security of people on an everyday basis. The frequent calls of strike, closures and blockades crippled the cities causing immense difficulties to people.

The conflict also impacted the vulnerable sections of people; poor, women and children. Trafficking in women increased in the wake of aggravated violence, disorder and atrocities. Often the women were persecuted by the police for their alleged complicity with the Maoists. The Maoist cadres too harassed hapless women to get shelter and other favors. A number of displaced women have resorted to distilling alcohol and some have reportedly resorted to sex work. The conflict has displaced over 1,00,000 people many of them sought shelter across Indian borders particularly in Uttarakhand. The Maoist said to have recruited around 12,000 young students below the age of 16 years. The rural families were reportedly pressured to depute at least one child to serve in the Maoist army.[25]

Despite the abysmal neglect of human rights standards during the war, the human rights and human security concerns were accorded a high premium in the CPA and in the Interim Constitution of January 2007. The legal framework to protect the human rights was expanded manifold as compared to the 1990 Constitution.[26] It included rights such as the presumption of innocence and the right to legal assistance upon arrest, as

---

[24] According to critics, the Maoists adopted this tactic from Peru's Shining Path to galvanising their own ranks and also to instilled fear among the public at large. See "Nepal Struggles to Cope with Diehard Maoist Violence" www.asiapacificms.com/articles/nepal_maoism

[25] B .C. Upreti, *Maoists in Nepal*, (Delhi: Kalpaz Publications, 2008) ,137

[26] The CPA, in its preamble, commits all signatories "to create an atmosphere where the Nepali people can enjoy their civil, political, economic, social and cultural rights and ... to ensuring that such rights are not violated under any circumstances in the future."

well as the prohibition of untouchability. The Interim Constitution also recognizes the right of traditionally marginalized groups to participate in State mechanisms on the basis of "inclusive principles". The induction of the Right to Information Act, Citizenship Act, the Constituent Assembly Electoral Act, and the Human Trafficking Act also deepened the scope of human security in the post conflict era.

However, the rhetoric of human rights and human security seldom got translated in practice. The post conflict era found a political consensus to evade accountability for serious human rights violations and abuses committed either during or after the conflict. The United Nations Office of the High commissioner for Human Rights in Nepal, reported in Dec 2007 that: "Not one member of the security forces or of the CPN-M has been held criminally accountable and convicted for killings, disappearances, torture or other abuses by the civilian courts".[27] The armed groups in southern Nepal seeking justice and inclusion have often engendered serious human rights violation.

Admittedly, there is a general improvement in the human rights climate in the post conflict phase allowing greater freedom to activists and agencies working around human rights and civil society issues activists but still there is no succor to the common masses who undergo human indignity and insecurity in their quotidian existence.

Maoists Specter

The growing influence of Maoism and the declaration of 'people's war' in 1996 raised India's security anxieties endlessly.[28] The Maoists never

---

[27] United Nations Office of the High Commissioner for Human Rights in Nepal. One year after the Comprehensive Peace Agreement , Dec 2007, http://nepal.ohchr.org/en/resources/ Documents/English/reports/HCR/CPA%20Report.pdf ; United Nations Office of the High Commissioner for Human Rights, Nepal, April 2007.Findings of OHCHR-Nepal's Investigations into the 21 March Killings in Gaur and Surrounding Villages. http://nepal.ohchr.org/en/ resources/Documents/English/reports/IR/Year2007/Gaur.pdf (accessed 20 July 2007)

[28] Despite a reformist agenda to attain a plural, inclusive, just, decentralized and secular democratic polity, Maoists preferred armed resistance as per the Ultra Left ideology. Starting with few Khukris and vintage rifles, they soon acquired automatic weapons, SLR, and AK-47 mostly through their cross border links in bordering states.

concealed their distrust for India as a stumbling block in their ambition of 'regional popular revolution'.[29] Their 40 point demand of 1996 included the demand to remove the unequal stipulations and agreements in the 1950 Treaty of Peace and Friendship, nullification of 1996 Mahakali Treaty on water resources, control of Nepal-India border, banning of Indian vehicles and stopping the 'cultural pollution of expansionist power like India'. In February 2001 in the National Conference of CPN (M) a declaration was made that any successful insurgency (in South Asian region) would eventually have to fight with India.

Although India had weathered the anti-Indian tirades on several past occasions, it never felt as challenged as it did during the Maoists insurgency and its aftermath. Despite India's countenance to the formation of the Maoist Government in 2007; the relationship between the Maoists and India remained strenuous. The Maoists' increasing political sway also allowed the Chinese to expand their diplomatic and trade ties with Nepal much to India's disadvantage. The Maoist led government also played the Chinese card to seek concessions from India. For instance it projected the Chinese offer of extending the Tibet Railway to Kathmandu to elicit a concrete offer from India for the extension of the railway from India to Kathmandu.[30]

Once ousted from the government, the Maoists made a no holds barred propaganda against India. They saw an Indian conspiracy in promoting Madhav Kumar Nepal led coalition as an alternative to CPN (M). During the month of January-February 2010 the Maoists unleashed a high pitch polemical war against India. Indian national symbols were desecrated and the walls of the Capital city were painted with abusive slogans against

---

[29] Seemingly, the Maoists formed a live connection with their counterparts in India and elsewhere: The Revolutionary International Movement, (RIM); Coordination Committee of Maoist Parties and Organization in South Asia (CCOMPOSA). See, Winne Gobyn, "From War to Peace: The Nepalese Maoists's Strategic and Ideological Thinking" in *Studies in Conflict and Terrorism*,32 no. 5 (2009), 420-438

[30] Landlocked Nepal has hitherto largely been dependent on India for imports. With trains from China soon reaching its border, Nepal will find importing from its northern neighbor easier. Sino-Nepal trade will expand exponentially, at India's expense. Sudha Ramachandran, "Nepal to get China Rail Link", *Asia Times,* May 15, 2008, http://www.atimes.com/atimes/South_Asia/JE15Df01.html (accessed on 19 June 2010)

India. In the beginning of 2010, the Maoists launched an aggressive anti-India campaign, declaring India as expansionist power, burning effigy & flags and threatening local residents. This in fact led to a series of local protests by the Indian inhabitants warning of serious retaliation to their Nepali counterparts. In a Seminar organized by the India Ministry of External affairs in Patna on 26-27 Feb 2010, the Maoists representatives were conveyed the utmost displeasure of India against such vicious campaign and cautioned that it could set into motion a chain of events that would not be under anyone's control. "Protests by locals in bordering Indian towns against the desecration of Indian national symbols by the Maoists were cited as proof of the hardening of Indian public opinion."[31]

Upheavals in Southern Nepal

One of the cascading ramifications of the ten years conflict was the eruption of political upheavals in Terai - the lowlands spread in southern Nepal up to Indian border. Also known as Madhes, this geopolitical sensitive region has been in the throe of political discontent for a while before the Maoists brought it its present precipice.

The Madhesis have nursed a long history of discrimination by the hill people (Pahadis) who held the reins of political power during the long decades of Panchayat regime from the nineteen sixties onwards. The simmering tensions came out in open against the discriminating state policies which sought to assimilate diverse ethnicities of Nepal into an ostensible pan-Nepali identity drawing from the cultures of upper caste Pahadis. The 1964 Citizenship Act and 1990 constitution imposed stringent criteria, based on descent and created huge hurdles for Madhesis to acquire Nepali citizenship. What disaffected the Madhesi's the most was the state sponsored resettlement program in the mid-1980s which encouraged an en mass migration of Pahadis to the Terai to take control the precious agricultural and industrial resources.

---

[31] Prashat Jha, "Indian Skepticism", *Nepal Times*, no. 491 (26 FEB 2010 - 04 MARCH 2010), http://nepalitimes.com/issue/2010/02/26/Nation/16848 accessed on 26 June 2010)

During 1950s and 1960s, the region became the common ground of pro-democratic movement and Madhesi activism. The notion of the "internal colonization of Terai" was construed in a number of ways ranging from their inadequate representation in the assembly to the denial of citizenship for all Madhesis.

It was the Maoist led conflict which infused militancy in the Madhes region leading to violent protests soon after the CPA was signed in 2006. The feeling of discrimination, relative deprivation and negligent attitude of the Nepal State was well exploited by the Maoists during their early mobilization. Many disgruntled factions in Southern Nepal were magnetized to join their armed struggle to undo the monarchy seen as a stumbling block for the Madhesis to seek their just political and economic share in new democratic Nepal.

However the end of conflict in 2006 did not bring any relief to the Madhesi unrest. Soon after the CPA was announced, the Terai found itself in the grip of violent demonstrations and clashes between political rivals which left several dozen dead. Beginning with the protracted public protests against the state sponsored discrimination, the Madhesi movement soon acquired a violent temper leading to violent clashes with the police and other political groups. Disassociating themselves from their Maoist past, the increasingly militant Madhesi leadership sought to transform the Terai region into a single autonomous province of Madhes. It saw armed Madhesi groups targeting both the state and the Maoists. The movement also acquired communal overtones with rallies of people armed with spears and khukris attacking police, government offices and homes, CPN-M groups, businesses, and the Pahadi (hill people).

The magnitude of violent upheavals shocked one and all concerned with Nepal. Though the government offered to negotiate the Madhesi demands for increased electoral representation, affirmative action for marginalized groups and federalism, the leaders in Terai were not content with these measures.

The major political parties currently in an alliance under the Unified Democratic Madhesi Front (UDMF), are currently pressing hard for a

Madhes autonomous province' with the right to self-determination and reservation for Madhesis in the state bodies in an inclusive manner. There are also some renegade Maoist leaders who are not content with the regional autonomy and have waged an armed secessionist movement. Prominent among such leaders are Jai Krishna Goit, who formed the Janatantrik Terai Mukti Morcha (People's Terai Liberation Front/JTMM), and Jwala Singh (head of a splinter faction with a similar name). These two former comrade –in –arms have declared their mission to establish a new independent state of Terai. These secessionist leaders were distraught by the Maoists leadership which according to them let down the Madhesi concerns. Maoist Chairman Prachanda, however refuses to engage with the militant Madhesis: "Negotiation is done with political forces, not with criminals and gangsters." The post conflict Terai has thus become the most instable site of lawlessness and criminality having a natural spillover effect on India.

Rising Frontier Insecurity

The conflict in Nepal has worsened the already brittle security environment across its long border with India. The post conflict surge of militant regionalism in Terai and its conflictual engagements with other political groups as well as with the Maoists have undermined the already frail law and governance in the area.[32] The security vacuum in the Terai districts marked by a feeble presence of police and other border regulating agencies known for their corruption has made this uniquely open border as one of the most illegally trafficked borders in the world. The scantly guarded open borders are increasingly tempting unscrupulous parties to engage in a range of criminal activities. The post conflict uncertainties and the erosion of law and governance have indeed raised the specter of criminal activities engendering security of both India and Nepal. Unsurprisingly, there is an increasingly strident demand from various quarters to review the unique provisions of a visa less travel between the two countries.

---

[32] Narad N Bharadwaj ,Shiva K Dhungana et al., "Nepal at a Crossroads: The Nexus between Human Security and Renewed Conflict in Rural Nepal", *Friends for Peace and International Alert*, Kathmandu, Nepal, September 2007, 44-45, http://www.internal-displacement.org/8025708F004CE90B/(httpDocuments)/6931A722625045CBC12573B50034D2E8/$file/Nepal (accessed on 10 July 2010)

From India's point of view most worrisome is the growing evidences of transnational operations of the anti-Indian terrorist groups. Terai has long been a favourite spot for the Pakistani intelligence agencies to foment trouble for India. Operating through their henchman Dawood Ibrahim and other transnational mafia groups, the Pakistani agencies have over time developed entrenched interests in illegal trade across Indo-Nepal borders which provide them space to engage in their anti-India activities. The killings of suspected criminals like Mirza Dilshad Beg in 1998 to the more recent murder of Majid Manihar in 2009 and of Jamim Shah and in 2010 indicate the continuing jostling between the criminal traders, cross border Mafias and intelligence agencies.[33] India's Ambassador to Nepal, Rakesh Sood has recently said in an interview to the Nepalese media that nearly 20 terrorists slipped into India from Nepal in 2009, and currency worth Rs 2 crore was seized in the country that is a major security concern.[34]

The increasing vulnerable security situation in Terai was unraveled in the aftermath of the hijacking of an Indian Airlines flight between Kathmandu and New Delhi in 1999. In a subsequent report leaked to the press Indian intelligence sources accused ISI and LeT of Pakistan to sponsor 26 criminal organizations operating in the Terai with 66 ISI-funded, LeT-run madrassas along the Indo-Nepal border.[35] According to the report, while the steady migration of Bangladeshi Muslims to the Terai considerably contributed to this increase, the influx of Pakistanis was also seen as a major factor.[36]

---

[33] "TNN;'Gang war looms large over Nepal after tycoon's murder'", *Times of India*, Feb 8, 2010, http://timesofindia.indiatimes.com/world/south-asia/Gang-war-looms-large-over-Nepal-after-tycoons-murder/articleshow/5549764.cms

[34] "Nearly 20 terrorists entered India via Nepal: Indian envoy", *NDTV News*; April 29, 2010, Kathmandu, http://www.ndtv.com/news/india/nearly-20-terrorists-entered-india-via-nepal-indian-envoy-21997.php (Accessed on 8 July 2010)

[35] Harinder Baweja, "Terrorism :The Kathmandu Nexus" , *India Today*, 12 June, 2000 at http://www.india-today.com/itoday/20000612/nation2.html

[36] Ibid., Adding credibility, several Nepali politicians, smugglers, and officials at the Pakistani Embassy in Kathmandu were later arrested on various charges related to the report. See Jason Miklian, "Illicit Trading in Nepal: Fueling South Asian Terrorism", *South Asia Briefing Paper no.3*, (27 January 2009), http://www.prio.no/sptrans/-352548431/Illicit%20Trading%20in%20Nepal%20(South%20Asia%20Briefing%20Paper%203).pdf

Murder of Mirza Dilshad Beg in Nepal, considered as the right hand man of ISI and arrest of many ISI trained terrorist in Madhubani (Jaynagar) near the Nepal border in Bihar in 2009, some of them are Nepali, is the clear indication of growing nexus between ISI and anti Indian people active in India and Nepal. The rise in criminal activities in frontier areas has also impacted the security concerns in Nepal. The condition of unrest and insecurity in many of the Terai districts are construed to offer incentives for the smuggling of arms from India into Nepal.

The unholy alliance between the illicit traders, criminals and terrorist in Terai thrives on a range of connected activities i.e. hawala system, fraudulent letters of credit and the distribution of counterfeit Indian currency. The illegal trading and the circulation of fake currency is protected by the transnational criminal syndicates such as like LeT which in turn facilitate their cross border operations including money laundering.

The easiest avenue to make money is to operate the *hawala* system along the instable border areas.[37] Given Nepal's remittance based economy, the unscrupulous money launders find a huge catchment of migrant workers who serve as their easy prey. The post conflict uncertainties in Terai region has made things less perilous for the clandestine operations of running hawala banking operations often times with the support of counterfeiting currency. Close on the heels of the 26/11, the Nepal police uncovered a terror link between Kathmandu and Karachi with the arrest of members of a fake currency gang known to be funding extremist groups in Jammu and Kashmir in India.[38]

The unabated circulation of counterfeit currency notes from across the Indo-Nepal border has lately become a critical challenge for the India security.[39] Trader networks in Terai deal with fake Rs 500 and 1000 Indian

---

[37] The Hawala system is a informal form of money laundering operated by an organized groups of money brokers often in tandem the international mafias and is used extensively in Nepal by the migrant worker to remit money home.

[38] Sudeshna Sarkar Kathmandu , "Nepal Police Bust Karachi-Kathmandu Terror Link", *Sulekha News,* December 21, 2008, http://newshopper.sulekha.com/nepal-police-bust-karachi-kathmandu-terror-link_news_1012387.htm

[39] It has also been said that the fake currency notes are of higher quality than the ones manufactured in India. Of late, any amount bigger than the 100 currency note of India has been declared an illegal tender.

notes trading them at a 2-1 rate in the grey market.[40] Flow of this currency has multiplied at least five times even since the Peace agreement has been signed. The fake currency comes in handy to procure arms from the international market as well as to promote other illegal transactions.

Reports also suggest that the Pakistani intelligence agencies in order to have a favorable sway in Terai are financing the illegal infiltration of Bangladeshi and Pakistani Muslims to offset the demographic imbalance in the region. There are reportedly over 300 madrassas and 343 mosques within 10 k.m. of the boarder in Indian side while 181 madrassas and 282 mosques are in Nepal side.[41]

The growth of armament culture in southern Nepal has ominous security implications for India. The rise of armed groups in Terai has led to undesirable cross border transaction including arms supply through the bordering states of UP and Bihar. Many of these groups reportedly engage in illicit trade and counterfeit currency to sustain their armed activities. There are suggestions that both the factions of Jharkhand Tarai Mukti Morcha (JMM) led respectively by Jai Krishna Goit and Nagendra Paswan (Jwala Singh)[42] and 'Terai Cobra'[43] led by Nagraj engage in the racket of fake Indian currency. Similarly the pro-King and pro-Hindu militant group Nepal Defense Army has plans to train several hundred armed men causing security anxieties on both sides of borders. The Nepal Janatantric Party (NJP) is a royalist outfit led by Rana Bahadur Chanda alias Samrat. Its objective is to retain constitutional monarchy and multiparty democracy in Nepal. Then there are groups like Chure Bhawar Ekata Samaj (CBES) allegedly backed

---

[40] A PRIO report has cited an Indian official claiming that the amount of fake currency flowing from Nepal has quadrupled in the last five years alone, and is of a much higher quality than fakes made in India. Jason Miklian, "Illicit Trading in Nepal: Fueling South Asian Terrorism", *South Asia Briefing Paper no.3,* (27 January 2009)

[41] R. Upadhyay, "Muslims of Nepal: Becoming an Assertive minority", October , 2007, http://madhesi.wordpress.com ?s=Muslims+of+Nepal:+ Becoming+an+ assertive +minority&searchbutton=Go! (Accessed on 04 October 2007)

[42] A successor of the Madhesi Rastra Mukti Morcha established in 2000, the JMM was created in 2004 by the disillusioned Maoists.

[43] *Terai Cobra* that fights against the Pahadi domination in Terai operates from around Birgunj in the border districts of Bara, Parsa, Rautahat, Sarlahi etc.

by the Maoists. There are many other militant organizations in Terai which operate with impunity due to ongoing political turmoil and complete breakdown of the law and order situation.[44]

Other Consequences

The long years of conflict marked by the willful negligence of the state to address the socioeconomic needs of people saw a spurt in the involvement of international aid and relief agencies. Currently over one hundred agencies are operating in Nepal to restore and stabilize peace and democratic governance through what is often described as 'peace-funding'. Despite tangible contributions of many such agencies, they are sometimes blamed to influence the course of governance and development as per their own agenda.[45] In any case, there has erupted a culture of donor dependency in Nepal that does not seem to be contributing to the progression of advance political culture.[46] The conflict also affected Nepal's tourism industry which is reported to have gone down from being the tenth most popular destination among adventure travelers, to the twenty-seventh.[47]

Yet another ramification of the conflict was the significant increase of the young and able people seeking work abroad due to the stagnant employment situation along with the persecution threats from both the warring parties.[48] While the regular flow of remittances from these migrant labors significantly helps the national economy, there are allied anxieties

---

[44] Some of the other militant outfits of the Terai region are: *Janatantrik Tarai Mukti Morcha (JTMM)* – Leader Bishfot Singh faction; *Madhesi Mukti Tigers*-Maoist splinter, leader Sher Singh Rajput and Rajan Mukti; *Terai Tigers* -leader alias 'Arjun';*Tharu Mukti Morcha* - leader Laxman Tharu, President ;*Samyukta Janatantrik Tarai Mukti Morcha* (SJTMM) - leader Mr. Pawan; *Liberation Tigers of Terai Elam*-President Ram Lochan Singh; *Madhesi Virus Killers*- Sanket .

[45] Madan Kumar Dahal, "Foreign Aid in Nepal: The Changing Context", *Telegraph Nepal,* May 14, 2008; http://www.telegraphnepal.com/news_det.php?news_id=3417

[46] See Tone Bleie, "The Decade of Violent Destabilization in Nepal: An Analysis of its Historical Background and Trajectory", *Occasional Papers in Sociology and Anthropology,* 10 (2007), http://www.nepjol.info/index.php/OPSA/article/viewPDFInterstitial/1147/1553. http://www.nepjol.info/index.php/OPSA/article/viewPDFInterstitial/1147/1553

[47] "Top Ten World Travel Destinations in 2004". *iExplore,* Chicago, January 9, 2006 , http://www.iexplore.com/about/pr_2006-01-09.jhtml (accessed on August 25, 2010)

[48] Most migrant Nepalese work as laborers/domestic help etc. work in the Gulf (Qatar, Saudi Arabia) and Southeast Asia.

and social concerns associated with such large scale migration.

The conflict has also displaced approximately 1,00,000 people and a sizeable number have found an abode in India. They have left due to targeted attacks and also due to economic hardships. The hardships that are being faced by women in this situation are enormous. Though the position of Nepalese women has undergone a major change due to the violence that for them, has not been negative in totality, but the brunt of displacement, anxieties concerning missing persons, challenges of rehabilitation of those who were directly involved in armed insurrection has impacted the entire Nation.

The neglect of women in the peace process has further pushed the post conflict achievement back to where it was initially struggled for. The Constituent Assembly has a sizeable number of elected women representatives as well as several Committees of the CA were headed by Women, their status still remains subordinate in the Society as well as family. They have toed the party line while serving as members and have been only marginally successful in their struggle for equal rights in all spheres. They continue to be discriminated against in rights concerning citizenship and also in rights of inheritance.

Conclusion

The internal conflict in Nepal waged on the noble grounds of justice and inclusion is yet to be over in its entirety. There is hardly any doubt that the decade long violent struggle embodying people's desperate assertion for democracy and development succeeded in demolishing the hitherto dominant structures of clientele and patronage. However the post conflict uncertainties and political jostling have marked the formative phase of the institution. The Maoists are still ambiguous about their commitment to democratic institutions and how are they going to reconcile their revolutionary perspectives in the current course of political restructuring. The long years of armed insurgency has diminished the already frail structures of law and governance including the police and army. The ongoing dynamic of distrust and discord has made difficult the evolution of a national consensus on the template of internal security which remains in shambles. The continued conflictual impulses in Nepali political milieu have led to several unanticipated faultlines endangering serious internal and transnational consequences.

Unsurprisngly the simmering disaffection of the Madhesi people found the post conflict phase a ripe moment to break out in open. While the Madhesi quest for identity, security and development is hard to ignore, the way it is being played out by a number of protagonist is rather perilous. Dozens of armed groups espousing secession and ethnic cleansing in violent overtones is hardly comforting in a sensitive frontier area already a play field of transnational crime syndicates. This has ominous security repercussions for both India and Nepal. The two Himalayan neighbors with a long lineage of cordiality must put their act together to redeem the overall security environment in Terai region. They need to look beyond nabbing the individual criminals and work in concert to reform the border management as well as develop a zero tolerance policy for corruption. It is only through the raising of punishment barriers that the illegal trading and allied criminal activities can be curbed in the region. While the positive conflicts may lead to progress, if unmanaged they may spell disaster for the security and development. Obviously the heightened insecurity and lawlessness in present day Nepal has raised doubts about the very *raison d'être* of the people's conflict. But one must reckon with the long drawn process of systemic reforms needed to rectify the structural imbalances and social injustice. However this requires at least some stability in governance which is proving to be a chimera in the crisis ridden state.

INTERNAL CONFLICT IN NEPAL:
IMPLICATIONS FOR INDIA

Padmaja Murthy

Since the end of Cold War most conflicts are not contests between countries but rather internal disputes as disparities among their citizens have become increasingly evident.[1] Nepal too has been a witness to this state of affairs.

The present phase of instability can be traced to the mid 1990s. The extreme concentration of political, social, economic power in a few and the refusal of the governments to effectively address this inequality had led to discontent among the excluded majority. Like all conflicts, the internal conflict in Nepal has not been static. With the passage of time it has changed its apparent external face while the root causes remain the same. During the mid 1990s, it was the Maoist insurgency which was the violent expression of this exclusion. Post Jana Andolan II 2006, the rise of the marginalized sections and their movements have added another dimension to the internal conflict. In fact, this discontent was clearly visible, though not in a violent manner, for those who sought to see it during the 1990 Jana Andolan I. As long as change is not visible on the ground and in people's lives, Nepal will continue to be in a state of conflict, which will be expressed in multiple ways with a degree of violence inbuilt into it. Post Jana Andolan II there has been a national consensus to prioritize mechanisms and policies to move away from exclusion and strive for an inclusive society. Since then these

---

[1] United Nations Development Programme, *Nepal Human Development Report 2009: State Transformation and Human Development*, Kathmandu, 2009, 15.

issues have had a permanent place in the national agenda of Nepal. This is a very significant historic development but intent has to be matched with implementation.

Post Constituent Assembly (CA) Elections a new unstable situation has arisen in Nepal. New set of issues, totally unanticipated, have completely changed the trajectory of the peace process. As seen in some other conflict situations in other parts of the world, a new dynamic situation arises after the conflict reaches a certain stage wherein the original conflict and the real core issues are sidelined. A new set of problems have taken over the original issues negating the progress made so far. These now need to be necessarily addressed first and resolved.

The conflict is primarily an internal development of Nepal which arose from within the grievances rooted in that country, with the leaders emerging from among the people and with strategies which were suited to Nepal. However, the internal conflict in Nepal has had significant external consequences. As the internal conflict went through various phases, so have the trans-border consequences with the greatest impact naturally on India. This is not only because of the compulsions of geography wherein security concerns are interlinked but also due to the close historical, social and cultural relations which the two countries share. The external factor – India – is inbuilt into the internal conflict of Nepal in many ways. This was specifically visible during the Maoist insurgency days because - i) some of the demands reflected discontent with India; ii) the war infrastructure of the Maoists in terms of men, material and ideas had linkage with similar Maoist/Naxal elements in India; iii) the official response mechanism in Nepal took assistance from India to meet the challenges arising from the Maoist insurgency and iv) the instability in Nepal easily spills over into India in innumerable ways, specifically through the open Indo-Nepal border effecting its internal security.

The different phases of the conflict situation show how security and stability is intertwined for both the countries. Indian foreign policy has been under stress right through this conflict situation. At every stage either India is being influenced or is influencing directly or indirectly events in Nepal.

However, there are limits to this influence and India too has realized that it too finally has to bow before the wishes and aspirations of the people of Nepal. While dealing with Nepal's internal conflict, India too has its own agenda of ensuring security and stability in its own country. Sometimes a section of the opinion in Nepal converges with India's views on the affairs in the country. In a situation where there is no consensus within the Nepalese polity and India is seen as aligning with a particular party, the convergence of opinions becomes a source of friction effecting bilateral relations and dragging India into the domestic politics of Nepal.

In this background this chapter briefly outlines the root causes of the conflict and in doing so revisits the 'exclusion debate' since Jana Andolan I. It is important to revisit the nature of this 'exclusion' so that correct policy responses will be formed by actors and stakeholders both external and internal. The paper argues that given the extent of 'exclusion' in the society, polity and economy of Nepal, a conflict was waiting to happen. The internal conflict is a consequence of exclusion. If not for the Maoist insurgency it would have taken another form. Post Jana Andolan II, there were multiple movements from the marginalized sections expressing their discontent and asserting their rights. The Maoists were not the sole champions. The paper argues that despite the many discussions and the debates there is still a definite gap in understanding the intensity of the problem which is reflected in the momentum of the peace process.

The Maoist insurgency raised some issues which directly relate to India. Thus, India is perceived as a problem and also as part of the solution. The conflict resulted in multiple challenges for Indian Foreign policy and new security concerns have arisen. This chapter examines India's responses both official and unofficial to address these challenges. It assesses India's role during the conflict period and argues that on certain occasions short term considerations took precedence over long term goals of the peace process.

The chapter examines the post CA elections scenario where the internal conflict in Nepal has decisively thrown up a new set of issues which have derailed the actual programme of drafting the Constitution and the process of integration and rehabilitation of the Maoist combatants. The paper argues that the UCPN (M) agitations to uphold civilian supremacy are actually undermining it. Actors both internal and external are responsible for this unfortunate state of affairs. Unless these concerns are resolved, the real issues stand neglected. It clearly reflects that the politicians and leaders are once again, like in the years following Jana Andolan I, failing the people.

The internal conflict has been characterized by loss of life and property. It has affected Nepal's economy in a major way. The continuing instability even after the CA elections does not create an environment conducive to foreign direct investment in Nepal. The paper spells out the grievances of the business community in Nepal and the manner in which it impacts Indo-Nepal economic relations.

Lastly, the paper looks into the possible future scenarios that are likely to emerge in Nepal.

Exclusion: Understanding the Root Causes of the Conflict

The long period of violent internal conflict has highlighted the extent of exclusion in Nepal – politically, economically and socially – where power lies in a few. The root causes of the conflict lie in prevalence of a system which does not seek to address this exclusion. It is essential to understand the nature of this exclusion for only then can corrective measures be formulated within Nepal and by stakeholders outside to end the state of conflict and move towards state transformation. The inability to bring about change can keep Nepal in a state of continuous instability.[2] The nature of this exclusion has been highlighted over the years and has its imprints in the Jana Andolan I too. It took a violent form in the Maoist insurgency and later Post Jana Andolan II in the various movements by the marginalized.

The Extent of Exclusion

This section spells out some aspects of the extent of exclusion in Nepal to

---

[2] The former Secretary General of the United Nations, Kofi Annan wrote, "Roughly half of all countries that emerge from war lapse back into violence within five years" in United Nations Development Programme, *Nepal Human Development Report 2009: State Transformation and Human Development*, Kathmandu, 2009, 52.

bring out how it permeates every aspect of society. Thus those who remain in the margins continue to remain in the margins and those holding power continue to do so. Some tables are presented to bring out these aspects more clearly.

a) The representation of various castes/ethnic groups in various sectors of society brings out how the Brahmin/Chhetri and Newar group occupy the space which is much more than their share in population. It is seen that these groups who form 30 percent of the population have a disproportionately high share of 60 percent. On the contrary, the Madhesis who form 30 percent of the population account for only 15 percent of the total representation. This trend is repeated in the state judiciary and council of ministers. These aspects are brought out in the two tables which show that access to state institutions is limited to a few and others are not able to participate in policy formulation and implementation to make any difference to their conditions. The democratic government which followed Jana Andolan I too did not make any difference to this state of affairs and the same scenario continued in the years that followed. This is again reflected in Tables 1 and 2[3].

---

[3] All Tables and Figures in this chapter are sourced from the Nepal Human Development Report 2009, see, United Nations Development Programme, *Nepal Human Development Report 2009: State Transformation and Human Development*, Kathmandu, 2009.

Table 1: Representation of Caste and Ethnicity in Different Sectors of Society, Nepal 1999 and 2005

Sector	BCTS		Nationaliti-es		Madhesi		Dalits		Newar		Others		Total	
	1999	2005	1999	2005	1999	2005	1999	2005	1999	2005	1999	2005	1999	2005
Public sector	235	82	42	7	56	9	4	2	36	14	-	-	373	114
Political sector	97	93	25	20	26	11	-	1	18	14	-	-	166	139
Private sector	7	21	-	3	15	30	-	-	20	42	-	-	42	96
Civil society	69	94	3	9	8	18	-	1	16	19	-	-	96	141
Total	408	290	70	39	105	68	4	4	90	89	-	-	677	490
Perce-ntage (a)	60.3	59.2	10.3	7.9	15.5	13.9	0.6	0.8	13.3	18.2	-	-	100.-0	100-.0
Caste in total popula-tion - %(b)	31.6	30.9	22.1	23.1	30.9	31.5	8.8	7.9	5.6	5.5	1.1	1.2	100.-0	100-.0
Ratio (a/b)	1.9	1.9	0.5	0.3	0.5	0.4	0.1	0.1	2.4	3.3	-	-	-	-

Note: The public sector includes Supreme Court, constitutional bodies, cabinet secretariats, lower and upper houses, whereas political sector includes leaders of political parties. Similarly, private sector refers to leadership of Federation of Nepali Chamber of Commerce and Industry (FNCCI) and Chamber of Commerce. Civil society includes the chiefs of different professional groups and media house. BCTS refers to Hill Brahman, Chhetri, Thakuri and Sanyasi. Source: Nepal Human Development Report, 2009, 161

Table 2: Representation of Caste and Ethnicity in State Organs, Nepal, 1999 and 2005

Sector	BCTS		Nationalities		Madhesi		Dalits		Newar		Others		Total	
	1999	2005	1999	2005	1999	2005	1999	2005	1999	2005	1999	2005	1999	2005
Supreme Court	16	11	0	0	0	0	0	0	0	0	0	0	16	11
Council of Ministers	20	8	4	1	5	1	-	-	5	2	-	-	34	12
Total	38	19	4	1	5	1	0	0	5	2	0	0	50	23
Percentage (a)	72.0	82.6	8.0	4.3	10.0	4.3	-	-	10.0	8.7	-	-	100.0	100.0
Caste in total population - % (b)	31.6	30.9	22.1	23.5	30.9	31.5	7.9	-	5.6	5.5	1.1	1.2	-	100.0
Ratio (a/b)	2.3	2.7	0.4	0.2	0.3	0.1	-	-	1.8	1.6	0.0	-	-	-

Note: Lower and upper houses of two-chamber legislature are not included because there was no lower house in 2005. BCTS refers to Hill Brahman, Chhetri, Thakali and Sanyasi. Source: Nepal Human Development Report, 2009, 161

b) Just before the onset of Jan Andolan II the scenario of the various castes in the leadership positions of the judiciary, executive and legislature shows a negligible share for the marginalized sections and domination by the Brahmin/Chettri and the Newar castes.

Table 3: Participation of Caste and Ethnic Groups in the Leadership Positions of Judiciary, Executive, Legislature and Constitutional Bodies, Nepal, 2005

Sector	BCTS	Nationaliti-es	Madhesi	Dalits	Newar	Others/Total
Supreme Court	11	-	2	-	2	15
Commission for Investigation of Abuse of Authority	3	1	-	-	1	5
Election Commission	3	-	-	-	1	4
Office of the Attorney General	1	-	-	-	-	1
Office of the Auditor General	1	-	-	-	-	1
Public Service Commission	2	1	1	-	2	6
Council of Ministers	8	1	1	-	2	12
Central Administration-Secret-ary or its equivalent	28	1	1	-	3	33
Lower House	-	-	-	-	-	-
Upper House	25	4	4	2	3	38
Total	82	8	9	2	14	115
Percentage	71.3	7.0	7.8	1.7	12.2	100.0

Note: BCTS refers to Hill Brahmin, Chhetri, Thakuri and Sanyasi.

Source: United Nations Development Programme, *Nepal Human Development Report 2009: State Transformation and Human Development*, Kathmandu, 2009, 162

c) The various important associations of professional bodies like those of the press, bar, teachers, medical and nurses also show the continuing domination of the Brahmin/Chettri group.

Table 4: Participation of Caste and Ethnic Groups in the Leadership Positions of Civil society Organizations, Nepal, 2005

Organisation	BCTS	Nationalities	Madhesi	Dalits	Newar	Others Total
Nepal Press Federation	18	1	1	.	1	21
NGO Federation	11	-	2	1	2	16
Nepal Bar Association	14	2	-	-	1	17
Nepal Professor Association	14	-	3	-	2	19
Nepal Teacher Union	12	1	5	-	6	24
Nepal Medical Association	7	1	5	-	1	14
Nepal Engineering Association	9	1	2	-	3	15
Nepal Nursing Association	9	3	-	-	3	15
Total	94	9	18	1	19	141
Percentage	66.7	6.4	12.8	0.7	13.5	100.0

Note: BCTS refers to Hill Brahmin, Chhetri, Thakuri and Sanyasi.

Source: United Nations Development Programme, *Nepal Human Development Report 2009: State Transformation and Human Development*, Kathmandu, 2009, 163

d) Politically, there has consistently been domination of the Brahmin/ Chhetri groups in Parliament.

Table 5: Representation of Different Caste/Ethnic Groups in Parliament, Nepal, 1959–1999

Caste/ ethnicity	1959		1967		1978		1981		1986		1991		1994		1999	
	No	%	No	%	No	%	No	%	No	%	No	%	No	%	No	%
Brahman	30	27.5	30	24.2	27	21.9	14	12.5	23	20.5	77	37.7	86	41.9	77	38.7
Chhetri	34	31.2	47	37.9	46	37.4	41	36.6	43	38.4	39	19.1	40	19.5	44	22.1
Newar	4	3.7	15	12.1	10	8.1	9	8.0	7	6.2	14	6.9	13	6.3	14	7.0
Janajati (except Newar)	21	19.3	21	16.9	28	22.8	36	32.1	29	25.9	48	23.5	38	18.5	35	17.6
Tarai high and middle castes	18	16.5	11	8.9	11	8.9	10	8.9	10	8.9	21	10.3	24	11.7	27	13.6
Muslim	2	1.8	-	-	1	0.8	2	1.8	0	0	5	2.4	4	2.0	2	1.0
Dalits	-	-	-	-	-	-	-	-	-	-	-	-	-	-	-	-
Total	109	100-.0	124	100..0	123	100-.0	112	100-.0	112	100-.0	204	100-.0	205	10-0.0	199	100-.0

Note: Percentages may exceed hundred because of rounding up the decimals.

Source: United Nations Development Programme, *Nepal Human Development Report 2009: State Transformation and Human Development*, Kathmandu, 2009, 160

e) In the state bureaucracy too, there is again a complete domination of the Brahmin/Chhetri groups who account for 70 percent of the gazette level employees. There is also a significant presence of the Newars. The complete marginalization of the Madhesis, Janajati and Dalits is starkly evident in the following table.

Table 6: Class-wise Caste and Ethnic Composition in Gazetted Level Employees

S.No.	Caste/ethnic groups		Gazetted level			Total	
		Special class	First class	Second class	Third class	Number	%
1	Brahman	24	230	1,161	3,306	4,721	58.3
2	Chhetri	6	63	283	728	1,080	13.3
3	Dalit	0	3	11	60	74	0.9
4	Newar	7	68	374	703	1,152	14.2
5	Janajati (excluding Newar)	1	3	70	190	264	3.3
6	Madhesi, Muslim and Marwari	0	30	237	538	805	9.9
	Total	38	397	2,136	5,525	8,096	100.0
	Percentage	0.5	4.9	26.4	68.2	100.0	

Source: United Nations Development Programme, *Nepal Human Development Report 2009: State Transformation and Human Development*, Kathmandu, 2009, 163

Thus, the marginalized majority do not have a say in policy formulation and implementation. In the various pressure groups of society too their presence is negligible. Thus, their problems and concerns never come to the limelight. Their various agitations propose to change this skewed concentration of power through various affirmative actions. Their discontent is reflected in the Jana Andolan I of 1990, the Maoist Insurgency, Jana Andolan II of 2006 and the Madhesi Agitations.

Jana Andolan I of 1990: The Political Class Ignores Signals of Discontent

Jana Andolan I of April 1990 has been projected as a successful movement which put an end to the Panchayati regime and brought in multi-party parliamentary democracy and Constitutional Monarchy. Nepal also had a new Constitution prepared by not an elected constituent assembly but a Constitutional Recommendation Commission (CRC) which was promulgated in November 1990. However, behind the apparent consensus lay deep discontent by multiple sections of the society. These groups have had a historic sense of marginalization from the national centre of power, a grievance that dates to the century long Rana era. [4]

Some of the demands forwarded to the CRC were:

- That suppressed classes be represented in the Constitution Commission.[5]

- The Nepal Sadhbhavana Party put forward demands of people of Terai region with regard to their language.[6] The party stated that people of Terai had been neglected from the political point of view and many had been denied citizenship.[7]

- Mongol National Organization demanded that Nepal be declared a secular state and that powers be restored to the Limbus. It also demanded equality for all languages.[8]

- Nepal National Peoples Liberation Front submitted a 21 point memorandum to the CRC. The demands included the provision for local autonomy, full democracy and freedom from exploitation in all forms in the new Constitution, that the central government should

---

[4] Deepak Thapa, "Day of the Maoist", *Himal South Asian*, 14 no.5 (2001): 4

[5] Nepal Press Digest, 34 (1990): 216

[6] Nepal Press Digest, 34 (1990): 238

[7] Ibid., 238

[8] Nepal Press Digest, 34 (1990): 261

be responsible for only foreign relations, nation-level plans, industry, security and foreign policy, the executive and legislative bodies at both district and central levels should provide for development of all local ethnic communities and their languages, culture and traditions.[9]

- All Nepal Women's association spelt out the need for reservation for women and proper representation of women in all Constitutional bodies.[10]

A very interesting and significant observation was made by the CRC Chairman on the above demands. He said that they dealt primarily with the questions of religion, language, and community and not the institutionalization of democracy on which very few representations had been made. He warned that it would be a tragedy if the country was divided on the issue of language, religion and community.[11] He failed to understand as did many of the political leaders that these groups were demanding an inclusive agenda. Thus, there was no appreciation of their demands and the deep discontent that it reflected. The focus of political movements had always, primarily, been establishing democracy and the multi-ethnicity of Nepal with more than 100 caste/ethnic groups and the grievances of these groups were never on the political agenda.

This discontent was further reinforced upon promulgation of the 1990 Constitution when dissenting notes were expressed by ethnic and other organizations.[12] The Nepal Rashtriya Janajati Party decided not to accept the new Constitution but launch an armed movement as the Constitution had recognized Nepal as a Hindu state, the interim government had ignored that the country be divided into 12 provinces and ethnic communities were neglected.[13] The Mongol National Organization held demonstrations saying

---

[9] Nepal Press Digest, 34 (1990): 311

[10] Nepal Press Digest, 34 (1990): 285

[11] Nepal Press Digest, 34 (1990): 293

[12] Nepal Press Digest, 34 (1990): 471-475

[13] Nepal Press Digest, 34 (1990): 471

that they were not Hindus and was determined to establish a Mongol State in Nepal. They opined that they would boycott elections if the new Constitution did not protect the interests of the Mongols.[14] The National Peoples' Liberation Front described the Constitution as –vague, undemocratic and revivalist.[15] Nepal Rashtriya Dalit Jana Vikas Parishad pointed out that the new Constitution contained no provisions to promote the interests of the depressed class people, who constituted 20 percent of the population of Nepal.[16] It demanded the formation of a Constitutional Commission consisting of representatives of depressed communities to protect their rights and solve their problems.[17] The Nepal Sadhbavana Party declared that by rejecting the demands for a constituent assembly, the interim government had undermined the efforts to maintain a balance among different classes, ethnic groups and communal forces in the country. Further, that the Constitution had failed to reflect the aspirations of half of the population of ethnic groups in the hills and no attention had been paid to their demand for a federal state.[18] The Nepal Jana Jatiya Mahasangh (Nepal Ethnic Groups Confederation), a central organization representing fifteen ethnic organizations criticized the new Constitution for having granted special recognition to one religion (Hindu), one language (Nepali) and demanded that Nepal be declared a secular state.[19] The Utpidit Jatiya Utthan Manch (Oppressed People's Upliftment Front) regretted that their demands had been ignored.[20] Similar grievances were expressed by other groups and organizations.

The run up to the writing and promulgation of the Constitution was thus filled with great discontent. Many of the provisions of the Constitution were clearly looked upon as denying rights to the marginalized and the

---

[14] Nepal Press Digest, 34 (1990): 472

[15] Ibid., 472

[16] Ibid.

[17] Nepal Press Digest, 34 (1990): 482

[18] Nepal Press Digest, 34 (1990): 472

[19] Nepal Press Digest, 34 (1990): 482

[20] Nepal Press Digest, 34 (1990): 492

minorities.[21] Jana Andolan I gave immense opportunities to democratic governments that followed for course correction but they all overlooked these critical issues. [22] The 1999 pattern of representation in legislature did not basically differ from that of the National Panchayat during the party-less era. Brahman/Chhetri and Newar domination continued after 1990 in the three parliamentary elections of 1991, 1994 and 1999, giving these three groups disproportionate representation at the expense of the excluded caste and ethnic groups. Thus the latter lagged behind in influencing polices conducive to their development.[23] The following table brings out the marginalization of the caste/ethnic groups in the House of Representatives of Nepal for successive years.

Table 7: Representation of Different Caste/Ethnic Groups and Gender in the House of Representatives, Nepal, 1991, 1994 and 1999

Caste/ ethnic groups	Population	Percentage of population	Representation of different caste and ethnic groups		
			1991	1994	1999
Hill caste groups	702,320	30.89	114 (55.6%)	129 (62.9%)	122 (59.5%)
Brahman	-	-	37.6	42.0	46.3
Chhetri	-	-	18.1	19.5	17.1
Dalit	1,692	7.11	1(0.5%)	-	
Kirat/Mongol Ethnic groups	501,131	22.04	34(16.6-%)	24 (11.7%)	28 (13.7%)

Contd/-

---

[21] For details see Michael Hutt, "Drafting the Nepal Constitution, 1990", *Asian Survey,* 31 no.11 (1991): 1020-1039 and Narayan Khadka, "Democracy and Development in Nepal: Prospects and Challenges", *Pacific Affairs* 66 no.1(1993): 44-71

[22] C K Lal , "Nepal's Maobaadi", *Himal South Asian,* 14 no.11 (2001): 39-47

[23] UNDP, *Nepal Human Development Report 2009,* 71; Thomas Meyer and Suresh C. Chalise, "Legislative Elite and the Nepalese Parliament : A Study of their Class Characteristics", *Contributions to Nepalese Studies,* 26 no. 1(1999): 27-64.

Newar	124,532	5.58	14 (6.8%)	12 (5.8%)	14 (6.8%)
Ethnic groups of inner Madhes	251,117	1.11	1 (0.5%)	-	-
Madhesi castes	3,464,249	15.24	18 (8.7%)	22 (10.7%)	29 (14.1%)
Madhesi Dalits	904,924	3.99	-	-	-
Madhesi ethnic groups	2,814,927	8.11	18 (8.8%)	14 (6.8%)	10 (4.9%)
Muslim	971,056	4.27	5 (2.4%)	4 (1.6%)	2 (1.0%)
Female	11,377,556	50.04	7 (3.4%)	7 (3.4%)	12 (5.8%)
Male	11,359,378	49.96	198 (96.6%)	198 (96.6%)	193 (94.1%)

Source: United Nations Development Programme, *Nepal Human Development Report 2009: State Transformation and Human Development*, Kathmandu, 2009, 160

The 1990 Constitution and the democratic governments that followed did not change in any major way the position of the marginalized politically, economically or socially. [24] Their multiple grievances were left unheard. The political class was busy with internal power politics, that they had neither the inclination nor the time to look into these issues. The important stage of conflict prevention, sadly, had been allowed to pass by.

---

[24] In 1991 37 percent of the Nepali Congress candidates and 48 percent of those of the CPM-UML were Bahuns and another 22 percent and 16 percent respectively were Chetris, even though these groups have only a share of 13 percent and 16 percent respectively in the population of the country according to the census of 1991. In 1999 elections, almost 40 percent of the MPs selected were Bahuns. The rest were dominated by Chetris or some elitist Newar castes. Thus the ethnic groups are clearly underrepresented compared to their over 40 percent share in the total population. Karl-Heinz Kraemer, "Resistance and the State in Nepal: How representative is the Nepali state?", *Resistance and the State in Nepal,* 16th European Conference on Modern South Asian Studies, Edinburgh, 2000; Karl-Heinz Kraemer, "The Janajati and the Nepali state: Aspects of Identity and Integration", *First Annual Workshop of the Himalayan Studies Network,* C.N.R.S., Meudon, 1998

The Maoist Insurgency: Setting the Agenda, the Violent Way

The Maoist insurgency in Nepal which began in February 1996 with over forty demands to the government covering social, political, economic and foreign policy issues rose on the multiple grievances clearly articulated since 1990, which only got accentuated with their neglect by successive democratic governments. It began in three or four mid-western districts and then spread to almost the entire country. What began as arson, looting, attacking district headquarters, rapidly reached to the extent of challenging the police forces, burning police stations and taking their arms and ammunition, looting banks, abducting individuals, businessmen and police personnel and then demanding ransom. On occasions elections too were effected in the districts where the insurgents had influence as the political workers did not accept tickets even when security was promised. The 40 demands which they submitted to the government in 1996 were as follows.

Table 8: Maoist 40-point Demand, Nepal, February 1996

Nationalism (7)	Political (13)	Economic (13)	Socio-cultural (7)
Abrogation of 1950 treaty	Republican constitution	End capital aggrandizement	Secular state
Abrogation of Mahakali treaty	End royal privileges	Self-reliant economy	Equality to women
Border regulation	Civil authority over army	Land to the tiller	End ethnic oppression
Discontinue Gurkha recruitment	Repeal repressive regulations	Nationalization of dubious property	Abolish untouchability
Introduce work permit system	Release prisoners	Employment generation	Equality of languages
End cultural invasion	End state terrorism	Set minimum wage	Access to education and health services
Stop imperial elements (INGO)	Enquiry on actions against Maoists	Resettle squatters	Protection of the disabled
	Recognition on martyrs and penalty to perpetrators	Debt relief and credit provision	
	Ethnic autonomy	Cheap inputs, fair price for agriculture products	
	Freedom of speech	Control price	
	Freedom of thought	Provide road, electricity, water supply to rural areas	
	Regional devolution	Promote cottage industries	
	Local governance	Control corruption	

Source: United Nations Development Programme, *Nepal Human Development Report 2009: State Transformation and Human Development*, Kathmandu, 2009,140

These demands clearly indicate their agenda of social, political and economic transformation. A close look shows that some of these were spelt out by other groups in Jana Andolan I of 1990 also. The paper argues that, if not for the Maoist insurgency, the accumulated grievances among the majority of the population would have been articulated in some or the other manner given the consistent mis-governance by the elected governments.

In negotiations between the government and the Maoists, their three core demands were interim government, elected Constituent Assembly to frame a new Constitution and a republic state. These were considered non negotiable by the government and peace talks broke down around these very demands. The immediate disapproval of some of these demands was understandable because it would have meant the end of monarchy which had major influence and control over the Army too. However, later the political events in Nepal post April 2006 took a turn such that the Maoists were successful in getting wide acceptance to these very demands.

Their demands also show that they made India as a factor in the internal conflict. However it was not the first time that such demands targeting India were being raised. Notably during 1989-90, the relevance of the 1950 Treaty was raised. It does make them anti-Indian to a certain extent. Being anti-India when out of power is a strategy in Nepali politics which is followed by all the political parties. Thus, it is not a new phenomenon. It is, however, important to stress that Maoist insurgency was primarily regarding grievances within the country – their inequitable society, economy and polity. It was this discontent which sustained it. Direct grievances with India though important did not drive the insurgency and garner wide support from the people. Given the close relations between the two countries, instability within Nepal has a direct impact on India and has led to cooperation and coordination in policies to address security concerns common to both countries. These cooperative measures harmed the Maoists interests and invited their ire towards India.

Since 1999 the Maoists set up parallel governments in many districts denying the government its legitimate control. In November 2001, they attacked the army barracks and fled with the army's weapons. This led to branding them as terrorists and the army was deployed in various parts of the country to respond to the new worsening situation. The Maoist insurgency had claimed over 13,000 lives and destruction worth crores of rupees by the time the Comprehensive Peace Agreement was concluded in November 2006. Apart from other factors, their successes in negating legitimate government rests on three factors – geography (rugged terrain and mountains), a weak central government and a sympathetic population. [25]

Jana Andolan II of April 2006: Assertion by the Marginalized

Jana Andolan II of April 2006 unleashed three important developments in Nepal. First, the beginning of the end of monarchy; second, bringing the Maoists into the political mainstream and with them their agenda of an elected constituent assembly which would draft a new inclusive Constitution that would undo the political-social-economic concentration of power resting in a few and third and the most unexpected, the assertion of rights by the marginalized sections for an inclusive society which changed the very nature of Jana Andolan II.[26] The Comprehensive Peace Agreement concluded on 21 November 2006 explicitly has provisions which relate to political and

---

[25]A country's physical and cultural geography will force the government of that country to confront certain strategic imperatives no matter what form the government takes. For example, Imperial Russia, the Soviet Union and post-Soviet Russia all have faced the same set of strategic imperatives. Similarly, place can also have a dramatic impact on the formation and operation of a militant group, though obviously not in quite the same way that it affects a government, since militant groups, especially transnational ones, tend to be itinerant and can move from place to place. From the perspective of a militant group, geography is important but there are other critical factors involved in establishing the suitability of a place. While it is useful to have access to wide swaths of rugged terrain that can provide sanctuary such as mountains, jungles or swamps, for a militant group to conduct large-scale operations, the country in which it is based must have a weak central government — or a government that is cooperative or at least willing to turn a blind eye to the group. A sympathetic population is also a critical factor in whether an area can serve as a sanctuary for a militant group. In places without a favorable mixture of these elements, militants tend to operate more like terrorists, in small urban-based cells. See Scott Stewart, "Jihadism and the Importance of Place", *Startfor Global Intelligence Review*, March 25,2010,http://www.stratfor.com/weekly/20100324_jihadism_and_im portance_place?u tm_source=SWeekly&utmmedium=email&utmcampaign=100325&utm_content= readmore &elq= 3cef261351034bb586b574ef74d4884e

[26] Dev Raj Dahal, in analyzing the social transformation in Nepal, says that following Jana Andolan II of April 2006 Nepal has seen transformation at five levels – discourse

socio-economic transformation apart from other aspects.[27] When these provisions are implemented there will be state transformation where in power and resources are concentrated not in a small minority but in the hands of the people in general.

However the marginalized groups wanted specific assurances. During Jana Andolan I, the marginalized made their presence felt but did not occupy any significant political space. The Maoist insurgency had politicized people and propagated their agenda of change. They had internalized in them the importance of the CA. Post Jana Andolan II, various marginalized groups organized themselves more effectively and put forward their demands assertively. The Maoists through the use of violence had challenged the government. This had now become a demonstrative effect leading to the belief that resort to violence will draw the government's attention to their grievances and concessions will ensue. Post Jana Andolan II, the political experiment in Nepal has become that much more complex and difficult. Most of these groups were demanding complete proportional representation for elections to the CA. The demand on the nature of federalism, autonomy and self determination varied from group to group. They wanted assurances on all these aspects before the CA elections were held and most of them used violent means to put forward their demands.

The agitations in Terai in January and February following the adoption of the interim Constitution in 2007 saw unprecedented violence.[28] Parliament proceedings were also stalled by members belonging to the Terai to press their demands. The first amendment of the interim Constitution was a result of these agitations. The Madhesi outfits demands included a fully proportional

---

transformation, context transformation, actor transformation, issues transformation, rules transformation. See Dev Raj Dahal, "The Paradox of a Weak State: Distributional Struggles and Social Transformation in Nepal", *Readings on Governance*, IX, 2007, http://www.fesnepal.org/reports/2010/seminar_reports/Statepercent20andpercent 20Socialpercent 20Transformationpercent20inpercent20Nepal.pdf.

[27] The other provisions of the CPA are - management of armies and arms, ceasefire provisions, protection of human rights and fundamental rights.

[28] "Nepal's Troubled Tarai Region", *Asia Report* no. 136 (2007), International Crisis Group, http://www.crisisgroup.org/~/media/Files/asia/south-asia/nepal/136_nepal_ s_troubled _tarai_region.ashx

representation based election system and federal autonomy with the right to self-determination before Constituent Assembly elections.[29] Following the sixth round of talks a 22-Point Agreement was reached between the two sides. This includes compensation to those killed during the Terai movement, guarantee of inclusion of Madhesis and other marginalized groups in the constituent assembly, autonomy to the states in the federal system to be designed by the constituent assembly among others.[30]

The Janatantrik Mukti Morcha (Jwala Group) ordered officials hailing from hills to leave the Terai plains, thereby vitiating the already tense atmosphere by bringing the hills versus plains division. Some of these groups have violent conflicts among themselves and also with Maoist affiliated Madhesi groups.[31] On the other hand the Chure Bhawar Ekta Samaj has been demanding security and protection of the rights of people from the hilly region in Madhesi areas and an autonomous status for Chure Bhawar region.[32]

Government held several rounds of negotiations with the Nepal Federation of Indigenous Nationalities (NFIN). The government had agreed to ensure at least one representation of the 59 listed ethnic communities. The NFIN also agreed to accept the mixed election system if the government guarantees proportional representation of various communities and regions

---

[29] "MJF Dismisses Addition of Constituencies", *Nepalnews.com,* April 13, 2007, http://www.nepalnews.com/archive/2007/apr/apr13/news03.php.

[30] "MJF Presents 26 Demands", *Nepalnews.com,* June 1, 2007, http://www.nepalnews.com/archive/2007/jun/jun01/news12.php; "MJF to Allow CA only if their Demands are Met", *Nepalnews.com,* July 1, 2007, http://www.nepalnews.com/archive/2007/jul/jul01/news01.php; "Govt-MJF reach 22-pt Agreement: MJF Withdraws Protests" *Nepalnews.com,* August 30, 2007, http://www.nepalnews.com/archive/2007/aug/aug30/news11.php

[31] "JTMM Goit Kills Maoist Activist in Siraha", *Nepalnews.com,* July 16, 2007, http://www.nepalnews.com/archive/2007/jul/jul16/news06.php; "Security to Govt Employees is Top Priority: Minister Gurung", *Nepalnews.com,* July 23, 2007, http://www.nepalnews.com/archive/2007/jul/jul23/news09.php; "Killings, Intimidation Continue in Terai", *Nepalnews.com,* July 8, 2007, http://www.nepalnews.com/archive/2007/jul/jul08/news08.php; "Goit Withdraws Talks Offer, Launches Divisive Campaign", *Nepalnews.com,* January 19, 2007, http://www.nepalnews.com/archive/2007/jan/jan19/news02.php.

[32] "Govt-Chure Talks Put Off till Friday", *Nepalnews.com,* July 26, 2007, http://www.nepalnews.com/archive/2007/jul/jul26/news06.php

through this system.[33] The indefinite bandhs called by Sanghiya Limbuwan Rajya Morcha and Khumbuvan Rashtriya Morcha (KRM) paralysed life in eastern districts. They were demanding autonomy, federal state and equal representation in the constituent assembly. The organizers demanded that the region beyond Arun river be declared 'Limbuwan state' in a federal system while the KRM has demanded a 'Khumbuwan state' mostly comprising the same districts.[34] There were agitations by the Dalit Civil Society Movement calling for 20 percent of reservation for people of Dalit community in CA.[35]

Thus many violent agitations took place before CA elections by various groups and organizations demanding specific assurances. The government too concluded agreements with some of these groups meeting their demands. However, many of these assurances would take definite shape following discussions in the CA only.

The Madhesi Agitation - Emergence of Identity Politics

Madhesis have been defined as non-pahadis (non-hilly people) with plains language as their mother tongue regardless of their place of birth or residence. The term encompasses caste hindus, and muslims and in some definitions indigenous Terai groups. Madhesis are underrepresented in all areas of national life. They have lower education and health indicators than hill communities.[36] Terai contributes over $2/3^{rd}$ of GDP. It has 60 percent of agricultural land. Though it is the backbone of national economy, commensurate investments are not made in the region to serve the local

---

[33] "NFIN Climbs Down from PR Demand: Close to Sealing Deal with the Govt", *Nepalnews.com*, August 4, 2007, http://www.nepalnews.com/archive/2007/aug/aug04/news03.php; "Government says No to Ethnicity Based PR", *Nepalnews.com*, June 14, 2007, http://www.nepalnews.com/archive/2007/jun/jun14/news01.php

[34] "Bandh Continues to Hit Normal Life in Eastern Region", *Nepalnews.com*, August 8, 2007, http://www.nepalnews.com/archive/2007/aug/aug08/news08.php; " Limbuwan in Extortion Drive", *Nepalnews.com*, August 1, 2007, http://www.nepalnews.com/archive/2007/aug/aug01/news03.php

[35] "Dalits Demand 20 percent Seats in CA", *Nepalnews.com*, August 18, 2007, http://www.nepalnews.com/archive/2007/aug/aug18/news05.php

[36] "Nepal's Troubled Tarai Region" , International Crisis Group, 5

population. The Madhesi agitation has a special place in the struggles of the marginalized groups with respect to the participation of the people, the violence it unleashed and the issues it introduced into the inclusive agenda. It again showed what people's power could achieve and the extent to which society had been awakened. It was a reflection also of the extent of exclusion in the Nepalese society.

It is generally assumed that half of the population in Nepal lives in the Terai. Even going by official statistics, it is inhabited by 33-34 percent of the population of Nepal. The agitations in Terai are about people living in bordering areas. Their first problem is that of 'identity' which was questioned by successive governments of Nepal in the past. Since their culture, language, dress, manners and customs were similar to those of the Indians living across the border areas their very Nepali identity was questioned. However, the people of Terai assert that it was wrong of the government to question their indigenousness or originality. Second, many were denied 'citizenship' because of which they could not exercise their basic rights, such as selling or buying their own land as they did not have any valid identity card. Third, as their language, culture, dress, differed from the rest and they faced further discrimination. Thus, they want their language to be recognized as one of the local languages and the other aspects as part of Nepal's diverse national culture. Not more than five percent are in the police, none in the Army and less than five percent in the bureaucracy despite their population. The Madhesis sought to correct these imbalances in the national polity and bureaucracy for more than 15 years in a peaceful manner but had no positive response. Seeing the attention the Maoists got following their violent insurgency, the Madhesis also felt that only an armed revolt will be given attention.[37] They seek to play a role in national politics by demanding for proportional representation based on the strength of their population and their domination in regional power structure through a federal system.[38]

---

[37] Rajendra Mahato, "The Madhesi Movement: Prospects for Peace in Nepal", *Nepal Monitor*, September 2, 2007,http://www.nepalmonitor.com/2007/09/the_madhesi_ movement_ prospects_for_peace_in_nepal_.html

[38] Krishna Hachhethu , "Madheshi Nationalism and Restructuring the Nepali State", *Constitutionalism and Diversity in Nepal*, Seminar Centre for Nepal and Asian Studies, Kathmandu, 22-24 August 2007, www.uni-bielefeld.de/midea/pdf/Hachhethu.pdf.

Following the promulgation of the interim Constitution in January 2007, the Madhesis were disappointed to see that the interim Constitution excluded issues of marginalized groups, was silent on issue of a federal democratic republic and did not have provisions for adopting an election system that would be based on proportional representation. Their leader Upendra Yadav said that "even in the new, so called democratic structure, we don't have adequate representation in police, army, judiciary or the political establishment"[1] and stated that their armed struggle would not end till the government ensures them proportional representation at all levels of governance. After 21 days of intense violence which saw anti Maoist sentiment and antagonism between the Hills People and those in the Plains, an agreement was concluded where in the eight parties agreed to embrace federal democratic system through the CA; adopt mixed electoral system and also to undertake fresh delimitation of existing constituencies based on latest census.[40] The Madhesi movement is not just about dignity and respect but also about substantive change in power sharing arrangements and representation.[41]

Prior to the CA elections in April 2008, Nepal saw another violent Madhesi agitation which again saw great loss of life and property. Three Madhesi parties – the Terai Madhesi Loktantrik Party (TMLP), the Madhesi Janadhikar Forum and the Nepal Sadbhavana Party (NSP) together formed the United Democratic Madhesi Front (UDMF). The result was an Eight Point Agreement and some of the issues included the following:-

  i) Nepal will be a federal republican democratic state accepting the wish of the Madhesi people for an autonomous Madhesi state and that of the people of other regions for a autonomous state with

[39] Nalin Verma, "Fire Next Door - Why India Should Worry when Passions are Aflame in Nepal", *The Telegraph,* February 5, 2007, http://www.telegraphindia.com/1070205/asp/nation/story_7351637.asp

[40] "8-parties Reach Understanding to Resolve Terai Unrest; PM to Address Nation on Wednesday", *Nepalnews.com,* January 30, 2007, http://www.nepalnews.com/archive/2007/jan/jan30/news17.php

[41] Prashant Jha, "Nepal at the Crossroads", *Seminar,* no.584 (April 2008), http://www.india-seminar.com/2008/584/584_prashant_jha.htm

federal structure. There will be distinct power sharing between the centre and the regions in the federal structure on the basis of lists. The regions will have complete autonomy and authority. The elected Constituent Assembly will devise a way to apply the formation of such states and the rights attributed to the region and the centre while keeping national sovereignty, unity and integrity intact;

ii) The government will compulsorily appoint, promote and nominate Madhesi, indigenous communities, women, Dalits, backward areas and minority communities to ensure proportional participation in security bodies and all organs of the state;

iii) The entry of Madhesi and other groups into the Nepal Army will be ensured to give the army a national and inclusive structure. [42]

These movements are apart from the other aspects about ethnicity and identity that have become a social and political force and a means to mobilize and organize members of the community as its leaders advance claim for full participation in the affairs of the state. A new politics of identity has become a means to empower these marginalized and oppressed sections.[43] Following the Madhesi uprising, federalism has been firmly put on the national agenda; changes have been made in the electoral system enabling them to have additional political representation, access to citizenship cards has been made easier and reservations and quotas in the civil service and the army have been legislated. Marginalized groups while united in their opposition to the present dispensation are divided on what remedies and policies must be pursued. [44] Thus, despite these gains, the pursuance of Madhesi objective of 'one madhes, one pradesh' could again divide people and lead to a new set of internal conflicts.[45] Many issues still need to be

---

[42] S. Chandrasekaran, "Nepal: Terai Agitation Ends: Update No. 152", *South Asia Analysis Group*, Note 431, February 29, 2008, http://www.southasiaanalysis.org/percent5Cnotes5percent5Cnote431.html

[43] United Nations Development Programme, Nepal Human Development Report 2009, p 85

[44] United Nations Development Programme, Nepal Human Development Report 2009, p 87

[45] "TMLP Proposes Single Madhesh Province", *Nepalnews.com*, March 12, 2008, http://www.nepalnews.com/archive/2008/mar/mar12/news11.php

resolved and lack of accommodation in the present unstable political scenario could result in the marginalized losing the historical gains because only in an atmosphere of peace can the benefits be experienced.

India's Role in the Madhesi Agitation

The Madhesi agitation is an internal movement of Nepal that emerged from a deep sense of exclusion at all levels in polity and society by the Madhesis. The opinion among the people, politicians and the intelligentsia in Nepal is divided regarding the extent of Indian influence. Some opine that it has been minimal and that there has not been any direct Indian official role in fomenting the trouble in Terai. The influence is alleged to have come from people close to the Rashtriya Swayamsevak Sangh (RSS) and Vishwa Hindu Parishad (VHP) in India. During the assembly elections in the Indian state of Uttar Pradesh (UP), the agitations become an issue in Gorakhpur. However the issue was not just religion and had deep undertones of protecting land property in Nepal by vested interests in India who feared that the Maoists land reform agenda would harm their interests. It is also alleged that criminals from UP and Bihar were increasing their activities in Nepal especially with a weak government there and the breakdown of institutional machinery.[46] The support for the Madhesi cause is limited to the border towns where people have relatives across the border in India. However, this does not get translated into active support. On the contrary, there is another opinion that India has never actually used its influence in Kathmandu for redressing the grievances of the Madhesis and that it was

---

[46] Prashant Jha, "The Gorakhpur Connection", *Nepali Times,* no. 365, September 7-13, 2007, http://www.nepalitimes.com/issue/365/Nation/13941; Other reports speak of assertion by the Maoists where they have stated , "We request India and all Indian political parties not to allow hooligans from Bihar and UP to enter Nepal and indulge in looting and arson. As far as the problem of the Terai is concerned, we are capable of dealing with it," For details refer Verma, "Fire Next Door", *The Telegraph*; The Maosit Chief Prachanda has also said that, "While we respect the aspirations of the Terai people, we can't ignore that India's Hindu fundamentalist group, the RSS and its ally—the palace—are behind the current disturbance in Nepal. The entire conspiracy to foment trouble in the Terai was hatched at Gorakhpur (Uttar Pradesh) by the RSS as it does not feel comfortable with Nepal becoming a secular country." For details refer Manoj Dahal, "No Fringe Folks", *Outlookindia.com,* February 12, 2007, http://www.outlookindia.com/article.aspx?233867

more interested in cultivating the elite hill people. Also if India had actually supported the Madhesi agitation it would have created more problems by vindicating the stand of those who feel that Madhesis are Indians. There is another view which holds that India wields a considerable influence over the Madhesi political parties. That India will use this influence to keep certain parties from coming to power and in this manner influence domestic politics of Nepal. Whatever might be the truth, instability of any kind in Terai will harm India as much as it does Nepal.

Peace in the bordering towns is essential for India too. The Terai agitation has imposed stress on its security forces who have had to be on the alert for movement of arms and criminal elements. This is also a strategic region because every major highway, custom point, industrial, economical, and other fertile resources of Nepal lies in Madheshi region.[47] Instability affects both countries and the economic cost is also substantial as the revenue is lost both sides when trade comes to a standstill.

Constituent Assembly Elections: Marginalized Make Their Presence Felt

All these agitations, the violence, the discussions, negotiations and agreements did bring in legislation which sought to ensure the increased participation of the marginalized in the polity and in other governmental institutions. Quotas were introduced to ensure that the marginalized have access to power. With this the beginning of an inclusive agenda was made. Figure 1 brings out the details of this policy. It was evident in the constituent assembly elections that the quota policy made a difference in terms of making the assembly representative of the population as shown in Figure 2.

---

[47] Krishna Hari Pushkar, "Seeds of Ethno-Civil War in Terai", *Nepal Monitor,* December 2007, http://www.nepalmonitor.com/2007/12/seeds_of_ethno-civil_war_in_nepal_Terai.html

Figure 1

Quota for Excluded Caste and Ethnic Groups and Region in the Constituent Assembly, Nepal, 2008

Figure 2

Social Representation in Constituent Assembly, Nepal 2008

Source: Figure 1 and 2, United Nations Development Programme, *Nepal Human Development Report 2009: State Transformation and Human Development*, Kathmandu, 2009, 73

The actual figures clearly show that the constituent assembly is in fact a representative body. From being marginal, insignificant and inconsequential to the politics in Nepal, the Madhesis have become indispensable for government formation. It is significant to note that both the President and Vice-President following the elections are Madhesis.

Table 9: Social Representation in the Constituent Assembly, Nepal, 2008

Population groups	FPTP result	PR result	Nomination	Total
Hill Dalits	6	30	-	36
Madhesi Dalits	1	12	0	13
Hill Janajati	66	89	9	164
Madhesi/Tarai Janajati	13	30	7	50
Madhesi	48	76	4	128
Muslim, Churaute	7	9	1	17
Others (Hill Brahman, Chhetri)	99	89	5	193
Total	240	335	26	601
Women	30	161	6	197

Source: United Nations Development Programme, *Nepal Human Development Report 2009: State Transformation and Human Development*, Kathmandu, 2009, 74

With specific reference to the FPTP system of voting, Table 10 brings out the details of the results of each party caste/ethnic wise. The advent of Unified Communist Party of Nepal –Maoist (UCPN-Maoist) that came out as the biggest political party from the elections has provided it an opportunity to transform its wartime ideology, structures and goal into a mass-based competitive party. It has also given opportunity to old parties – Nepali Congress Party (NC), Communist Party of Nepal-Unified Marxist Leninist (CPN-UML), Rashtriya Prajatantra Party (RPP), Rashtriya Janshakti Party (RJP), etc to foster democratization of party structures and leadership. The emergence of new political parties - UCPN (Maoist), Madhesi Jana Adhikar Forum (MJAF), Tarai-Madhes Loktantrik Party (TMLP) and Sadbhavana Party (SP) - has provided mobility to new social groups in politics. It has substantially increased the representation of various social groups— women, youth, Dalits and ethnic groups in the 601-member CA as shown in Table 10.[48]

Table 10: Representation of Caste /Ethnic Groups and Gender in the FPTP Electoral System of the Constituent Assembly, Nepal, April 2008

Party name	Hill Brahman-/Chhetri /Thakuri	Janajati excluding Tharu	Madhesi including Tharu	Hill Dalits	Muslim	Female	Male	Total
Unified CPN (Maoist)	56	40	16	8	0	23	97	120
Nepali Congress	21	8	7	0	1	2	35	37
CPN (UML)	18	10	4	0	1	1	32	33
Madhesi People's Rights Forum, Nepal	1	1	25	0	3	2	28	30
Tarai Madhes Loktantrik Party	0	0	9	0	0	1	8	9

Contd/-

[48] Dev Raj Dahal, "The Constituent Assembly Election and Challenges Ahead", *Kurzberichte aus der Internationalen Entwicklungszusammenarbeit: Asien und Pazifik* (Reports from International Development, Asia and Pacific) June 2008, Friedrich-Ebert-Stiftung, http://library.fes.de/pdf-files/iez/05481.pdf

Sadbhawana Party	0	0	4	0	0	0	4	4
Janamorcha Nepal	1	1	0	0	0	0	2	2
Nepal Workers and Peasants Party	0	2	0	0	0	0	2	2
Independents	0	0	1	0	1	0	2	2
Rastriya Janamorcha	1	0	0	0	0	0	1	1
Total	**98**	**62**	**66**	**8**	**6**	**29**	**211**	**240**
Percent (a)	40.8	25.8	27.5	3.3	2.5	12.1	87.9	100.0
Proportion of caste/ethnicity in total population (b)	30.9	23.1	31.5	7.9	4.3	50.5	49.5	
Representation ratio (a/b)	1.3	1.1	0.9	0.4	0.6	0.2	1.8	

Source: United Nations Development Programme, *Nepal Human Development Report 2009: State Transformation and Human Development*, Kathmandu, 2009, 158

The winner in the elections was a party which championed the cause of the marginalized sections while the established parties which had many opportunities since 1990 came a far second and third as shown the following table.

Table 11: Number of Seats of Political Parties in CA Election, Nepal, 2008

No	Political parties	FPTP result	PR result	Total	Nominees*	Grand total
1	Unified CPN (Maoist)	123	105	228	10	238
2	Nepali Congress	36	73	109	5	114
3	CPN (UML)	34	70	104	5	109
4	Madhesi People's Rights Forum	29	22	51	2	53
5	Tarai-Madhes Loktantrik Party	9	11	20	1	21
6	Sadbhawana Party (Mahato)	4	5	9	1	10
7	Rastriya Prajatantra Party	0	8	8	-	8
8	CPN (ML)	0	8	8	1	9
9	CPN (United)	0	5	5	-	5
10	Nepal Workers and Peasants Party	2	2	4	1	5
11	Rastriya Janamorcha	1	3	4	-	4
12	Rastriya Prajatantra Party Nepal	0	4	4	-	4
13	Rastriya Janashakti Party	0	3	3	-	3
14	Rastriya Janamukti Party	0	2	2	-	2
15	CPN (Unified)	0	2	2	-	2

Contd/-

16	Nepal Sadbhawana Party (Anandi Devi)	0	2	2	-	2
17	Nepali Janta Dal	0	2	2	-	2
18	Sanghiya Loktantrik Rastriya Manch	0	2	2	-	2
19	Samajbadi Prajantantrik Janta Party Nepal	0	1	1	-	1
20	Dalit Janajati Party	0	1	1	-	1
21	Nepal Pariwar Dal	0	1	1	-	1
22	Nepal Rastriya Party	0	1	1	-	1
23	Nepal Loktantrik Samajbadi Dal	0	1	1	-	1
24	Chure Bhawar Rastriya Ekata Party Nepal	0	1	1	-	1
	Independents	2	0	2	-	2
	Total	240	335	575	26	601

* Refers to 26 members nominated from various sections of society to make a 601-member CA.

Source: United Nations Development Programme, *Nepal Human Development Report 2009: State Transformation and Human Development*, Kathmandu, 2009, 159

At this juncture, a mention of some of the changes brought out in Nepal through legislation and other measures brings out the change that has taken place in the national agenda of Nepal. When implemented they bring into the mainstream the marginalized by ensuring their presence in various institutions of society. Some of the important measures taken to further the inclusive agenda following the Comprehensive Peace Agreement are as follows:

Inclusive Provisions after the CPA[49], Nepal, November 2006

1. **Citizenship Act. 26 November 2006:** removed some aspects of gender-based discrimination, e.g. permitting both father and mother to transmit citizenship to their children, further enabled Madhesi/Terai people to obtain citizenship among other progressive steps.

2. **Ratification of Protocols of Convention on the Rights of the Child, 2007:** concerned the protection of children in armed conflict and prohibited the sale of children and child prostitution.

3. **Interim Constitution 2007, 15 January 2007:** pronounced Nepal a secular state recognized the right of traditionally marginalized groups; provided the right to non discrimination and the right not to be subjected to untouchability as fundamental rights.

4. **Amendment Bill of Interim Constitution, 9 March 2007:** amending Article 33 (D) the Bill has stated that Madhesis, Dalits, ethnic Janajatis, Women, labourers, peasants, the disabled, backward classes and regions will be provided with a proportional representation in the state. Similarly, amending Article 138, the Bill said that the present centralized and unitary model of the state will be restructured so as to make it inclusive and democratic, with a federal system in place.

5. **Election to Members of the Constituent Assembly Act 2007:** adopted a mixed electoral system with both the FPTP and PR systems. Right to Information Act, 18 July 2007, guaranteed access to official documents to any citizen, excluding only those papers related to the 'investigation, inquiry and prosecution' of crimes and those which jeopardize the "harmonious relationship between various castes or communities".

6. **Agreement with Bonded Labourers (Kamaiya), 25 July 2007:** Government signed an agreement that sets out a timetable for the allocation of land and other support measures to ex-Kamaiyas.

---

[49] United Nations Development Programme, Nepal Human Development Report 2009, 71

7. **Civil Service Bill, 3 August 2007:** amended the Civil Service Act 1993. Among others it provided seat reservation to excluded people and backward regions and trade union rights. The reservation quotas in the civil service are as follows: women (33 percent). Janajatis (27 percent) Madhesi (22 percent). Dalits (9 percent) persons with disabilities (5 percent) and backward regions (4 percent).

8. **Working Journalists Bill 2007, 6 August 2007:** among other this has made provision of provident fund, minimum salary, treatment compensation, capacity building, and limiting media houses to keep only 15 percent journalists on contract.

9. **Ratification of ILO Convention 169, 22 August 2007:** this will ensure the rights of Janajati with regard to culture, land, natural resources, education, traditional justice, recruitment and employment conditions, vocational training, social security and health, as well as the development of a mechanism for consultation and participation in governance.

10. **Ratification of ILO Convention 105, August 2007:** It banned forced labour.

11. **Provision of Quotas of Posts in the Nepal Police and Armed Police Force, October 2007:** This reserved quotas for women and marginalized groups.

12. **Memorandum of Understanding between Ministry of Peace and Reconstruction and the Badi Community, 16 October 2007:** It made the provision of the right to take citizenship with the surname of their choice, an end to the forced use of derogatory surnames; and free schooling for children of the Badi community.

13. **12th amendment to the Nepal Police Regulations, 8 November 2007:** It amended the regulation to provide for recruiting 32 percent indigenous nationalities, 28 percent Madhesis, 15 percent Dalits, 20 percent women and 5 percent from the "backward regions".

14. 90-point Government's Programs and Policies, 10 September 2008: the main priorities included Constitution making, the peace process, socio-economic transformation, role of private, public and cooperative sectors in economic progress and special plans for the Karnali region.

15. Ordinance on Social Inclusion, 2009: It makes the public service inclusive. The proposed ordinance reserves 45 percent of posts to women, Adivasi Janajati, Madhesi, Dalit, people with disabilities and residents of "backward regions", while filling vacant posts through free competition.

Nepal's Transformation Begins but Instability Remains

The process of bringing the issues of the marginalized to centre stage of Nepali politics has been both a difficult and violent struggle. The credit for giving these issues a permanent and a prominent place in Nepal's politics rests primarily on the Maoists. They have been consistent and uncompromising in their demand for a CA which they believed was an essential ingredient to redraw the power equations. Significantly, this is what they exactly did through participation in the CA elections and emerging as the largest party. The dominant discourse in Nepali politics will be what should constitute an 'inclusive agenda' and how to implement it. The credit for the representative character of the CA goes to all the marginalized sections and it is indeed a great achievement for the polity and society of Nepal. As seen, with the passage of time, the excluded majority have become effective in organizing themselves, leaders coming from within, articulating and asserting their demands so as to ensure their direct participation in setting the agenda.

These changes however have come on the bedrock of intense violence and agitations. This is not a constructive development. Peace is needed to sustain the change so that it can take deep roots and for this violence has to be taken out of the society. Recourse to violence undermines legitimate, peaceful and democratic means of grievance redressal. The consistent failure of democratic governments to correct their course led to this situation. The signals for the impending events were clearly there in the Jana Andolan

I of 1990. A multiethnic society of over 100 caste/ethnic groups needs rules which are adhered to and respected by all. A system of checks and balances is required so that there is legitimate space for all and no one group or caste dominates the other.

The gains of 1990 were wasted away and this led to the Maoist insurgency and then Jana Andolan II 2006. Are huge gains made Post Jana Andolan II and the CA elections also getting wasted? Having reached the CA, what are the leaders for the marginalized sections doing now? How influential and effective have they been in taking forward the agenda? Sadly, a rigidity has crept in which has the potential to undo the historic gains made so far. The task is still incomplete and only a beginning has been made. The marginalized groups while united in their opposition to the present dispensation are divided on what remedies and polices must be pursued. Debating what constitutes an 'inclusive agenda' has become controversial and pits these groups against each other. Thus, while uniting for expressing 'exclusion' was easy, deciding and implementing an inclusive agenda will be more difficult.

Accommodation and consensus have become rare features in Nepal's politics. Does this reflect in any sense the political culture of Nepal? This is the same political culture which led to Jana Andolan I and II. The same political culture which gave rise to the various marginalized groups and their assertion. Have the leaders, keeping in view competitive politics, failed the people? The civil society and intelligentsia in each of these groups need to come forward and talk of practical solutions which can accommodate all in the 'inclusive agenda'. An inability to do so will result in the continuation of the unstable phase

The internal conflict has unveiled before the external world a new agenda of change for Nepal. The external world has to change its policies to support, sustain and encourage this state transformation as this will address the root causes of conflict. For, otherwise, again another conflict will break up to fight the exclusion. The external stakeholders have to formulate their policies keeping in view these multiple uncertainties and these parallel features of progress and status quo.

What do these movements Post Jana Andolan II indicate to the external stakeholders especially India. It is seen that:-

i) Extreme violence spills over its borders so there is rise of security concerns.

ii) It has got used to conducting relations with established political parties with whom relations go back to decades. Now, it has to build relations with new parties, new leaders and their new agenda. This brings in uncertainty in the relations. Nobody knows how they will react to events and issues because there is no past record and experience with them to draw conclusions. The foreign policy has to be flexible enough to factor this element of unpredictability in relations.

iii) These new groups have become part of mainstream politics through the path of violence and they represent a constituency which is restless and rigid with high expectations and quick results. 'Accommodation' is not something they are thinking of presently. More so because, having become part of democratic politics, electoral gains could force them to pursue competitive politics. They could be posturing in important foreign policy issues too which might not be in India's interests. Bilateral relations will be under stress in this transitional period till the process of change is complete in Nepal. Dealing with them will be a challenge for India's foreign policy.

iv) India will get inter-twined in the politics of these innumerable groups as has been seen during the Madhesi agitations.

v) Decisions on foreign policy for Nepal too will be difficult because now building consensus will be a difficult process. Once the federal structure is decided the external stakeholders will have to deal with the demands of the federal units too. This will be a completely new experience for both India and Nepal.

vi) It is in the external stakeholder's interest to see that these issues are resolved quickly for continuous state of conflict and instability deepen divisions bilaterally too.

vii) India's policy has to be based on supporting these groups who pursue the 'inclusive agenda'.

India is an important player for stability in Nepal. Change has taken place and is taking place in Nepal, but in India there is continuity in those who formulate and implement foreign policy. Do they understand the change that is taking place in Nepal? Have they understood the whole debate of exclusion and the need for state transformation? There seems to be a gap in India's perception and the demands of the situation on the ground. The need of the time now is to view Nepal completely from a different holistic perspective to adopt and implement policies which balance strategic considerations and the requirements of the peace process. Only then will peace and stability prevail in Nepal and benefit India in the process. The harsh consequences of not doing so will not be limited to Nepal only but the brunt will have to be borne by India too.

Implications of the Internal Conflict on India

In trying to understand the trans-border consequences of the internal conflict in Nepal, this paper seeks to focus on India exclusively. India, the most important external stakeholder is directly influenced by this instability politically, socially and most importantly in terms of security.

India has always stated that its stature and strength cannot be divorced from the quality of its relations with the immediate neighbors[50] and that a stable and peaceful neighborhood provides the positive external environment which enables it to focus on the primary task of its socio-economic development[51]. Nepal is an important country in India's immediate neighborhood. Their close historical, socio-cultural and economic relationship is symbolized by, among other things, the open 1,800 km-long border that they share which provides for the free movement of people and the fact

---

[50] I.K Gujral, *Continuity and Change: India's Foreign Policy*, (Delhi: MacMillan, 2003); Padmaja Murthy, "The Gujral Doctrine and Beyond", *Strategic Analyses*, 23 no. 4 (1999): 773-796.

[51] Shiv Shankar Menon, "The Challenges Ahead for India's Foreign Policy", Speech delivered at the Observer Research Foundation, New Delhi, April 10, 2007, http://www.indianembassy.org/prdetail780/—%09—andquot;the-challenges-ahead-for-india's-foreign-policyandquot;—speech-by-foreign-secretary,-shri-shivshankar-menon-at-the-observer-research-foundation,-new-delhi

that the two countries also provide national treatment to each other's citizens.[52] With regard to the security context, Nepal's geopolitical importance for India has been stressed by both British India[53] and independent India.[54]

India-Nepal relations have for most of the period since Independence been difficult. Nepal under the monarchy always looked upon India with suspicion for encouraging democratic forces and sought to build extra-regional linkages especially with China. In this context the difficult period of 1988-90 marked a new low in India-Nepal relations under the monarchy[55]. Normalcy was restored in 1990 following Jana Andolan I which ended the party-less panchayat system under the monarchy.

---

[52] The Text of the Treaty of Peace and Friendship, 1950 between India and Nepal spells out the special relations between the two countries. Articles 6 and Article 7 of the 1950 Treaty specifically spell out the details regarding national treatment provided to each other's citizens. For the text of the Treaty of 1950 refer Appendix in Verinder Grover ed, *Encyclopedia of SAARC Nations, Nepal, Vol 5* (New Delhi: Deep & Deep, 1997) 684.

[53] The 1815 Treaty of Segouli and the Treaty of 1823 defined British India's relations with Nepal. For details on British India's security concerns arising from Nepal refer Kanchanmoy Mojumdar, *Political Relations Between India and Nepal* (New Delhi: Munshiram Manoharlal, 1973)

[54] Following Independence, a critical dimension of the importance of the neighbourhood to India and the anxieties concerning it comes out in a statement made by Prime Minister Jawaharlal Nehru with regard to Nepal in Parliament on 6 December 1950. He pointed out, "... [India's] interest in the internal conditions of Nepal becomes still more acute and personal, if I may say so, because of the developments across our borders, because of the developments in China and Tibet to be frank. And regardless of our feelings about Nepal, we are interested in our own country's security, in our country's borders. Now so far as the Himalayas are concerned, they lie on the other side of Nepal, mostly, not on this side. Therefore, the principal barrier to India lies on the other side of Nepal and we are not going to tolerate any person coming over the barrier. Therefore, much as we appreciate the independence of Nepal, we cannot risk our own security by anything going wrong in Nepal which permits either the barrier to be crossed or weakens our frontiers." Quoted in MD Dharmadasani, "Democratic Experiment in Nepal: India's Role and Attitudes," in *Encyclopedia of SAARC Nation.* Verindar Grover *ed,* 1997. While these conventional security concerns remain, some of the new concerns which have arisen are India's concerns regarding fake Indian currency entering India through Nepal, the country being used for terrorist activities directed at India, and the use of Madarsas for anti –India activities. These are discussed at regular bilateral forums of the two countries.

[55] A complete dilution of the spirit of the 1950 Treaty was observed. Nepal bought arms from China which included anti-aircraft guns and medium range SSMs besides assault rifles etc.

The Scenario before the Onset of the Internal Conflict

The new multiparty democracy under a Constitutional Monarchy resulted in a clearly positive bilateral India-Nepal relationship. While there were stresses and strains, and misunderstandings too, with new security challenges from non-state actors and the misuse of the open borders, overall there was a marked improvement in India-Nepal relations from what existed till the beginning of the 1990s.

Jana Andolan I of 1990 and the subsequent developments set in great optimism in Indo-Nepal relations. **First**, India believed that stability in Nepal was based on the twin principles of Constitutional Monarchy and Multiparty Democracy, the two principles which were incorporated in Nepal's Constitution of 1990. This policy continued till Jana Andolan II of 2006. **Second**, India was hopeful that the new political leaders would conduct Nepal–China relations in a manner which would be appreciative of India' security concerns, unlike the period which preceded it. [56] **Third**, bilateral relations after 1990 were marked by regular high level meetings between

---

that entered Nepal through the Kathmandu-Kodari road. The differences that followed extended the entire gamut of bilateral relations. For details of India's views on the manner in which India-Nepal relations had eroded, refer to Narasimha Rao, Statement in Parliament, April 26, 1989, in *Nepal's Relations with India and China, Documents 1947-1992 Vol. 2* ed. Avtar Singh Bhasin, (Delhi: Siba Exim, 1994), 998. India's official reason was, "...strains surface in Indo-Nepal relations, especially after the lapse of the Indo-Nepal Treaties of Trade and Transit in March 1989.This was consequential on the non-fulfillment by Nepal of the commitments made when a new trade treaty was negotiated and initialed in October 1988." For Details refer, Ministry of External Affairs, Annual Report 1989-90, Government of India, 1990.

[56] The positive development began with the visit in June 1990 of Prime Minister Krishna Prasad Bhattarai and interestingly the issue of security was referred to in a veiled manner. The joint communiqué of June 1990 set the tone for great optimism. It restored status quo ante in bilateral relations to April 1, 1987, a period before the emergence of bilateral tensions. Both sides undertook to fully respect each others security concerns, not to allow activities in the territory of one that would prejudice the security of the other and to have prior consultations, with a view to reaching mutual agreement on such defence related matters which in view of either country could pose a threat to its security. This was clearly with reference to Nepal conducting its relations with China after taking into consideration Indian sensitivities. For details refer, Ministry of External Affairs, Annual Report 1990-91, Government of India, 1991. Nepal –China relations become a major concern for India after King Gyanendra took over powers and later with the Maoists coming to power in 2008.

leaders and senior officials. The relations were institutionalized with the formation of various commissions and committees so that there could be continuity despite change of individuals at the helm. In 1991, for the first time, an Indo-Nepal High Level Task Force was formed which prepared a comprehensive programme for bilateral cooperation. **Fourth,** the focus was cooperation in the spheres of industrial and human resources development; harnessing of the waters of the common rivers for the benefit of the peoples of the two countries; protection and management of the environment. Various possibilities of widening bilateral economic cooperation were also considered. Many new agreements were also signed in this direction.[57] This included trade, transit, agriculture, cooperation in water resources etc.[58] Subsequent years saw further expansion of economic cooperation.[59]

However, soon bilateral relations were to come out of this comfort zone with the rise of new security concerns.

The Scenario after the Onset of the Internal Conflict

By 1998, the Joint Working Group on Border Management had held its second meeting in Delhi on 16th and 17th June. A number of decisions with the objective of preventing misuse of the open border between India and Nepal by undesirable elements were taken by the two sides. Institutional mechanisms were also set up to deal with the economic crimes and combat smuggling activities across the open India-Nepal border. [60]

The hijacking of Indian airlines flight IC-814 with 178 passenger and 11 crew members on board which took off from Kathmandu to Delhi decisively brought issues concerning security to the forefront. These include

---

[57] Ministry of External Affairs, *Annual Report 1990-91,* Government of India, 1991

[58] Ministry of External Affairs, *Annual Report 1991-92,* Government of India, 1992

[59] Ministry of External Affairs, *Annual Report 1993-94,* Government of India, 1994; Ministry of External Affairs, *Annual Report 1996-97,* Government of India, 1997.

[60] Ministry of External Affairs, *Annual Report 1998-99,* Government of India, 1999. The focus of economic cooperation till then was trade, transit, and cooperation in economic activities and water resources. To these were added efforts to combat economic crimes.

Pakistani ISI's activities in Nepal which are reported to have begun in the initial year of the nineties. They were using Nepal to carry out their anti-India activities taking advantage of the open borders between India and Nepal to gain easy access into India. Some reports brought out the nexus among ISI agents, the bureaucrats, smugglers and politicians of Nepal which enabled the ISI to carry out its activities.[61] Thus, even before the concerns arising out of Maoist insurgency assumed centre stage the misuse of the open Indo-Nepal borders was a cause of concern. Since then mechanisms to fight new security challenges which included the Maoist insurgency and terrorism have been incorporated and institutionalized in the bilateral mechanism.

The July 31, 2000 visit of PM Koirala focused on a wide range of issues encompassing security, energy, economic development, boundary demarcation, terrorism, trade, border management and many other issues. During the visit, one of the long standing demands of Nepal for a review of the 1950 Treaty was agreed upon and India and Nepal decided to undertake a review of all issues pertaining to the Treaty. Certain realism was noticed in the bilateral relations.

Border Management assumed importance in the bilateral relationship. By the year 2000, the 5th meeting of India-Nepal High Level Task Force to review ongoing projects and initiate new ones, recommended focus on border infrastructure. The home secretary level talks on security for cooperation in combating activities of criminals and terrorists called for improved management of Indo-Nepal borders to stop cross border crime, combating terrorism and managing the fallout of the Maoist insurgency. Both the countries agreed not to allow each other's territories for prejudicial activities directed against the other. During this period India completed the building of 22 bridges in Nepal which opened up new possibilities of trade and

---

[61] For further details see The Kathmandu Nexus by Harinder Baweja , *India Today,* June 12, 2000. pp 26-29 http://www.india-today.com/itoday/20000612/nation2.html.. For a Nepali viewpoint on the report in India Today about ISI's activities , refer Prakah Dahal, "Nepal Game Plan – Pathalogocally Malicious", The Rising Nepal, June 19, 2000. Nepal officially stated that it is committed to its policy of not allowing Nepal's territory to be used against any friendly country. For details refer The Rising Nepal June 7, 2000.

investment.[62] There was now a clear assertion of the need to focus on combating security concern arising from the open borders. However it needs to be stressed that though the activities of non-state actors emanate from Nepal, they do not emanate from the Government of Nepal. These activities do not have state patronage.

Since 2004-2005, in order to streamline security related cooperation between India and Nepal a network of bilateral institutional mechanisms evolved, comprising Bilateral Consultative Group on Security Issues, Home Secretary level talks and Joint Working Group on Border Management, which proved to be very effective in addressing mutual security concerns.[63] Recognizing that the growth of Maoist insurgency in Nepal is a shared security concern, India provided assistance as to Nepal.[64] Measures have been taken to enhance cooperation with Nepal for effective border management and intelligence sharing. Sashastra Seema Bal (SSB) personnel have been deployed along the Indo-Nepal border with a view to ensure peace and security along the border and prevent unfriendly elements from exploiting the open border for cross border subversive activities. Discussions were also concluded on a bilateral agreement on Mutual Legal Assistance in Criminal Matters and an updated Extradition Treaty which would strengthen the institutional legal arrangements between India and Nepal for effectively combating crime and terrorism. With a view to facilitate trade and transit, strengthen security and efficient management of the border, India took up several new projects to improve border infrastructure along the India- Nepal border. These projects include development of border check-posts, improvement of road infrastructure in the Nepalese Terai to

---

[62] Ministry of External Affairs, *Annual Report 2000-01*, Government of India, 2001

[63] Ministry of External Affairs, *Annual Report 2004-05*, Government of India, 2005

[64] Dev Raj Dahal, "Nepal: Supporting Peace Process through a Systemic Approach", Berghof Foundation for Peace Support, September 2005, 15-17, http://www.berghof-peacesupport.org/publications/NEP_Supporting_ Peace_Processes_ Through_a_ Systemic_ Approach.pdf. This report spells out the cooperation among USA, UK and India in giving military assistance to Nepal Army. Also see Rita Manchanda, "New Guns in an Old Bottle", 20 no. 3 (2003),http://www.hinduonnet.com/fline/fl2003/stories/200302140011053 00. htm. The author is of the opinion that the strengthening of the Kings army in military terms does not point to the health of multi-party democracy, rather it points to the possible rise of autocratic forces.

strengthen connectivity of towns and villages with the East West Highway, improvement in the roads and highways on the Indian side of the border which connect to the towns in Nepal and bringing broad-gauge railway connectivity to Nepalese towns in the Terai from the nearest points in India where broad-gauge already exists. Once implemented, this infrastructure would enable movement of people and goods and also help in efficient management of the border.[65] The Indian Consulate in Birgunj also started functioning. Border security concerns were reiterated when Indian External Affairs Minister SM Krishna visited Nepal from 15-17 January 2010. Four MoUs were signed including strengthening roads in Terai with Indian assistance. India agreed to assist Nepal in developing infrastructure in border areas through development of integrated check posts; cross border rail links; feeder and lateral roads in Terai area of Nepal. [66]

Simultaneously, concerns emanating from the activities of the Maoist insurgents came to occupy much larger space in bilateral relations. Indian paramilitary forces were soon deployed along the border to prevent miscreants from misusing the open border between the two countries. India's consistent position during this difficult period was that a national consensus needs to be evolved based on the principles of Multiparty Democracy and Constitutional Monarchy to effectively address the challenges posed by the Maoist insurgency and that only a representative government, with the participation of all parliamentary parties, working in close cooperation with the monarchy, could help in evolving a sustainable solution to the conflict. Last, India strongly condemned the recourse to violence by Maoists and supported all efforts of Government of Nepal to restore normalcy and order in the country.[67] India was also of the opinion that the Maoist problem could not be overcome by military alone.[68]

All the above stress the point that security had occupied centre stage and efficient border management and improving border infrastructure

[65] Ministry of External Affairs, *Annual Report 2007-08*, Government of India, 2008

[66] Ministry of External Affairs, *Annual Report 2009-10*, Government of India, 2010

[67] Ministry of External Affairs, *Annual Report 2003-04*, Government of India, 2004.

[68] "India has "very very high stakes" in Nepal: Saran", *Nepalnews.com*, November 17, 2005, http://www.nepalnews.com/archive/2005/nov/nov17/news06.php

became the key elements. This new scenario was the result of the internal conflict and instability in Nepal. The open borders were no longer 'open' and security concerns persist.[69]

The Maoist insurgents of Nepal had multiple links with India. Some ex-servicemen from the Indian army and the ex-Gorkha soldiers are reported to have trained the Maoist Peoples' Liberation Army (PLA) in the initial days. The Maoists set up camps along the forested area of India-Nepal border. Indian Maoists also trained their Nepali counterparts in the forest of Jharkhand. The Maoists obtained weapons through smuggling from illegal markets in India and Tibet apart from grey markets in other areas. The open India-Nepal border facilitated this and on various occasions Indian security personnel had confiscated huge cache of arms and explosives intended for the Nepali market.[70] The relations between Indian Naxals and the Nepali Maoists took the form of attending each other's meetings, helping in propagating each other's views, having joint views on certain issues and providing safe havens.

The Annual Reports of the Ministry of Home Affairs clearly state the nature of relations between the CPN (M) and similar groups in India. According to these reports the MCCI (Maoist Communist Centre of India) is reported to have provided logistic support including arms, shelter and manpower to the CPN(M). The Maoists from Nepal are reported to have received military training in MCCI camps and Communist Party of India – Marxist Leninist (People's War) (CPML –PW) camps.[71] These interactions posed new security challenges that were hitherto unknown to India, at a time when the Maoist/Naxal movement in India was at resurgence and spreading its reach. It needs to be stated that the Maoist insurgency of Nepal did not depend on their Indian connection to sustain their movement. While these interactions definitely helped them and aided in having a regional perspective, their insurgency was homegrown.

---

[69] For details of India's security concerns on the open border refer, Rakesh Sood, Interview, *Republica,* April 29, 2010, http://myrepublica.com/portal/index.php?action=news_details& news_id=18049

[70] Paul Soren, "Maoist Warfare Strategy", *World Focus, 331 (2007)*

[71] Ministry of External Affairs, *Annual Report 2003-04,2004-05, 2005-06*

They were both part of international groups too.[72] Nepal's Maoists had links with similar elements at the international level who were very appreciative of their people's war and their success in setting up parallel government structures. Its international allies included the Revolutionary Internationalist Movement (RIM) which played an important role in encouraging them to go ahead with their people's war strategy. Nepal's Maoists acknowledge that as a part of the RIM, they learnt from the experiences of similar groups and movements in other parts of the world. [73] These experiences were passed on to their Indian counterparts. Then there was another important grouping for the formation of which the Nepal's Maoists took a major initiative. This was the Coordinating Committee of Maoist Parties and Organizations of South Asia (CCOMPOSA) formed in July 2001 by nine Maoist outfits from India, Bangladesh, Nepal and Sri Lanka. This regional confluence helped smoothen the path for the September 2004 unification of India's two major Naxalite organizations – the CPI-ML (PW) and the MCC-I - as the Communist Party of India (Maoist). This helped in reuniting a movement which was for sometime divided in India. Earlier in February 2001 National Conference Resolution on 'a new Soviet Federation for South Asia', the CPN (M) had developed a regional perspective. The conference concluded that India was a major obstacle to any regional popular revolution and any successful insurgency would eventually have to fight with India. CCOMPOSA's twin aims were "struggling for the achievement of people's power in one's own country" and "fighting against American imperialism and Indian expansionism".[74]

The Maoists had expanded their reach and presence throughout Nepal and had put a good defense against the Nepal Army too. They had demonstrated their ability to disrupt life in major towns including in the Kathmandu valley. Growth of Maoist insurgency in Nepal was a matter of serious concern to India because of its adverse fall-out for India due to the

---

[72] PV Ramana, "Comrades in 'Arms': India-Nepal Maoist Ties", *World Focus*, 331(2007)

[73] "Nepals Maoists: Purists or Pragmatists?", *Asia Report no.132* (2007), International Crisis Group http://www.crisisgroup.org/en/regions/asia/south-asia/nepal/132-nepals-Maoists-purists-or-pragmatists.aspx

[74] Ibid.

open and unregulated border as well as the links between Nepal's Maoists and the Indian Naxalite groups.

By 2005 new security concerns arose to the ones already existing. On 1 February 2005, the multi-party Government led by Prime Minister Sher Bahdur Deuba was dissolved by the King of Nepal. An emergency was declared and fundamental rights were suspended. Political leaders, media personnel, intellectuals, human rights activists and student leaders were under house arrest/detention. There was strict censorship on both print and electronic media. These developments in Nepal constituted a serious setback to the cause of democracy, benefiting the anti-Constitutional forces and undermining both democracy as well as the institution of monarchy. India reiterated that the challenges being faced by Nepal could be addressed effectively only on the basis of national consensus. In this context, India called for a return to democratic processes at the earliest. India also called for immediate release of all arrested political leaders, media personnel, intellectuals and human rights activists. While India continued to support all efforts for the restoration of political stability and economic prosperity in Nepal, it was critical of the Kings actions.[75] The King overlooked suggestions of India and the international community that the maoist insurgency should be tackled with the involvement of the political parties. India,[76] along with

---

[75] Ministry of External Affairs, *Annual Report 2004-05*, Government of India. Before the emergency was declared, the bilateral relations saw a series of interactions. A comprehensive review of bilateral issues was undertaken during the visit of Prime Minister of Nepal to India. In addition, several important bilateral meetings were held including the Home Secretary-level Talks (19-20 January 2005), Joint Working Group on Border Management (17-18 January 2005), Meetings of India- Nepal Bilateral Consultative Group on Security Issues, Joint Committee on Water Resources (7-8 October 2004), the Joint Group of Experts Meeting on the Pancheshwar Project (6 October 2004), Secretary-level Telecommunication Coordination Meeting 1-2 (November 2004) and Joint Secretary-level Trade Talks (1-2 November 2004). As a result, significant progress was achieved on several bilateral issues which received a set back after the emergency was declared.

[76] For a detailed analyses of India's immediate response and options towards Nepal during this phase following King Gyanendra's undemocratic action refer S.D.Muni , Neighbourly Concerns, *Seminar*, April 2005, No.548 ,http://www.india-seminar.com/2005/548/ 548%20s%20d%20muni.htm ; S.D.Muni Indo-Nepal, A Himalayan Shift , http:// www.outlookindia.com/article.aspx?225119 ; B.C.Upret , Will the Monarchy Survive ? *Seminar*, April 2005 , No.548 , http://www.india-seminar.com/2005/548/ 548%20b%20c%20upreti.htm

US and the UK, stopped their military assistance in protest of the royal takeover.

In his search for legitimacy and his actions being criticized by India and other countries, the King sought support from China. In 2005-2006, there were a series of interactions between Nepal and China militarily, economically and politically. Compared to earlier decades the cooperation during this period was extensive. There were high-level military exchanges and visits between Nepal and China. These visits affirmed the strengthened military cooperation between Nepal and China. They were taking place at a time when the traditional arms suppliers to Nepal had stopped military cooperation. China however was of the view that the royal takeover was an internal matter of Nepal and that there should be no interference in Nepal's internal affairs by outside forces.[77] It was reported that China supplied 4.2 million rounds of 7.62 mm rifle ammunition, 80,000 high explosive grenades and 12,000 AK-series rifles to Nepal in last week of November 2005.[78] Reports in Nepal media said that China sent 18 truckloads of arms and ammunition to Nepal via the Kodari highway (northeast of Kathmandu). China had been providing Nepal with non-lethal equipment like telecommunication sets in the past and this was the first time it has provided guns and ammunition to Nepal.[79] Initially, there was no official comment on reports of arms import from China by the Nepal Army. Some reports speak of Army officials confirming that Nepal has received few truckloads of arms and ammunition from China as per the agreement reached during

---

[77] "China to Promote Military Cooperation with Nepal: Report", *Nepalnews.com,* October 22, 2005 http://www.nepalnews.com/archive/2005/oct/oct22/news09.php; "China Grants Rs 72 million as Military Aid to Nepal", *Nepalnews.com,* October 25, 2005, http://www.nepalnews.com/archive/2005/oct/oct25/news10.php.

[78] Shishir Gupta, "China Arms Shadow Over Indo-Nepal Treaty", *Indian Express,* November 30, 2005, Also see "China Backs Nepal Against Maoist Insurgency", Daily Times, November 26, 2005, http://www.dailytimes.com.pk/default.asp?page=2005/11/26/story_26-11-2005_pg4_8;

[79] "Chinese 'Deliver Arms to Nepal", *BBC News,* November 25, 2005, http://news.bbc.co.uk/2/hi/south_asia/4469508.stm; "Import of Arms from China as Per the Agreement: RNA", *Nepalnews.com,* November 25 2005, http://www.nepalnews.com/archive/2005/nov/nov25/news16.php

the visit to China by chief of the army staff, General Pyar Jung Thapa.[80] Later it was officially stated that Nepal has not received any lethal arms from China.[81] Thus, there is a lack of clarity on this issue but some movement of arms seems to have definitely taken place.

During King Gyanendra's period, China with the support of Nepal could secure 'observer status' in the SAARC during the 13th SAARC summit held in Dhaka during 12-13 November 2005.[82] A significant feature of King Gyanendra's addresses abroad was regarding Nepal's desire to be a transit point between her two neighbors - China and India and enhance economic ties between them. The King was of the view that its role as a transit point would contribute to welfare of Nepal, India, China and the region as a whole. Further the King took actions against the Tibetan refugees in Nepal which continues be a cause of concern for China.

At this juncture it is essential to spell out briefly China's security and foreign policy objectives in Nepal. At the minimum, China requires Nepal's cooperation to safeguard its interests in Tibet as that region is dependent on neighboring countries for border trade and also there is a regular flow of thousands of Tibetan refugees into Nepal and India every year. China would like to nullify any negative fallout of Tibetan refugees from these countries. At the maximum, China would like support on its 'one China' principle either supporting its efforts at unification with Taiwan or preferably declaring against independence of Taiwan. With regard to economic interests the Western Development Campaign in its Tenth Five Year Plan (2001-2005) of opening up its backward western provinces and developing the infrastructure in the region is seen as crucial for China. Thus stability in the neighborhood would be paramount for Chinese national interests and China could ill afford to see failed states in the region. China called the Maoists 'anti-government guerrillas' and it was apprehensive of the increasing Maoist influence not only in Tibet but also in other parts of China.[83]

---

[80] "Import of Arms from China as per the Agreement: RNA", *Nepalnews.com*, November 25, 2005,   http://www.nepalnews.com/archive/2005/nov/nov25/news16.php

[81] "No Lethal Arms from China: RNA", *Nepalnews.com, November 25, 2005*, http://www.nepalnews.com/archive/2005/nov/nov25/news20.php

[82] Anil Kumar Mohapatra, "China's Inroad into Nepal", *World Focus*, 345 (2008)

[83] Srikanth Kondapalli, "China's Forays into Nepal", *World Focus*, 317 (2006)

Post Jana Andolan I of 1990, India felt assured that Nepal's governments would be sensitive to India's concerns arising from China. This was to be short lived. The China factor once again arose in the horizon.

Changes in Indian Foreign Policy

The disturbing security scenario from the Maoist insurgency along with continuing instability following the negation of the democratic process by King Gyanendra brought in major changes in Indian foreign policy, some of its own initiative and some forced. These were:-

i)   12 Point Agreement.

ii) Abandoning support to Constitutional Monarchy.

iii) Policies to ensure secure borders following agitations by the marginalized.

The 12 Point Agreement: Courting the Maoists

In November 2005, the political parties in Nepal and the Maoists concluded a 12 Point Agreement in New Delhi. [84] This was the culmination of the process which had begun in 2001-2002 when both sides started establishing contacts and got accelerated in 2005 following the Kings undemocratic actions. It was an important agreement which later led to the historic Jana Andolan II of 2006. Apart from setting the stage for Maoists to enter the political mainstream, it was a joint alliance against the monarchy.[85] The discussions before reaching the agreement were never done under public

---

[84] The 12 Point Agreement was concluded between the Seven Party Alliance (SPA) and the CPN (M). Some of the provisions were – commitment to democracy, ending autocratic monarchy, CA elections; the Maoists committed to new peaceful political line and to multiparty democracy; the Maoists agreed to return of seized properties and facilitate return of displaced people; all committed to peaceful relations with India and China; arms of Nepalese Army and the Maoist Army would be supervised by the United Nations or a similar neutral authority.

[85] G.P. Koirala said that the objective of the 12 Point Agreement with the Maoists was to end the autocratic regime. For details refer, "NC will Continue its Fight Against Absolute Monarchy: Koirala", *Nepalnews.com,* November 30, 2005, http://www.nepalnews.com/archive/2005/nov/nov30/news03.php

glare and secrecy was maintained. India too has never acknowledged that it played a role in bringing the Maoists and the other political parties together.[86] However, there are enough indications that India had a role to play.[87]

There was a denial by the Nepali leaders that they were in Delhi to hold talks with the Maoist leaders or that they had met them.[88] However it is believed that they must have met in Delhi for secret parleys.[89] There were a series of visits by leaders from Nepal to India prior to the 12 Point Agreement for, as they said, moral support from the Government of India, its people and political leaders for restoring democracy and peace in the country. The Nepal Democracy Solidarity Committee, headed by CPI (M) leader Harkishan Singh Surjit invited some of these leaders. It is suspected that the leaders from India's communist parties had a significant role to play and in this Sitaram Yechury is believed to have played an important role with the approval of the Government of India. [90] Many of the leaders from Nepal insisted that they were Delhi for health checkups. However all

---

[86] There is an opinion that the excessive covert approach of India to the 12 Point Agreement did not help. That analysts and retired officials from India complain that the Indian government's strategic shift in 2005 was neither well explained nor well implemented through usual diplomatic means. For details refer, "Nepal's Future: In Whose Hands?" *Asia Report No. 173* (2009) International Crisis Group, 22 http://www.crisisgroup.org/en/regions/asia/south-asia/nepal/173-nepals-future-in-whose-hands.aspx

[87] "India played behind-the-scenes role in Parties-Maoist understanding: TOI", *Nepalnews.com,* November 26, 2005,   http://www.nepalnews.com/archive/2005/nov/nov26/news09.php

[88] "Martin and Tamrat in New Delhi", *Nepalnews.com,* November 20, 2005, http://www.nepalnews.com/archive/2005/nov/nov20/news01.php; "We don't need to visit Delhi to meet Maoists: MK Nepal", *Nepalnews.com,* November 17, 2005 http://www.nepalnews.com/archive/2005/nov/nov17/news18.php

[89] Shirish Pradhan, "Maoists Agree to Lay Down Arms", *The Tribune,* November 20, 2005, http://www.tribuneindia.com/2005/20051120/world.htm#1; Bharat Bhushan, "Maoists, Parties in a Secret Pact", *The Telegraph,* November 19, 2005, http://www.telegraphindia.com/1051119/asp/foreign/story_5496002.asp

[90] " UML Gen Secy to seek Moral Support from India for Democracy", *Nepalnews.com,* October 23, 2005, http://www.nepalnews.com/archive/2005/oct/oct23/news11.php; Sitaram Yechury, the CPI(M) Polit Bureau member from India is supposed to have played a key role on behalf of the Government of India. For details see , "Nepal Maoists Committed to Peace Talks:Yechury", *The Hindu,* July 2, 2006, www.hinduonnet.com/2006/07/02/stories/2006070206541000.htm.

were in denial that they had met the Maoists in Delhi. [91] Even the US Ambassador to Nepal denied any knowledge of the meetings. [92]

However, a press statement released by the Maoist Chairman Prachanda, apart from spelling out the understanding reached, mentioned that his party welcomed international mediation in the process of peacefully resolving the crisis.[93] In subsequent interviews the Maoist leaders acknowledged that the 12 Point Agreement could be reached only because of India's support. This marked a change not only in India's policy towards the Maoists but also in that of the Maoists towards India.[94] However, the agreement had many shortcomings. It was not a real meeting of minds. The mainstream parties neither agreed to the Maoist agenda nor were the Maoists commitment to democratic means beyond doubt. It was the animosity towards the monarchy which brought them all together and led to the concessions which they offered to each other. Despite this, the agreement had an important critical role to play and help streamline events and give direction to them as was seen Post Jana Andolan II. For India working with limited options the agreement was a mechanism to put a break on King Gyanendra's undemocratic regime and create an environment to bring normalcy in Nepal so necessary for its own security and stability.

India's official reaction to the agreement was, "We have seen newspaper reports about an understanding between the Maoists and the political parties in Nepal for the restoration of multi-party democracy and

---

[91] Rabindra Mishra, "India's Key Role in Nepal's Affairs", *BBC News*, November 22, 2005, http://news.bbc.co.uk/2/hi/south_asia/4456036.stm

[92] " I am Completely Unaware about the 'Delhi Talks': US Envoy", *Nepalnews.com,* November 21, 2005,   http://www.nepalnews.com/archive/2005/nov/nov21/news05.php

[93] " Parties, Maoists Agree to End 'autocratic monarchy' to Establish 'total democracy'", *Nepalnews.com,* November 22, 2005, http://www.nepalnews.com/archive/2005/nov/nov22/news13.php

[94] Prachanda has said that, "India allowed a 12 Point Agreement between the seven party alliance and the Maoists in Delhi...which created ground to launch the joint peoples movement against the autocratic monarchy to establish democracy. Had India not allowed, the accord could not have been signed in Delhi and it was not possible to deal within the country ...". For details see Ameet Dhakal, "Historic Beginning to New Nepal", *The Hindu,* November 9, 2006, http://www.thehindu.com/2006/11/09/stories/2006110916981400htm

the return to political normalcy...........It remains to be seen whether the Maoists are genuinely prepared to live up to their commitments and refrain from acts of violence and extortion,......". MEA spokesperson also said that the Maoists should "accept the discipline of multi-party democracy" and work for a political settlement that contributes to political stability. [95]

India, the mainstream political parties of Nepal and external stakeholders like USA were all expressing ignorance of events leading to the 12 Point Agreement and India's role in it. Why were all of them in a denial mode? Most likely, first, they wanted to project the agreement as an entirely internal development of Nepal as it was a very crucial development that involved bringing Maoists into the mainstream and the political parties taking a step forward towards the agenda of the Maoists.

Second, India owning up to any of these far reaching decisions would have had implications for the Maoists in India too. Also, India still had doubts of the Maoists of Nepal. It could not guarantee that Nepal's Maoists, whom it had termed as terrorists a few years back, would not turn back. Further, India continued to maintain that it supported Constitutional Monarchy. [96] This despite his undemocratic credentials and it developing close ties with China. This could be because the monarchy has within it the loyalty of the Army and India did not want that institution to be disturbed. Openly supporting the 12 Point Agreement would mean that the issue of Constitutional Monarchy was debatable for India too, as the Maoists were fighting for a republic. India was not as yet ready for a change of its policy in that direction. Thus contradictions were inherent in the policy.[97]

---

[95] "Wait & Watch MEA Stand on Nepal Maoists" *Indian Express* , 24.11.2005 accessed through http://nepalresearch.com/coup_2005/articles/articles_2005_11.htm (accessed on January 17, 2010)

[96] Ministry of External Affairs, *Annual Report 2005-06,* Government of India. India's stated position was that multiparty democracy as enshrined in Constitution of Nepal 1990 should be restored and Constitutional forces which include both the institution of monarchy and the political parties should work together to confront the challenge facing Nepal including Maoist insurgency and that there could be no military solution to the problem facing Nepal. It reiterated that it stands by all efforts towards a peaceful settlement for the problems facing Nepal.

[97] "India Cautiously Welcomes Party-Maoist Agreement", *Nepalnews.com,* November 24, 2005, http://www.nepalnews.com/archive/2005/nov/nov24/news06.php .

We now come to some important uncomfortable questions. Did India want to bring the Maoists overboard because they believed in at least some of their demands or was it for strategic reasons? The answer seems to be the latter. What were the strategic concerns to reverse the policy towards Nepal Maoists? First, there was a stalemate on the ground between the Maoists PLA and the Nepali Army. The Nepali Army was holding their positions but the Maoists had set up parallel governments in most of the 75 districts. There was a fear that the Nepali Army could face reversals in the future. Legitimate government control and democracy was being made irrelevant. This had to be stopped and reversed as soon as possible. Second, stability in Nepal so essential for India's security called for revival of the democratic process in which the mainstream political parties had to be included. Third, increasing influence of China under King Gyanendra could be curtailed only with the anti-monarchy forces joining hands which included the Maoists and the mainstream political parties. Fourth, by bringing the Maoists overboard into the political mainstream, their links with similar groups in India could be weakened and severed too. Also the success of the Maoist insurgency in denying the government its control in Nepal was not setting a good example for similar elements in India. Thus, it was purely strategic considerations and not because they felt that the agenda for change of the Maoists had merit, that India opened channels of communication with the Maoists reversing its earlier policy.

It definitely would not have been an easy decision for India because built into some of Maoists basic 40 demands was a strong dose of taking stands which are anti-India. Circumstances forced India to change its view. With the changing conflict situation, India too had to change its policy towards issues arising out of the conflict.

Similarly the question arises as to what made the Maoists enter mainstream politics? Within five years of launching the armed struggle in 1996, the Maoists influence had grown at an unprecedented rate. Despite all the gains made by the Maoists there was a military stalemate with the Nepal army. While the Army could not re-establish control over the entire country, it could hold its minimum defensive position even if it meant only district headquarters and the capital. The Maoists realized that the urban areas were out of its reach. The need thus arose to re-examine the strategy so that Peoples' War in the villages could be complemented by a push for People's rebellion in the towns. The new strategy called for focus on urban insurrection while continuing to build up in rural areas and working to surround towns. They realized that in a centralized country like Nepal, pressure on the state could be built only when people in the urban areas were mobilized. Entering mainstream politics was necessary for this. The 12 Point Agreement helped to fulfill this need.[98]

Did India's role in the 12 Point Agreement change the Maoists view of India? Yes, it did change Maoists view towards India and this has been acknowledged by them many times. The changes towards India were also driven by necessity. It is difficult to say whether this was because they really believed that there was no need to be anti-India any longer or was it also for strategic concerns. The latter seems to be true because time and again they seem to be going back to anti-India slogans and standpoints. However the Maoists are under no illusion and they know the importance of India for Nepal too well and there is immense clarity in this context.

Ironically, everybody entered into the 12 Point Agreement to preserve their influence and power. None was aware that the subsequent events would actually strike at status quo and re-draw the power structure of Nepal like never before. The long term impact of the 12 Point Agreement was never factored in.

The pro-democracy movement in which the signatories to the 12 Point Agreement participated was primarily directed against the monarchy in Nepal and the King reacted by using force. The movement was supported and in some sense led by the civil society, the business community and the

---

[98] "Nepals Maoists: their Aims, Structures and Strategy", *ICG Report* No. 104, October 27, 2005, International Crisis Group, http://www.crisisgroup.org/~/media/Files/asia/south-asia/nepal/104_nepal_s_Maoists_their_aims_structure_and_strategy.ashx; Also see "Nepals Maoists: Purists or Pragmatists?, Asia Report No. *132*, May 18 2007, International Crisis Group, http://www.crisisgroup.org/en/regions/asia/south-asia/nepal/132-nepals-Maoists-purists-or-pragmatists.aspx

marginalized sections of society. [99] During Jana Andolan II, India misread the support the monarchy enjoyed in Nepal. As a result, its policies faltered one after the other. While agitations had intensified and spread, India sent Karan Singh, a friend of the Nepali Royals to Nepal. In the midst of the agitations, he said that the multiparty democracy and monarchy were two pillars for Nepal's political system. He was in fact just reiterating what was India's policy consistently since 1990, during the insurgency days and even when the King took over powers in 2001 and later in 2005. However, this statement was made when it was crystal clear that the people of Nepal were not ready for a compromise with the monarchy. [100] The Kings initial offer of reconciliation was welcomed by India but the political parties and people of Nepal rejected it and there were demonstrations against it. [101] It was then that India realized that it had made a wrong assessment of the situation. It understood that India's support for Constitutional Monarchy as

---

[99] For details on the wide nature of participation, see "NC calls for Wider Participation on Thursday's rally: 3 Killed, over 100 Injured in Kathmandu Demonstrations; Protests Continue Nationwide", *Nepalnews.com,* April 20, 2006, http://www.nepalnews.com/archive/2006/ apr/apr20/news14.php; "Civil Society Leaders Call for Unconditional 'constituent assembly'", *Nepalnews.com,* April 21, 2006, http://www.nepalnews.com/archive/2006/apr/apr21/ news09.php; "Historic Demonstration" in Kathmandu, Hundreds of Thousands of People March along the Ring Road", *Nepalnews.com,* April 21, 2006, http://www.nepalnews.com/ archive/2006/apr/apr21/news10.php; "Demonstrations Against the Royal Proclamation; Hundreds of Thousands take to Street on Friday", *Nepalnews.com,* April 22, 2006, http:/ /www.nepalnews.com/archive/2006/apr/apr22/news01.php; "Seven Parties Reject Royal Proclamation, Vow to Continue Agitation", *Nepalnews.com,* April 22, 2006, http:// www.nepalnews.com/archive/2006/apr/apr22/news10.php; "Over 300,000 March in Dang Calling for 'total democracy'", *Nepalnews.com,* April 23, 2006, http://www.nepalnews.com/ archive/2006/apr/apr23/news10.php

[100] For details see, "King Grants Audience to Indian Special Envoy", *Nepalnews.com,* April 20, 2006, http://www.nepalnews.com/archive/2006/apr/apr20/news09.php; "Karan Singh Returns to Delhi with 'optimism'", *Nepalnews.com,* April 20, 2006, http:// www.nepalnews.com/archive/2006/apr/apr20/news12.php; "Karan Singh Briefs Indian PM on Nepal Crisis", *Nepalnews.com,* April 21, 2006, http://www.nepalnews.com/archive/ 2006/apr/apr21/news08.php

[101] For details see, "India Welcomes, NC 'dissatisfied' Protests Against Royal Proclamation", *Nepalnews.com,* April 21, 2006, http://www.nepalnews.com/archive/2006/apr/apr21/ news15.php; "Demonstrations Against the Royal Proclamation Hundreds of Thousands Take to Street on Friday", *Nepalnews.com,* April 22, 2006, http://www.nepalnews.com/ archive/2006/apr/apr22/news01.php; "India, US Welcome King's Step", *Nepalnews.com,* April 22, 2006, http://www.nepalnews.com/archive/2006/apr/apr22/news04.php

an important pillar of political system in Nepal did not have any takers and that it stood isolated. India thus made a retreat and amended its position[102]. Indian Foreign Secretary said that the future political arrangement in Nepal is "is really a matter for the people of Nepal to decide and not for India to decide." This changed position was welcomed by all in Nepal. [103]

India was more committed to 'Constitutional Monarchy' than were the political parties within Nepal. The Communist Party of Nepal (Unified Marxist-Leninist) led by Madhav Kumar Nepal opted for a democratic republic and for a Constituent Assembly at its Central Committee meeting on August 25. The Convention of the Nepali Congress (Koirala) adopted a resolution on August 30 deleting references to Constitutional Monarchy from its Constitution in 2005. Presumably it looked upon the King as holding the real power of the Army and the complete negation of the monarchy would make the army openly assertive. In 1990, the established political parties could tune in the peoples power in a manner which served India's interests too. The result was parliamentary democracy with Constitutional Monarchy. In 1990 the leaders led the movement. This was not the scenario in 2006. Sixteen years had given a completely new identity and force to the people's power. In 2006, the people led the leaders in not making any compromise with the monarch.

India's policy response was definitely lacking in understanding the ground situation in Nepal. What choices did India have? Its policy should have been based on balancing both its strategic concerns and the multiple

---

[102] http://www.indianexpress.com/news/a-policy-of-deception-on-nepal/3357/0 . The article spells out how India was attatched to its two pillar formulation : constitutional monarchy and multiparty democracy – even when the two entities were at daggers drawn.

[103] See "India Supports Democratic Forces in Nepal: Saran", *Nepalnews.com, April 23, 2006,* http://www.nepalnews.com/archive/2006/apr/apr23/news06.php, this report gives details of the press conference given by Indian Foreign Secretary Shyam Saran; "NC Hails Latest Indian Reaction on King's Address", *Nepalnews.com,* April 23, 2006, http://www.nepalnews.com/archive/2006/apr/apr23/news08.php; "UN Urged to Reconsider its Position", *Nepalnews.com,* April 23, 2006, http://www.nepalnews.com/archive/2006/apr/apr23/news13.php; "India, China Welcome New Political Developments in Nepal", *Nepalnews.com,* April 26, 2006, http://www.nepalnews.com/archive/2006/apr/apr26/news02.php

social undercurrent of discontent. It should have committed itself to supporting 'democratic elements' in Nepal. Thus, this could have broadly included the monarch if his actions were within the parameters of upholding democracy and excluded him when he crossed the boundary of democratic conduct. In this manner India would not have faced the displeasure of the people of Nepal and make a retreat in its policy.

After Jana Andolan II, India supported Nepal's efforts to hold the CA elections.[104] There was a convergence of efforts of India and the interim government of Nepal in this direction. In 2005-06, India announced an economic assistance package of around Rs. 1000 crore to address the immediate needs and priorities of the Government of Nepal. That year India's total aid to Nepal in comparison to those of other countries accounted for 16 percent.[105]

For the time being the influence of the monarch was curtailed, the Maoists were brought to the political mainstream, democratic process revived and China's influence was limited. However, security concerns in the open Indo-Nepal border increased. The unexpected rise of the violent

---

[104] Ministry of External Affairs, *Annual Report 2006-07,* Government of India, 2007, India acknowledged the far reaching changes in Nepal, welcomed the CPA as a significant step in Nepal's journey towards settled constitutional order in which the people of Nepal could realize their aspirations for peace and prosperity. The Government of India was of the view that the people of Nepal should have the right to freely choose and decide their future without the fear of gun. India's policy was to help in political stability and economic recovery of Nepal.

[105] Ibid. Normally aid to Nepal accounts for, on an average every year, 6 percent of India's total aid to the other countries. In 2005-06 it was 16 percent i.e. 210 Crores. Bhutan gets the highest accounting for 41.32 percent of the total aid disbursed by India. Bilateral trade with India accounted for 65.8 percent of Nepal's total external trade in 2004-05. India's share in Nepal's imports stood at 64.9 percent. India, on the other hand, absorbed about 67.7 percent of Nepal's exports. Under the Small Development Project Scheme India is undertaking development projects in the areas of infrastructure, health, rural and community development, education. There are more than 160 projects implemented or under implementation. Two big projects viz. Bir Hospital Expansion at the cost of Rs.65 crores and Manmohan Adhikari Polytechnic at the cost of Rs 20 crores were under implementation, while the Mahendra-Nagar Tanakpur Road Link and Hetauda Polytechnic projects were at take off stage. The Government laid particular emphasis on the improvement of border infrastructure as well as initiating work on other infrastructure projects in Nepal in consultation with the Government of Nepal.

agitations by the marginalized groups in Nepal required all the more patrolling of the border areas to control movement of criminal elements and arms. The agitation in the Terai where many armed groups had emerged only aggravated the situation. There were also allegations that criminals from India and some sympathizers belonging to the right wing Hindu groups were also involved.[106]

Constituent Assembly Elections: The New Power Equations

After Jana Andolan II, India supported Nepal's efforts to hold the CA elections. After being postponed twice the CA elections were finally held in April 2008.[107] The elections provided legitimacy to the whole peace process which had started after Jana Andolan II. Soon the country was declared a republic ending the 240 yr old rule of the Shahs. This was an issue which was considered non-negotiable by most political parties even in 2005.[108] Thus the final seal was put on this issue. After the successful holding of CA elections, India has stressed that the peace process should fulfill its goal of drafting the Constitution.[109] With a view to strengthen and expand cultural relations, an Indian Cultural Centre was opened in Katmandu in August 2007 while it continued with its economic cooperation with Nepal.[110]

The real power equations came to the forefront only after the CA elections. The unexpected victory of the Maoists brought discomfort and insecurity to many of the political players and stakeholders and changed their perceptions of the peace process.[111] The established parties of Nepal

---

[106] See section 2 in this chapter titled Exclusion: Understanding the Root Cause of the Conflict.

[107] "Polling Concludes, Voter Turnout around 60 percent; EC Describes Polling a Success", *Nepalnews.com,* April 10, 2008, http://www.nepalnews.com/archive/2008/apr10/news08.php

[108] Ameet Dhakal, "Nepal is Now a Republic", *The Hindu,* May 29, 2009, http://www.hindu.com/2008/05/29/stories/2008052950005010htm.

[109] Ministry of External Affairs, *Annual Report 2007-08,* Government of India, 2008

[110] Ibid.

[111] "India's Confidence in Maoists Considerably Low: Narayanan", *Nepalnews.com,* March 30, 2008, http://www.nepalnews.com/archive/2008/mar/mar30/news17.php "We have put a great deal of faith in Prime Minister (Girija Prasad) Koirala and the Nepali Congress. We're

were shocked and disappointed. The victory of the established parties would have ensured that India's interests were being looked after. Accommodation and flexibility took a back seat and short term goals dominated interactions. Consensus gave rise to confrontation. Many criticized India for facilitating the 12-Point Agreement which enabled the Maoists to come into the mainstream and later form a government after a very impressive performance in the CA elections.[112] Forgetting however that later events of Jana Andolan II of 2006 and the rise of the marginalized sections clearly show that the King could not have continued indefinitely and deep discontent among the people would have arisen with or without the 12 Point Agreement. The political parties and the Maoists were in consultation and would have formed some united front against the monarchy even if India had not facilitated the 12 Point Agreement.

Following Jana Andolan II, India has maintained that there is no physical link between the Maoists in Nepal and India[113]. However, there is an ideological link. Statements emanating from the Maoists speak of them putting priority to bilateral relations with India. At the same time they also talk of fighting Indian expansionism when they are in the midst of similar

---

unsure as to where we stand with regard to the Maoists despite professions on both sides that we can work together," India's National Security Advisor, Narayanan is reported to have made this statement before the CA elections.

[112] Indian opposition leader L.K.Advani said that the UPA government outsourced handling of Nepal affairs to communists who saw Maoist government in place, but now anarchy was prevailing in Nepal. For details refer "Advani sees Mishandling of Foreign Policy", *The Hindu, May 8, 2009,* http://www.thehindu.com/2009/05/08/stories/ 2009050855421200.htm; "Advani faults UPA's Foreign Policy on Lanka, Nepal", *Rediff.com,* May 08, 2009, http://election.rediff.com/report/2009/may/08/loksabhapoll-advani-faults-upas-foreign-policy-on-lanka-nepal.htm; "Nepal Crisis Result of UPA's Foreign Policy Failure: BJP", *OutlookIndia.com,* May 04, 2009 http://news.outlookindia.com/item.aspx?659397

[113] See Ministry of External Affairs, "Maoist Activities in the Country", *Parliament Question and Answers,* Q No. 5157, April 30, 2008, Government of India, http://www.mea.gov.in, When asked if the Maoist activities have increased in various parts of the country, particularly in the border areas adjoining Nepal, the External Affairs Minister said that - India-Nepal have an open border and visa free regime. There are no restrictions on movement of both nationals across the border. Sashastra Seema Bal (SSB) has been deployed along the Indo-Nepal border. There are no reports confirming Nepali Maoist activity in the Indian States bordering Nepal.

Maoist groups. India needs to understand this duality.[114] Maybe Nepal's Maoists want to keep all channels of communication open – with groups they have interacted in the past and those they want to interact in the present. Despite the Maoists being mainstreamed, the security concerns in the open borders remain and during high level visits these issues have come up again and again. [115]

Problems and misconceptions immediately arose between the UCPN (M) led government and India. This was with regard to the close relations the Maoists led government was building with China. The dominant perception was/is that Prachanda's moving closer to China is not in India's interest and that the Maoist government has been seeking closer ties with China at the cost of India. Breaking a tradition of first visiting India, the first Prime Minister of Federal Democratic Republic of Nepal Pushpa Kamal Dahal (Prachanda) just eight days after his election, preferred to go to China to attend the closing ceremony of the Beijing Olympic on 23rd August 2008. It is argued that Indian foreign policy needs to preserve its influence in South Asia and at the same time ensure a democratic Nepal that would deter China's inroad into Nepal. These views are based on the fact that the draft of the China-Nepal Friendship Treaty on the lines of the India-Nepal 1950 Treaty curtails India's special relations with China. That China's policy pronouncements towards Nepal stressing its independence try to obviate India's influence. Underscored in China's South Asia policy is the strategy to marginalize India's influence in Nepal.

Second, that infrastructure is being developed and upgraded and China has accepted Nepal's proposal in April 2009 to open up two more custom points in addition to the existing five in the Nepal–China border in Tibet. China is also building a 65 km second road link, the Syafrubesi-Rasuwagadi

---

[114] P V Ramana, "No Clarity on Nature of Naxalite Threat", *Deccan Herald*, October 24, 2006. Union Home SecretaryVK Duggal is quoted here. At the Sardar Vallabhai Patel National Police Academy he said that "There is no physical link between Maoists in Nepal and India. However, there is an ideological link".

[115] Ministry of External Affairs, *Annual Report 2008-09,* Government of India, 2009, When Prachanda visited India the stregthening of border infrastructure along the Indo-Nepal border was high on priority. Project related to development of check posts, road and rail connectivity between the two countries is under various stages of implementation.

road, which is the shortest route from Tibet to Kathmandu.

Third, that China is actively participating and promoting Nepal's hydro-power projects. In 2008, China's Assistant Minister for Foreign Affairs, He Yafei, pledged to provide Nepal a loan of $125 million for Upper Trishuli 3 'A' and $62 million for Upper Trishuli 3 'B'. The plants would start operating from 2012. Marginalizing Indian influence in Nepal would allow China not only to dominate South Asia but also provide easy access to Nepal's roughly 83,000 megawatts of hydroelectric potential.

Fourth, military cooperation under the Maoists has also moved forward with China. On December 7, 2008 during a meeting in Kathmandu between Nepal's Defence Minister Ram Bahadur Thapa and the Deputy Commander of China's People Liberation Army, Lieutenant General Ma Xiaotian China pledged to provide US $2.6 million as military assistance for Nepal's security sector. Earlier in September 2008, China had announced military aid worth $ 1.3 million, the first such assistance to the Maoist government in Nepal.

Fifth, China's inroads into Nepal are being greatly facilitated by the systematic promotion of China Study Centers (CSCs) which are completely funded by China. The number of CSCs in Nepal has increased in recent times. There are 33 China Study centres in Southern Nepal adjoining the Indian Border. Also there are multilayered Nepal–China associations of various kinds, all of which promote greater interaction among the various sections of people in Nepal and China and present a positive image.

Sixth, there has been an increase in the official interaction. 38 delegations from China visited Nepal in 2008 alone and China is strengthening relations with all the political parties.

Seventh, with growing tensions in Tibet, particularly after the March 2008 uprising, China's conception of Nepal as a new buffer acquired particular significance. Its policy towards Nepal came to be driven by the need to curb the clandestine activities of some 20,000 Tibetan refugees (the second largest Tibetan refugee community in the world) in Nepal. Consequently, China has been increasingly playing a significant role in determining the future shape of Nepali politics. During each of the high-level meetings China has extracted assurances from Nepal that it adheres to the one-China principle, acknowledges Tibet as an inalienable part of China, and will ensure that no anti-China activity is allowed on its soil.[116]

There is then an alternate view that opines that New Delhi would grossly err in drawing long term policy conclusions from Mr. Prachanda's visit to China.[117] This paper opines that while those cautioning against China do have a merit, there is a need for India to take a much holistic view. There is a marked difference between King Gyanendra's pro-China tilt and that of the Maoist Prime Minister. King Gyanendra was seeking legitimacy and military assistance and building relations with China at a time when he had the disapproval of his people and his actions clearly violated the letter and the spirit of the 1990 Constitution. It was legitimate for India to get concerned then. The Maoist leader on the other hand has been democratically elected and is the leader of the party which has won the most number of votes leaving behind the established parties at a far second and third place. His visit was not for seeking legitimacy for himself or his actions or for his party either. This complete difference in intentions needs to be noted. His party had entered mainstream politics after fighting a violent insurgency and one of the issues they had stressed was an independent foreign policy. Their entering mainstream politics had dissidents and disapproval within their own party. Prachanda's visit first to China would have silenced these dissents. The Maoist insurgency always had an anti-India ideology. Visiting India first could have negated all these arguments. New Delhi needs to remember that the Maoists are also fighting

---

[116] Abanti, Bhattacharya, "China's Inroads into Nepal: India's Concerns", *IDSA Comment,* May 18, 2009, http://www.idsa.in/node/756/117; Nihar Nayak, "Nepal: New 'Strategic Partner' of China?", *IDSA Comment,* March 30, 2009 http://www.idsa.in/idsastrategiccomments/NepalNewStrategicPartnerofChina_NNayak_300309; Nihar Nayak, "Maoist Rhetoric on Indo-Nepal Relations", *IDSA Comment,* January 13, 2010 http://www.idsa.in/idsacomments/MaoistsrhetoriconIndia-NepalRelations_nnayak_130110

[117] S.D.Muni, "Dealing With a New Nepal", *The Hindu,* September 15, 2009 http://www.hindu.com/2008/09/15/stories/2008091555521100htm Also refer http://lookandgaze.blogspot.com/2009/12/interview-with-sd-muni-indias.html and http://www.ekantipur.com/news/news-detail.php?news_id=300260 for interview with Prof S.D.Muni on need for change in India's policy towards Nepal.

for the same political space which is inhibited by other identity-based groups and this gives rise to competitive politics where breaking from past Nepalese government's actions is termed as being more independent and nationalistic.

Thus, this paper asserts that while India's concerns are legitimate, it should have waited till the Constitution was drafted before pronouncing the judgment on Maoists actions with regard to their relations with China. For India, the security concerns emanating from Nepal's relations with China dominated over the need of Nepal to have Constitution first. In case the Maoists had gone completely overboard and their actions reflected a complete negation of India's concerns, there were many peaceful options which could have been implemented as a last resort. These included negating or withholding the innumerable benefits in the Indo-Nepal Treaty of Trade and The Treaty of Transit. These are mechanisms which have been adopted by India in the past with varying degrees of success. Trade with third countries is done primarily through transit points in India-Nepal border and not Nepal-China border. When the Madhesi agitations took place, the curfew led to loss of revenue on customs points both in India and Nepal. By the end of the Nepalese fiscal year 2005-06, bilateral trade with India was of US$ 2.31 billion which accounted for 63.2 percent of Nepal's total external trade. India's share in Nepal's imports stood at 61.7 percent. India, on the other hand, absorbed about 67.6 percent of Nepal's exports.[118] 40 percent of this trade accounted for critical items like petroleum etc. The sheer size of economic relations, the movement of people across the 1850kms open border and the centuries old socio-cultural relations cannot compare India's relations with that of Nepal's relations with China or for that matter any other country.

Indo-Nepal relations are completely of a different nature. Almost half the population of Nepal lives in Terai which borders India and not China. Also, it is here that major industries are situated. Further, Post Jana Andolan II there are 109 armed groups operating in Nepal creating security

---

[118] Ministry of External Affairs, *Annual Report 2007-2008*, Government of India, 2008.

nightmares in the transitional period.[119] These groups use Indo-Nepal open borders for their activities. Relations with India and its cooperation become crucial for Nepal to meet the challenge posed by these non-state actors. Further, the major market for Nepal's power potential of 83,000 MW lies in India and not China.[120]

More important than all these facts is that the Maoists despite their anti-India postures and agitations have very clearly acknowledged the importance of India and have not negated its place, relevance and centrality to Indo-Nepal relations. In February 2006, the Maoists stated that while in the past India's role was not good as New Delhi had aligned with the King, India's role had been positive since February 2005. There remained the grievance nevertheless, that though India supported the democratic movement, India had not abandoned its two pillar policy. [121]

In April 2008, however, following India's clarification post-Jana Andolan II that it would respect the wishes of the Nepalese people, the Maoists declared their view that historically a very big change had taken place in Delhi's policy when it abandoned the twin-pillar policy and acknowledged

---

[119] "109 Armed Groups Operating in the Country", *Nepalnews.com,* July 31, 2009, http://www.nepalnews.com/main/index.php/news-archive/1-top-story/700-109-armed-groups-operating-in-the-country.html According to this report , Home Minister Rawal said the government is closely studying the situation to identify which of these armed outfits are political groups and which of them criminal gangs. He said government would take initiatives for talks with armed outfits with political objectives while those involved in criminal activities would face action. The Home Minister also said the government was planning to coordinate with the security agencies of the neighboring country [India] to check the movement of the criminal gangs.

Saying that the government was determined to implement the new security strategy, Rawal informed that the strength of police forces would be increased and they would be extensively mobilized to curb crime and disruptive activities such as highway blockades.

[120] For details on the proceedings of the Power Summit 2008 held in Kathmandu from 23rd - 24th September where various aspects of cooperation in the hydro power sector were discussed, see NICCI Newsletter, October 2008- March 2009, http://www.nicci.org/includes/downloads/newsletter/Oct_%20March_2009.pdf.

[121] For details see, Siddharth Vardarajan, " Transcript of the Complete Prachanda Interview", Reality, One Bite at a Time, comment posted on February 10, 2006, http://svaradarajan.blogspot.com/2006/02/transcript-of-complete-prachanda.html (accessed on August 20, 2010)

that the 12-Point Agreement could be reached only because of India's support. This marked a change not only in India's policy but also in that of the Maoists as they appreciated India's constant support for the CA elections and for taking the peace process forward.[122]

Interestingly, the Maoists have shown a great understanding of the special relationship between the two countries. They accept that without cooperating with India it is not possible to bring stability and prosperity in Nepal and that any leader who understands reality cannot be confused about it. Even when the Maoists refer to revisiting all treaties including the 1950 Treaty of Peace and Friendship, it is not with a view to undermine the bilateral relations but with a view to build a new relationship with India on a new basis". "Far from wanting to damage our relations we want to make it even better..."[123] They no longer talk of closing the open border but regulating it better so that criminal elements do not misuse the openness.

The Maoists have also clarified what they mean regarding maintaining equidistance between India and China – they say the term equidistance has been used in political terms to have an alliance and not go against anyone and violate the geopolitical conditions and the needs of Nepal. They accept that the ground reality indicates that the historical, cultural, geopolitical relationship with India is very different from that with China and this has to be acknowledged and factored in while the relationship is defined [124].

The Maoist Prime Minister's visit to India itself was a hugely positive one and Prachanda described the historic transition in his country as a collective accomplishment to which India had contributed. He said, if Nepal is failed, its repercussions would be felt in India too and thus there was a collective responsibility to ensure success[125]. Prachanda was also specific about the nature of cooperation he visualized, mentioning Nepal's need for

---

[122] Dhakal, "Historic Beginning to New Nepal", *The Hindu,* November 9, 2006.

[123] Siddharth Vardarajan, "We Want New Unity on a New Basis with India", Interviews, *The Hindu*, April 28, 2008, http://www.thehindu.com/2008/04/28/stories/2008042851511100.htm

[124] Ibid.

[125] Gargi Parsai, "Pact on Water Management Mechanism", *The Hindu* , September 17, 2008, http://www.hindu.com/2008/09/17/stories/2008091760901200.htm

a rail link going across the Terai region from East to West for which he wanted Indian help and talked about power projects that could generate 10,000MW with which Nepal could help energy-deficient India. He also referred to the problem of floods, being faced by Bihar and areas in Nepal and the need to look at possible solutions as well as the need to look afresh at the issue of water resources. During his visit, the two countries agreed to set up a three-tier joint water management mechanism.[126]

Addressing Indian industry interests he said that, without the presence of a vibrant private sector, the government alone could not accelerate Nepalese development efforts. He declared that his government remained committed to adopting every possible measure to provide investors the necessary security including repatriation of capital and profit earned by them in the country and to a fair and collaborative relationship between industry and labor. Admitting that the economy was sluggish in the transition period, he said additional opportunities for Indian industry lay in reconstruction of damaged facilities and building of infrastructure.

It is interesting to know that their decision to join the peace process and end the war in Nepal was criticized by their counterparts in India. The CPI (M) found it difficult to accept that having made substantial gains the CPN (M) had through the Comprehensive Peace Agreement (CPA) ended its war in Nepal and was participating in multi-party democracy. The CPI (M) was critical of CPN (M)'s participation in the democratic political competition, was against dissolving 'peoples governments' and peoples courts which they consider a major achievement, against cantoning the PLA and their proposed merger with Nepali Army, against inviting the UN which is essentially an instrument of imperialism particularly American imperialism and was particularly critical of CPN (M)'s relationship with the Indian government and the other mainstream parties. The CPI (M) objected to Nepal's Maoists urging their Indian counterparts to reconsider their revolutionary strategies and to practice multi-party democracy.[127] After

---

[126] Ibid.

[127] K.Srinivas Reddy, "The Situation in India and Nepal are completely Different", Interview, *The Hindu*, May 17, 2008, http://www.thehindu.com/2008/05/17/stories/2008051754771100.htm

the CPN (M) won the most number of seats in Nepal CA Elections the Indian Maoists termed the CPN (M)'s performance as a verdict against feudal monarchy, Indian expansionism and U.S. imperialism. While sending their fraternal revolutionary greetings, the Indian Maoists reminded the CPN leaders that very limited gains could be achieved by a government which came to power through elections. Thus, they should not overestimate the prospect of radical restructuring of society or economy through the Maoist government. Their suggestion to the Maoists in Nepal was that they should not become part of the government but that the class struggle should be continued. [128] The UCPN (M) however went ahead and formed the government.

Definitely for the Maoists who have openly declared their antagonism towards India right through the insurgency days, making a change in their stand towards India openly required courage. No doubt, the Maoists have given out mixed signals about desiring to develop close relations and at the same time overlooking certain issues about which India is very sensitive. However, Nepal is in transition and so are its political parties and the Maoists, in particular. The latter's open recognition of India's role in the 12-Point Agreement and of the special relationship between the two countries indicates two important aspects. First, that they agree that cordial and cooperative relations with India are essential for the New Nepal they want to build and second, that they look to India to play a positive constructive role in taking the peace process ahead. India should have built on these convergences, despite their relations with China to ensure stability till the Constitution drafting was completed.

This positive trend in relations between India and the Maoists which was slowly eroding saw a clear break by May 2009. The civilian supremacy issue created doubts and mistrust not only among the parties within Nepal, resulting in Prachanda's resignation and a new government being formed but also between the Maoists and Delhi. Prachanda said that India-Nepal

---

[128] K.Srinivas Reddy, "Nepal Maoists must Concentrate on Continuing the Class Struggle", *The Hindu*, May 5, 2008, http://www.thehindu.com/2008/05/05/stories/2008050560511300.htm

relations were not being redefined and improved upon according to the new changes and that there was a danger of the big brother-small brother kind of relationship returning. Further, that India's stand on the controversial actions of the Nepal's Army Chief had confused people of both countries whether relations were moving forward or backward. Prachanda said he wanted to redefine the relationship but added that the persistence of traditional mindsets affected the task.[129] The Maoist disappointment is evident when they say that they had expected India to take a consistent position in favor of civilian supremacy because of its own traditions and because it had supported the struggle for democracy. On the China tilt of the Maoist government and of several Chinese delegations visiting Nepal, which also contributed to the distance between India and Nepal, the response has been that such a tilt did not exist and that not a single delegation came to Nepal on the government's invitation. Further, it was the case that because of the Tibet situation, the Chinese side had gotten more sensitive about Tibet-related activities going on in Nepal.[130]

Instability in Nepal with several armed groups as compared to the pre Jana Andolan II days is not to the advantage of China too. This is, especially, given the difficult situation it faces in Tibet. A failed state is not in China's agenda or to its advantage. The Maoists did give conflicting signals of being friendly with India while not respecting issues on which India was sensitive. But, India definitely has the means to safeguard its security concerns, whether it was China's activities in Nepal or some other country. India, should have first made all efforts to sustain the consensus, however weak and fractured, among the political parties of Nepal to see that the Constitution was drafted by May 2010. This would have been as much a success of Nepal as of Indian foreign policy contributing to stability. India was hasty in passing a judgment on a group which had entered mainstream politics after controlling a significant area of the country and had put a

---

[129] Siddharth Vardarajan, "India Should have Defended Civilian Supremacy in Nepal", Interview, *The Hindu*, May 11, 2009, http://www.hindu.com/2009/05/11/stories/2009051154600900.htm

[130] Siddharth Vardarajan, "Perception that Nepal is Tilting is Exaggerated", Interview, *The Hindu*, May 12 2009, http://www.hindu.com/2009/05/12/stories/2009051252420900.htm

strong defense to the country's army. However, the Maoists need to realize that continuing with its anti Indian rhetoric will not benefit it either domestically, bilaterally or at an international level.

It is seen that an undercurrent of trust deficit has always been there between Nepal's Maoists and India. During the Maoist insurgency period, the anti-India agenda was openly stated. Their views took a positive turn post 12 Point Agreement in 2005. However, since Madhav Kumar Nepal took over as Prime Minister in May 2009, the Maoists have been openly anti-India. Thus, their views towards India have been very inconsistent.

Following Prachanda's resignation, India welcomed the formation of the 22 party-led government of Madhav Kumar Nepal. Anxiety about an uncertain future, distrust of the Maoists and suspicions about their perceived closeness with China led India to play safe by aligning with leaders familiar to it but who had failed to win the people's trust and who themselves are not focusing on the larger goals. An approach by New Delhi that does not have Maoists as important players will only result in accentuating India's security concerns.

The Maoists have been influential in Nepalese politics whether in government or in opposition. This was clearly visible during the new Nepalese Prime Minister's visit to India, in August 2009. Before Prime Minister Madhav Kumar Nepal embarked on his visit to India, the UCPN (Maoist) advised him not to sign any big agreement with India that required a broader consensus at home or had a far reaching effect on India-Nepal ties. The Maoists were bitter towards India for its stand in the 'civilian supremacy' issue.[131] Prime Minister Nepal asked them , not to be suspicious of his India tour, stating that there would not be any agreement on issues like

---

[131] "Defence Minister Clears Air Over Arms Row", *Nepalnews.com,* August 6, 2009, http://www.nepalnews.com/main/index.php/news-archive/2-political/794-defence-minister-clears-air-over-arms-row.html; "Maoists tell PM not to Sign Pancheshwar Agreement", *Nepalnews.com,* August 16, 2009, http://www.nepalnews.com/main/index.php/news-archive/2-political/954-Maoists-tell-pm-not-to-sign-pancheshwar-agreement.html; "Cabinet Finalises Team, Approves Agenda for PM's India Visit, *Nepalnews.com,* August 17, 2009, http://www.nepalnews.com/main/index.php/news-archive/1-top-story/962-cabinet-finalises-team-approves-agenda-for-pms-india-visit.html

water resources or arms deals that have a long-term impact without the consensus of major political parties[132] Nepal's visit was marked by caution and no major agreement was concluded. Earlier when India wanted to renew the defense ties which had been suspended in 2005, the UCPN (M) opposed it saying that it was against the Comprehensive Peace Agreement of November 2006. Such a situation where in the government in power in Nepal is favorably disposed towards India but is unable to take the relations forward because of an influential opposition, does not serve India's interests in the long term .

India needs to accept that there are now new important players in Nepal who have the legitimacy and the approval of the people at large. These players look at interdependence and bilateral relations in a different paradigm, but which need not necessarily be anti-India.

India's Policy: An Assessment

The continuing internal conflict in Nepal completely upset India's search for security and stability. While the 90s decade began on a euphoric optimistic note, which was later reinforced by the Gujral doctrine, it was to be short lived. India's foreign policy failed to understand the undercurrent of the intensity of domestic discontent in Nepal and the manner in which it could manifest itself with the potential to spill across the open borders.

India failed to infuse flexibility in its approach and visualize various scenarios. There is now neither peace nor security for India nor stability for Nepal. Why did this happen? i) India saw issues from status quo aspects. It stuck to its rigid reference points and made policy on its basis. Thus, the twin pillar policy of stability in Nepal being based on Constitutional Monarchy and Multi-Party Democracy had become sacrosanct to it. That is till it was forced to abandon it; ii) It did not create new reference points with changing situations. Thus, even after the CA election results, where the established

---

[132] "PM Nepal Arrives in New Delhi", *Nepalnews.com*, August 18, 2009, http://www.nepalnews.com/main/index.php/news-archive/1-top-story/975-pm-nepal-leaving-for-india-today.html

parties performed poorly and the peoples mandate was not with them, India was committed to them; iii) it failed to balance strategic considerations with that of the needs of the peace process and the historical changes taking place. UCPN (M) relations with China were looked upon as disturbing and thus cracks appeared in India's relations with the former. This had detrimental impact on the entire peace process itself bringing in more instability than ever before; iv) short term goals dominated over long term implications. Thus it supported the 12 Point Agreement without drawing possible multiple scenarios that could emerge, v) India, failed to correctly assess the influence and power of new leaders and parties. It did not realize that UCPN (M) would be equally powerful and influential while in opposition than in power; vi) It failed to understand that the world view of Nepal could change and it need not be detrimental to India; and finally vii) India failed to realize that continuing instability in Nepal will increase engagement of other countries in Nepal and reduce India's acknowledged prominent position in the peace process in Nepal.

The consequences of prolonging the peace process only increase uncertainty and instability which will not be beneficial to security of either India or Nepal. Issues need to be resolved at the earliest for otherwise delays result in lawlessness and positions becoming hardened and uncompromising.

The search for security since the two decades following 1990 has been elusive for India. It arrives at an arrangement confident that its interests will be secure, but soon unexpected developments take place and new concerns arise. Its foreign policy was not prepared to factor in and respond to the changing dynamic situation. Its power to influence events got severely reduced and it had to bow down to people's pressure. Despite intense patrolling of the borders, they are still unsafe. Given its naxal problem, the renegade breakaway elements of UCPN (M) could develop links with similar Indian elements challenging India's fight against the Maoists much more.

Also India has a significant economic assistance programme being implemented in Nepal. Under the Small Development Project Scheme, India is undertaking development projects in the areas of infrastructure, health, rural and community development and education. Already more than 160 projects have been implemented or are under implementation. Somewhere there is a policy gap because despite all these important steps what India gets over the years is consistent anti-India rhetoric.

New Dynamics of the Conflict Post CA Elections

The paper has argued that it was extreme concentration of political-economic-social power in a small minority, that forced the marginalized majority to support the Maoist insurgency in the first place and then later launch their own multiple movements for proportional representation, federalism, more reservation in government institutions, state apparatus etc. The Maoists three basic demands of a republic, interim Constitution, and a CA have been fulfilled. The marginalized sections too through their movements have achieved significant success and the CA so elected in 2008 is most representative so far. Then, why was there no forward movement in the peace process to complete the unfinished task of drafting the Constitution by 28th May 2010 and secondly complete the task of rehabilitating and integration of the Maoist combatants? Why is there obstruction in the working of the CA and confrontation in all forums among the political parties? Why is there a complete breakdown of consensus?

Post CA elections were not going to be easy times as the various provisions of the Constitution would be debated and contested. Further, prior to elections, agreements were concluded with various protesting marginalized groups that their interests would be protected and incorporated into the Constitution. Those relating to federalism, self determination and autonomy and that relating to the nature of the government were all going to be keenly discussed. However, none of this happened.

New Power Equations: Reinforcing Confrontation

Results of the Constituent Assembly (CA) elections held in May 2008 shook the established political parties as the UCPN (M) emerged with the most number of seats. They obtained 229 seats in a house of 601 members. The Nepali Congress Party won 109 and the CPN (UML) won 104 seats. The possibility of such a situation was not envisioned either by the domestic actors nor the external stakeholders, especially India, when the peace process commenced. The electoral politics not only re-set the power equations but doubts both real and imaginary arose regarding the agenda of the new winner. Fears arose regarding the possibility of the Maoists expanding their political space, by force, and consequently shrinking that of the other parties which had existed for decades. Instead of looking inward, analyze their disappointing performance and take corrective measures, these parties looked outward to artificially set right the balance of power.

Events that followed showed that neither were the established parties gracious losers nor were the Maoists sensitive winners. Confrontation was thus inbuilt in such a scenario. The situation was further aggravated as UCPN (M) had not only the most number of seats in the CA elections but unlike other parties it also had its combatants in the cantonments. Though they were being monitored by the United Nations Mission in Nepal (UNMIN) there were apprehensions about the democratic credentials of UCPN (M) and that it would not hesitate to use them. Even with the combatants in the cantonments, had one of the established parties won the CA elections, Nepal would not have seen the rigidity which exists presently among all the political parties. The Maoists failed to understand these insecurities and did nothing to allay their fears. They failed in their duty of building consensus among the political parties. Deviation from the peace process seemed imminent now. The all important duty, goal or task of drafting the Constitution was slowly being pushed backwards by everyone.

Breakdown of Consensus

As the Maoists did not win enough to form a government on their own, they needed the support of the established parties. Tough negotiations, bargaining and misunderstandings among the various political parties preceded government formation. The many discussions and debates that took place prior to the government formation broke down on sharing of the crucial sensitive ministries, especially the defense ministry.[133] The control of the defense ministry and other crucial ministries would raise the power and influence of the political party concerned whatever the verdict of the CA result might be. This was the time when external stakeholders should have as neutral players sought to preserve and protect the consensus. This was the stage of preventing conflict escalation. By the time the coalition government led by the Maoists was formed in August 2008 and much before the controversial issues relating to the Nepali Army broke out, the battle lines were already drawn. The NC (Nepali Congress), the main opposition party, followed a policy of obstructing the functioning of the legislative parliament till they were assured that the demands they raised relating to - return of the seized property to its rightful owners, abiding by the past agreements and understandings, scrapping of paramilitary structure of the Young Communist League (YCL) would be adequately addressed and implemented.[134] Some other parties too obstructed the legislative parliament on some or the other grievances.

The issues which triggered the crisis in Nepal in 2009 related to Nepal Army's recruitment of 3010 soldiers, reinstatement of eight retired Brigadier Generals, and their boycott of the National games[135] - all overlooking the

---

[133] Padmaja Murthy, " India and Nepal: Transitional Phase, Testing Times", IPCS Issue Brief, No 136, Feb 2010 available online at http://www.ipcs.org/pdf_file/issue/IB136-Padmaja-IndiaNepal.pdf accessed on 17 March 2011.

[134] "NC to Obstruct House if Progress not Made on its Demand", *Nepalnews.com,* April 13, 2009, http://www.nepalnews.com/archive/2009/apr/apr13/news07.php; "NC Leaders Speak their Mind on Army Integration", *Nepalnews.com,* January 1, 2009, http://www.nepalnews.com/archive/2009/jan/jan01/news08.php. According to this report, Nepali Congress (NC) acting-president Sushil Koirala has said that Maoist combatants can in no circumstances be integrated into the Nepal Army (NA). He also said that NC will continue to obstruct the legislative parliament session until the Maoists don't implement past agreements.

[135] For a detailed analysis of this crises refer S.D.Muni , The Civil Military Crises in Nepal , *The Hindu* http://www.hindu.com/2009/05/06/stories/2009050655151100.htm. This article in The Hindu ,argues that the stated issues involved in the Government –NA conflict are indeed trivial. They cannot be advanced as legitimate excuses either for NA's repeated defiance or for Maoists extreme decision. The article delves into the real issues behind the crises and argues that it is reflection of the unresolved conflict in Nepal between the discarded feudal order and the inclusive democratic new Nepal.

reservations and views of the elected government led by the UCPN(M).[136] Debates which took place on these three issues further polarized the political parties with UCPN (M) on one side and the other parties primarily the Nepali Congress leading them on the other. The NC boycotted the legislative parliament over the Maoists action of seeking clarification from the Army Chief on the three controversial issues.[137] The NC also warned that it would wage a strong nationwide protest movement against the government if the Maoist-led government were to sack Chief of Army Staff General Rookmangud Katawal.[138]

---

[136] "Katawal Might be Sacked, says Dr Bhattarai", *Nepalnews.com,* April 21, 2009, http://www.nepalnews.com/archive/2009/apr/apr21/news01.php; "PM meets President Amid Rumours of Govt. Preparing to Sack Army Chief", *Nepalnews.com,* April 20, 2009,http://www.nepalnews.com/archive/2009/apr/apr20/news12.php According to this report, PM Dahal met the President hours after the government asked the army chief to come up with a formal clarification. A cabinet meet on 19 April, 2009 concluded that the army chief had gone against a number of decisions of the government, "challenging the norms of civilian supremacy".

[137] "Army Chief Submits Written Clarification to Govt.", *Nepalnews.com,* April 21, 2009, http://www.nepalnews.com/archive/2009/apr/apr21/news04.php. According to this report, the Maoist controlled ministry, which is at odds with Nepal Army since the latter recruited 3010 soldiers by going against the government's orders to stop it, had accused General Katawal of challenging "people's supremacy" by repeatedly Disobeying the Government Orders; "MoD issues 24-hr Ultimatum to Army Chief to Clarify on Thorny Issues", *Nepalnews.com,* April 20, 2009, http://www.nepalnews.com/archive/2009/apr/apr20/news04.php; "NC Leaders Meet Prez to Oppose Govt'sddecision to seek CoAS Clarification", *Nepalnews.com,* April 21, 2009, http://www.nepalnews.com/archive/2009/apr/apr21/news08.php . According to this report, NC spokesperson Arjun Narsingh K.C said that the Maoist- led government's decision to seek clarification from the army chief on controversial issues related to the army was in line with the Maoist party's policy to attack all organs of the state by making various excuses; "NC set to be on war-path if Govt. sacks Army Chief", *Nepalnews.com,* April 26, 2009, http://www.nepalnews.com/archive/2009/apr/apr26/news08.php. According to this report, at the meeting, Koirala said the party should "strongly oppose" Maoists plan to "capture state power" and directed his party leaders and activists to be ready to wage a strong protest movement against the government if it removes Army Chief from his post.

[138] "NC Boycotts House", *Nepalnews.com,* April 20, 2009, http://www.nepalnews.com/archive/2009/apr/apr20/news16.php; "16 Parties Join Forces Against Maoists over CoAS Clarification Episode", *Nepalnews.com,* April 21, 2009, http://www.nepalnews.com/archive/2009/apr/apr21/news10.php. According to this report, a meeting of 16 political parties including a key partner in the government coalition, CPN (UML), concluded that the Maoist initiative to seek clarification from the Army Chief was against the spirit of peace process. At a meeting called by the main opposition Nepali Congress on Tuesday afternoon at its office in Sanepa, the parties slammed the Maoists for "attacking on all state agencies to destabilize democracy".

The Maoist-led government decision to sack the Army chief was a minority decision taken with all the major coalition partners including the CPN(UML) disagreeing. This decision was revoked by the President and the Army Chief was reinstated. This action led to Prachanda resigning as the Prime Minister in May.[139] This crises needs to be understood in the background of the civil-military relations in Nepal as they have existed and in particular the relations between the NA and the Maoists as it existed during the Maoist insurgency. The NA and the Maoists (through the PLA) had been adversaries during the ten years of maoist insurgency. When it all ended post Jana Andolan II in April 2006 there was no clear victor. Neither the NA could defeat the Maoists nor could the later capture power through violent means. This situation was considered a serious disadvantage to the NA. Under the CPA, both NA and PLA are treated almost equally and the United Nations through UNMIN managed the arms and armies of both the state and the Maoists. Agreements between the Maoists and the political parties also indicate to not only PLA's integration but also restructuring of the NA. This has not been appreciated by many sections within the NA, some political parties and also some stakeholders external and internal. It also needs to be noted that the political parties and the NA have had their share of suspicion and distrust post 1990 and also post 2006 peoples movements. It was their common distrust of the Maoists for different reasons which brought them together in 2008-2009.[140]

Madhav Kumar Nepal led the new 22 party coalition government which the Maoists termed as 'puppet of India'. The Maoists blamed India for the fall of their government. These extreme positions left little scope for

---

[139] "Prime Minister Dahal Resigns Slamming Prez's Move", *Nepalnews.com,* May 4, 2009, http://www.nepalnews.com/archive/2009/may/may04/news05.php. This report described President Yadav's move to override the government's decision to sack the Army chief as "unconstitutional", Dahal said it has dealt a serious blow to democracy, peace process and the newly established republican order and asked him to rectify his decision.

[140] For a detailed analyses refer S.D.Muni, State, Army and the aam admi in Nepal , *Seminar,* No.611, July 2010, http://www.india-seminar.com/2010/611/611_s_d_muni.htm. The article spells out why King Birendra refused to deploy the army against the Maoists ; the rise of Army's corporate interests; the background to the 2009 hostility between the Maoists and the NA and the manner in which the NA and mainstream political parties have found convergence – all of which has its repercussions to the peace process and developments taking place presently.

consensus and the deadlock continues even now on this issue and many others too.[141] The UCPN(M) have since implemented a four phase protest movement demanding that the President's action of reinstating the Army Chief they had sacked be termed as 'unconstitutional' as it challenges 'civilian supremacy'.[142] This only deepened the divide and polarized the views further. Both the sides put forward their hardened positions in such a way that compromise or a way out seemed difficult. The Maoists wanted the Presidents action to be termed as unconstitutional, forgetting that the Presidents action had the support of the rest of the parties. The political parties supporting a resolution indicting the President would have been indirectly passing a censure against their own actions and views. This was not to happen and no wonder the deadlock continues. However, this paper argues that if not the issues relating to the army, there would have been some other issue leading to the polarization of views among the political parties. The postures of all the political parties post CA elections were belligerent with no trace of the consensus for taking the peace process

---

[141] "Top Leaders to Meet Tuesday to End Deepening Political Crisis", *Nepalnews.com,* December 14, 2009, http://www.nepalnews.com/main/index.php/news-archive/1-top-story/2901-top-leaders-to-meet-tuesday-to-end-deepening-political-crisis.html According to this report, there is a serious dispute between the three parties on the contents of the resolution motion. "While the Maoists were adamant on their stance that the resolution motion should categorically mention about the "unconstitutional" move of the President on the Army chief row, the NC and UML were clearly opposed to the idea. However, lately, the Maoists have shown some amount of flexibility in this regard and want the resolution motion to symbolically state that the President's move of reinstating the former Army Chief by overturning the then Maoist government's decision was "erroneous". Although UML seems to be somewhat positive regarding this, Nepali Congress is not in favor of mentioning anything that even remotely suggests that the President's move on the Army chief case was wrong"; "Parties Remain Divided on Essence of Civilian Supremacy", June 30, 2009, http://www.nepalnews.com/archive/2009/jun/jun30/news06.php; "Maoists are Trying to Belittle Parliament: PM", *Nepalnews.com,* June 27, 2009, http://www.nepalnews.com/archive/2009/jun/jun27/news04.php . According to this report. Prime Minister Nepal said that in no way the President's move could be called unconstitutional, but the issue of civilian supremacy could be discussed among political parties.

[142] "President Tells Katawal to Stay in Position", *Nepalnews.com,* May 4, 2009, http://www.nepalnews.com/archive/2009/may/may04/news01.php . According to this report, President Dr Ram Baran Yadav has written to the army headquarters instructing Rookmangud Katawal to stay in position, despite sacking orders from the government. The President intervened in the issue following a memorandum submitted by 18 political parties including Nepali Congress and the CPN (UML).

ahead. [143]

Maoists Four Phase Protest Movement

Maoists did have certain genuine grievances. However, these protest movements which were carried to uphold 'civilian supremacy' as the Maoists claim, have done more harm than benefit this very cause. First, their protests have undermined the whole peace process. In fact, the drafting of the Constitution would have been the real triumph of 'civilian supremacy' for which the Maoists could have without doubt taken the major credit. Second, the Maoists periodically escalated their protest movements as no concrete success was forthcoming. National sovereignty became another issue along with civilian supremacy. Protests on issues, over which there was no unanimity, took place for almost a year. They have demonstrated that their actions can result in stalemate in national politics and bilaterally too. However, it has benefited neither them nor the peace process or the country. There is now introspection within the UCPN (M), if right strategies were adopted to put forward their grievances. [144]

In the first phase of their protest which began in May 2009, they decided to obstruct the functioning of the regular session of the parliament[145]; protest in the parliament and the streets; and obstruct all public programmes of the President, Prime Minister and other ministers[146]. In the second phase starting

[143] "CA Chair Saddened Over Culture of House Obstruction", *Nepalnews.com,* December 9, 2009, http://www.nepalnews.com/main/index.php/news-archive/2-political/2822-ca-chair-saddened-over-culture-of-house-obstruction.html

[144] "Dahal Under Fire at Polit Bureau Meeting", *Republica,* June 19, 2010, http://myrepublica.com/portal/index.php?action=news_details&news_id=20082; "Most Leaders Support Bhattarai's view", *Republica,* June 18, 2010,   http://myrepublica.com/portal/index.php?action=news_details&news_id=19998; "Dahal Blames 'foreign power' for Deadlock", *Republica,* June 20, 2010,   http://myrepublica.com/portal/index.php?action=news_details&news_id=20117

[145] "Maoists Disrupt House Proceedings",*Nepalnews.com,* May 5, 2009, http://www.nepalnews.com/archive/2009/may/may05/news13.php

[146] " Maoists Show Black Flags at President Yadav",*Nepalnews.com,* October 3, 2009, http://www.nepalnews.com/main/index.php/news-archive/2-political/1708-Maoists-show-black-flags-at-president-yadav.html; "Maoist Cadres Show Black Flag to State Minister, Pelt Stones at Him", *Nepalnews.com,* June 23, 2009, http://www.nepalnews.com/archive/

in November, they organized torch rallies, picketed the district administration office and village development committees across the country and blocked the office gates to prevent the employees from entering inside[147]. In the third phase which began on 11 December, they declared over a period of one week, 13 autonomous states based on ethnicity and region to uphold what they say civilian supremacy.[148] On 25 December, they launched the fourth phase of the protest movement where the party campaigned for national independence and sovereignty and for fighting 'Indian

---

2009/jun/jun23/news11.php; "Maoists Decide to Intensify Agitation", *Nepalnews.com,* August 30, 2009, http://www.nepalnews.com/main/index.php/news-archive/2-political/ 1187-Maoists-decide-to-intensify-agitation.html According to this report - Joint National People's Movement Committee of the Unified CPN (Maoist) has decided to intensify the party's ongoing agitation for civil supremacy. The committee also decided to organise mass assemblies in 18 places across the country from September 6 to 14 demanding for civil supremacy. They have decided to boycott all functions attended by Prime Minister Madhav Kumar Nepal from Monday as part of the agitation. Maoists lawmakers have continued obstructing normal proceedings of the legislative parliament demanding the President's move be allowed to be discussed in the parliament.

[147] "Maoists Begin Second Round of Protests Against President's Move", *Nepalnews.com,* November 1, 2009, http://www.nepalnews.com/main/index.php/news-archive/1-top-story/2186-Maoists-begin-second-round-of-protests-against-presidents-move.html; "Maoists Picket DAOs Across the Country", *Nepalnews.com,* November 4, 2009, http:// www.nepalnews.com/main/index.php/news-archive/1-top-story/2239-Maoists-picket-daos-across-the-country.html; "Violence and Vandalism Mark Maoist Protest", *Nepalnews.com,* June 21, 2009, http://www.nepalnews.com/archive/2009/jun/jun21/ news01.php; "Dr Bhattarai says Maoists' Ultimate Aim is State Capture", *Nepalnews.com,* November 1, 2009, http://www.nepalnews.com/main/index.php/news-archive/2-political/ 2183-dr-bhattarai-says-Maoists-ultimate-aim-is-state-capture.html; "Chand says 'civilian supremacy' Means Maoist-led Govt.", *Nepalnews.com,* November 15, 2009, http:// nepalnews.com/main/index.php/news-archive/2-political/2413-chand-says-civilian-supremacy-means-Maoist-led-govt.html. In this report, Standing Committee Member of the Unified CPN (Maoist) Netra Bikram Chand has defined 'civilian supremacy' as formation of a new government under his party's leadership. He said, if the largest party in the parliament is given the right to lead the government, it automatically rectifies the President's move and restore civilian supremacy.

[148] "Maoists to Declare Autonomous Federal Units from December 11", *Nepalnews.com,* November 26, 2009, http://www.nepalnews.com/main/index.php/news-archive/1-top-story/2609-Maoists-to-declare-autonomous-federal-units-from-december-11.html; "Maoists take Autonomous States Count to 12; Declare Magarat and Tamuwan", December 17, 2009, http://www.nepalnews.com/main/index.php/news-archive/1-top-story/2953-ucpn-m-declares-magarat-autonomous-state-from-palpa.html; "Peace Minister Cries Foul as Maoists Declare Two More States", *Nepalnews.com,* December 15, 2009, http://

expansionism'[149]. They said that an indefinite general strike would be launched if the coalition government fails to address the issue of civilian supremacy by 24 January 2010. The silver lining was that just before the launch of the fourth phase, the UCPN (M) decided to end the Parliament House obstruction and instead adopt a different strategy of protest inside the House for civilian supremacy.[150]

Fourth phase of UCPN (M) protest movement for 'civilian supremacy' which began in the last week of December 2009 targets India.[151] Divisive politics within Nepal have now drawn India into it. This not only affects relations between the two countries but also the public opinion which is a critical decisive element in policy formulation on relations between them.

www.nepalnews.com/main/index.php/news-archive/1-top-story/2918-peace-minister-cries-foul-as-Maoists-prepare-to-declare-more-autonomous-states.html; "Maoists Declare Kochila, Limbuwan Autonomous Provinces", *Nepalnews.com,* December 11, 2009, http://www.nepalnews.com/main/index.php/news-archive/1-top-story/2850-Maoists-declare-kochila-limbuwan-autonomous-provinces.html. According to this report various political parties have expressed their objection to the Maoist plan, saying that it undermines the supremacy as well as the significance of the Constituent Assembly (CA) itself. They also say that the Maoist plan has raised deep suspicion among the people on whether the country will have a new Constitution in the stipulated time. It needs to be noted that the boundaries of the proposed 13 states were not spelt out by the Maoists.

[149]" Maoists to Wage War Against 'Indian Expansionism'", *Nepalnews.com,* December 26, 2009, http://www.nepalnews.com/main/index.php/news-archive/2-political/3093-Maoists-to-wage-war-against-indian-expansionism.html; "UCPN (M) Dubs 3rd Phase Protest a Success: Announces Fresh Protests", *Nepalnews.com,* December 25, 2009, http://www.nepalnews.com/main/index.php/news-archive/1-top-story/3079-ucpn-m-dubs-3rd-phase-protest-a-success-announces-fresh-protests.html ; During India's External Affairs Minister SM Krishna's visit to Nepal in January 2010 there was a meeting held with Prachanda. The official spokesperson from India said that "EAM also conveyed his deep disappointment at the baseless attacks on India by the Maoist leadership which vitiate the age-old and time-tested friendly relations between India and Nepal and the people of the two countries. He emphasized that such baseless propaganda has a negative impact on Indian public opinion."

[150] "Maoists Decide to End House Obstruction", *Nepalnews.com,* December 23, 2009, http://www.nepalnews.com/main/index.php/news-archive/2-political/3046-Maoists-decide-to-end-house-obstruction.html; "Legislature-Parliament Back to Business", *Nepalnews.com,* December 23, 2009, http://www.nepalnews.com/main/index.php/news-archive/2-political/3053-legislature-parliament-back-to-business.html

[151] "Maoist Nationwide Protest to Concentrate on Protecting National Sovereignty", *Nepalnews.com,* http://www.nepalnews.com/main/index.php/news-archive/1-top-story/3273-Maoist-nationwide-protest-to-concentrate-on-protecting-national-sovereignty.html;

The UCPN(M) leaders have said that Nepal's sovereignty is in serious danger and is more important than civilian supremacy; that the present government in Nepal was acting at the behest of New Delhi and that Indian imperialism has been the main constraint to Constitution writing and peace process. The alleged comment by the Indian Army Chief, that they are against integration of the Maoist combatants in the Nepal Army, further created controversy.[152] The Indian embassy in Nepal issued a statement which intended to communicate that they were not the views of the Government.[153] The Maoists dispatched their leaders to different border points on the Indo-Nepal border where they alleged encroachment had taken place by the Indian side and organized mass gatherings in these places.[154] They also burnt Indo-Nepal treaties which they considered unequal. On the eve of the Indian Foreign Minister's visit, UCPN (M) said that Nepal Army had imported a large quantity of arms and ammunition from India by violating the peace accord. The Nepal Army clarified that it bought trucks and other vehicles as per requirement and no arms were in these vehicles. More recently the UCPN (M) raised concerns over the contract of the machine readable passports being given to India. The government of Nepal unsuccessfully tried to defend its decisions. The contract was finally cancelled. The fourth phase of protest movements reflects the Maoists frustration over the continued deadlock. They remain disappointed with several issues including not being able to play the lead role of heading the government in this critical transition period given the nature of results of the CA elections and the fact that hardliners in the party are gaining more ground besides being disappointed with India's role.

---

[152] "Maoist Chairman asks Govt. to Clarify its Position on Indian Army Chief's Comment", *Nepalnews.com,* December 24, 2009, http://www.nepalnews.com/main/index.php/news-archive/2-political/3064-Maoist-chairman-asks-govt-to-clarify-its-position-on-indian-army-chiefs-comment.html

[153] "Kapoor's Views on PLA Integration do not Reflect Indian Govt's Position: Indian Embassy", *Nepalnews.com,* January 4, 2010, http://www.nepalnews.com/main/index.php/news-archive/1-top-story/3247-kapoors-views-on-pla-integration-do-not-reflect-indian-govts-position-indian-embassy.html

[154] "Maoist Leaders to Visit 'encroached' Border Areas Including Kalapani", *Nepalnews.com,* January 2, 2010, http://www.nepalnews.com/main/index.php/news-archive/1-top-story/3212-Maoist-leaders-to-visit-encroached-border-areas-including-kalapani.html

During the Indian Foreign Minister's January 2010 visit, India expressed its concern over the UCPN(M) fourth phase of protest movement in its discussions with their leader Pushpa Kamal Dahal who also expressed their concerns on national sovereignty and civilian supremacy. The leaders were positive about the discussions and India seems to have conveyed that it wants to treat all the parties equally.[155] India is looked upon by many in Nepal including the academia as following a policy of isolating the Maoists which is detrimental to the peace process.

This paper argues that while the merit of their grievances can be debated, and benefit of doubt can be given to them on certain issues, their method of protest has discredited them. It has shown that they have been unable to put the need for drafting the Constitution *i.e.* the peace process above everything else. It is UCPN (M) which has been hurt the most by their very own protest movements. The very impressive mandate given to them during the CA elections has been wasted.

Impact on the Army: Long Term Implications

The sensitive issues relating to the Nepali Army, on which there ought to be consensus whether or not there is a peace process, has the potential to blow up at a future date with regard to two issues. First, the role of the Army in a fractured democratic polity; and second on the whole process of integration and rehabilitation of the Maoist combatants.

When, the Madhav Kumar Nepal led 22 party coalition government came to power, the balance of power had been temporarily and artificially reset. However, UCPN (M) is now an effective permanent player in electoral politics in Nepal. Almost all the political parties were in convergence with the Army's interpretation of events and issues and only the UCPN

---

[155] The Indian Minister had discussions with all the important leaders in Nepal. Towards the end of the visit a 20 point joint press statement was   issued wherein they agreed to cooperate closely to combat the threat of terrorism and extremism which was a threat to both countries; control cross border crimes such as smuggling of fake India currency, agreed to expedite the finalization of MoU for the construction of the Nepal Police Academy at Panauti with India's assistance, maintain peace and law and order along the Indo-Nepal border; review the 1950 Treaty of Peace and Friendship with a view to further strengthen bilateral relations.

(M) spoke against it. The confrontation was all about who controlled the Defense Ministry and the armed forces. One wanted to maintain status quo, the other wanted to bring change and both were impatient. Post peace process, the army felt that its interests will not be served by a particular party. If the Army were to take sides in the absence of political consensus in future, the first casualty would be democratic politics. The vacuum created by politics being polarized could be filled by the army directly or indirectly.

The UNSG (United Nations Secretary General) tabling its quarterly report in January 2010 on Nepal's peace process said that tensions and mistrust between UCPN (M), the government and the army threatened the peace process and there was a possibility that the peace process could collapse as major disagreements continue. All issues are now being seen through the fractured politics. For example, 98 key provisions to be incorporated in the new Constitution were finalized by voting in the Constitutional Committee as political parties failed to forge a consensus. There is a possibility that some provisions which have merit could have been voted out because they belong to a particular party.

Given the fractured consensus, deep divisions and polarization of views it is not surprising that two important aspects of the peace process – the Constitution drafting and the integration and rehabilitation of the Maoist combatants have remained incomplete. The integration and rehabilitation of the Maoist combatants relates to dismantling the infrastructure which was built to wage the insurgency and the writing of the Constitution is all about building the edifice on which the infrastructure of ideas, rules and regulations to build the New Nepal will be raised. Views differ on which action should precede first or whether both should happen simultaneously.

The Special Committee for Supervision, Integration and Rehabilitation of the Maoist Combatants headed by the Prime Minister deliberates on this issue. Differences arise on the number of people to be integrated and the criteria thereof for integration and at what levels.[156] Fears and doubts are

---

[156] "Extremists Want to See Peace Process Derailed., *ekantipur.com*, January 31, 2010 http://www.ekantipur.com/2010/02/01/oped/extremists-want-to-see-peace-process-derailed/307479/   . Refer to the interview of CPN-UML General Secretary Ishwor Pokhrel for more details (Accessed on February 2, 2010.)

expressed as to the possible influence of the highly politicized Maoist combatants into the professional national army. Some are of the view that there should not be any integration into the national army and that they should be integrated into other security sectors and into the society.[157] Then, the second view is that only some should be integrated into the national army after they meet certain criteria so as to maintain the standards set for a professional army. This is the middle ground which would most likely be acceptable to a wide section of society. The third view which is advocated by the Maoists is that all the Maoist combatants should be integrated into the national army. Another view is that the Maoist People's Liberation Army combatants should have been integrated into Nepal Army before the Constituent Assembly election which catapulted the Maoists into being the largest party in the Constituent Assembly.[158]

Maoists accuse the government of not being serious and that only a national government can solve this issue.[159] The Special Committee for the Supervision, Integration and Rehabilitation of Maoist combatants has finalized the organizational chart of the new chain of command that will bring Maoist combatants under government control.[160] The Prime Minister

---

[157] "No Integration of Maoist Combatants into Nepal Army: Sushil", N*epalnews.com,* January 1, 2010, http://www.nepalnews.com/main/index.php/news-archive/2-political/3200-no-integration-of-Maoist-combatants-into-nepal-army-sushil.html

[158] "Dahal takes Koirala to Task Over his Remark on Army Integration", *Nepalnews.com,* July 23, 2009, http://www.nepalnews.com/main/index.php/news-archive/2-political/568-dahal-to-take-koirala-to-task-over-his-remark-on-army-integration.html According to this report Koirala had told journalists in his hometown Biratnagar that the ex-Maoist combatants need to be rehabilitated into the society, not integrated into the Nepal Army. Koirala had earlier also lambasted ethnicity-based politics, which the Maoists championed, saying that his party instead believes in class-based politics where workers fight for their own rights.

[159] "Violence can Escalate if Army Integration Issue Not Taken Seriously: Bhattara", *Nepalnews.com,* September 11, 2009, http://nepalnews.com/main/index.php/news-archive/2-political/1393-violence-can-escalate-if-army-integration-issue-not-taken-seriously-bhattarai.html, According to the report Bhattarai said that the ongoing peace process cannot reach a logical conclusion without consensus and cooperation among the political parties, but added that violence can escalate in the country if the integration and rehabilitation of ex-Maoist combatants is not done properly; "Maoist Leader says UML Govt. Unable to Complete Integration Process, hopes Better Terms with New NA Chief", *Nepalnews.com,* September 10, 2009, http://www.nepalnews.com/main/index.php/news-archive/2-political/1380-Maoist-leader-says-uml-govt-unable-to-complete-integration-process-hopes-better-terms-with-new-na-chief.html

[160] "Special Committee to Form Secretariat for Chain-of-Command for PLA Fighters", *ekantipur.com,* January 26, 2010, http://www.ekantipur.com/2010/01/26/related-news/Special-Committee-to-form-secretariat-for-chain-of-command-for-PLA-fighters/307112/

had tabled at the Special Committee the 112-day army integration action plan which proposed to complete the integration and rehabilitation of the Maoist combatants within four months *i.e.* April 2010[161]. The committee was to debate this and garner consensus on the number of Maoist combatants to be integrated into state security agencies and forces and those who want to charter their own career in politics and those who just want to be rehabilitated back into society. [162] Progress had not been made on this proposal and the deadline has also passed.[163]

Thus, more than the issues for which the insurgency was waged, the dismantling of the infrastructure to wage the insurgency has become a tricky issue and very difficult one. Ironically, actions of all political parties are eroding the gains made since Jana Andolan II and civilian supremacy is the one factor which is being compromised.

The manner in which this issue is resolved will have implications regarding - the neutrality and professionalism of the armed forces of the country and the working of democracy in which the armed forces should be under the elected civilian leadership. It should act as a deterrent for any future groups to take up arms and wage insurgency.

The Conflict's Impact on the Economy

The following table gives an assessment of the damage done to physical infrastructure during the conflict. It indicates to not only the damage done

---

[161] For details see, "Govt. Maoist Agree to Finish Army Integration in 112 Days", *Nepalnews.com*, January 7, 2010, http://www.nepalnews.com/main/index.php/news-archive/1-top-story/ 3322-govt-Maoists-agree-to-finish-army-integration-in-112-days.html. According to this report - Prime Minister Madhav Kumar Nepal had tabled the action plan which proposes, among others, to garner political consensus on the number of Maoist combatants to be integrated in state security agencies and collect separate data regarding combatants who want to integrate into the state security forces, those who want to chart their own career in politics and those who just want to be rehabilitated back into the society.

[162] "PLA Combatants are Now Under Govt. Aegis", *ekantipur.com*, January 30, 2010, http:/ /www.ekantipur.com/2010/01/31/related-news/PLA-combatants-are-now-under-govt-aegis/307461/

[163] "Maoists Agree in Principle for Army Integration Within Four Months", *ekantipur.com*, January 7, 2010, http://www.ekantipur.com/2010/01/07/related-news/Maoists-agree-in-principle-for-army-integration-within-four-months/305933/

but most importantly the enormity of the task to rebuild all these and how peace is the most essential ingredient for it.[164]

Table 12: Estimates of Damage of Physical Infrastructures in Nepal by Mid May 2007 (in thousand NRs)

Ministry/department/organization	Estimated cost of damage	Percent	Cost of reconstruction	Percent
Ministry of Local Development	598,448	11.73	161.722	3.78
Ministry of Water Resources	342,703	6.74	297.243	6.94
Ministry of Health and Population	417	0.01	130.130	3.04
Ministry of Forest arc! Soil Conservation	354.461	6.97	377.123	8.80
Ministry of Education and Sports	20,980	0.41	44,984	1.05
Ministry of Agriculture and Cooperatives	260.755	5.13	-	-
Ministry of Industry and Commerce	72,768	1.43	69,709	1.63
Ministry of Environment, Science and Technology	3.209	0.06	-	-
Ministry of Information and Communication	741.555	14.58	145,166	3.39
Ministry of Culture and Civil Aviation	134.747	2.65	26,550	0.62
Ministry of Physical Planning and Works	25.174	0.49	19,746	0.46
Ministry of Land Reform and Management	32,215	0.63	361,181	8.43

CONTD/-

---

[164] Padmaja Murthy, " India and Nepal: Transitional Phase, Testing Times", IPCS Issue Brief, No 136, Feb 2010 available online at http://www.ipcs.org/pdf_file/issue/IB136-Padmaja-IndiaNepal.pdf accessed on 17 March 2011.

Ministry of Foreign Affairs	-	-	-	-
Ministry of General Administration	-	-	-	-
Ministry of Law and Justice and Parliamentary Affairs	-	-	-	-
Ministry of Defence	30.967	0.61	53,266	1.24
Ministry of Finance	4.666	0.09	2,270	0.05
Ministry of Home	2,428,646	47.75	2,428,203	56.69
Ministry of Women Children and Social Welfare	265	0.01	-	-
Ministry of Labour and Transport Management	524	0.01	524	0.01
Other organizations				
National Planning Commission	242	0.00	-	-
Supreme Court	27.489	0.54	165,555	3.87
Election Commission	2.946	0.06	-	-
Office of the Attorney General	201	0.00	-	-
Public Service Commission	4.781	0.09	1	0.00
Commission for the Investigation of Abuse of Authority	-	-	-	-
Office of Financial Comptroller General	-	-	-	-
Total amount in thousand	5,086,137	100.00	4,283,373	100.00

Source: United Nations Development Programme, *Nepal Human Development Report 2009: State Transformation and Human Development*, Kathmandu, 2009,139

Impact on Nepal's Economy

The internal conflict in Nepal since the Maoist insurgency began in 1996 has effected all economic activities in Nepal. The Nepalese business community itself is a dejected lot regarding the uncertainty in the economic environment due to continuing political instability even after the CA elections. They feel that continuous power cuts, ceaseless wage dispute between employees and employers, the frequent strikes, deteriorating law and order are all wrecking havoc with the business sector of the country. Highways are blocked for several days for trifle issues; the threats of extortions and the terror spread by the trade unions affiliated to the Maoists result in closure of industries. In this context, they feel that the chances of new investment internally as well as FDI in any productive avenue are bleak. On the contrary the country is witnessing capital flight because of volatile political situation. They emphasize that the internal problems are more inimical to national economy rather than the external ones.

Some suggested that it is necessary to declare the industrial estate or corridor as a peace zone. For otherwise the continuation of this pathetic state will not help in achieving double digit growth and generating the proposed 10,000 MW of electricity in ten years will be confined to the shelves only. They suggested that infrastructure should be improved upon and the joint ventures on hydropower should not be made into political issues for it deters investment in big projects. These grievances clearly bring out that the prospects of economic development in Nepal in a disturbed political environment are not bright. The enormity of the task ahead is clearly visible. Unless political transformation is accompanied by corresponding economic development, the former process will be hollow and incomplete and cannot sustain the political change too. For, economic deprivation will impact peace in the society too. [165]

Also according to government statistics, the country is likely to face a deficit of 132,000 tonnes of food grains by the end of this fiscal year. The

---

[165] NICCI Newsletter, October 2008- March 2009, http://www.nicci.org/includes/downloads/newsletter/Oct_%20March_2009.pdf.

central's bank report on macroeconomic situation based on nine months of the current fiscal year has painted a bleak outlook of the Nepal's economy. The inflation hovers around double digit, balance of payments (BoP) has recorded a deficit of Rs. 22.10 billion, exports have plummeted and imports have gone up pushing the trade deficit up to double compared to the same period last year. Also the revenue mobilization has been poor, while government expenditure has increased and the gross foreign exchange reserves continue to deplete.[166] The slowdown in remittances has added to the woes of the economy.

India – Nepal Economic Relations

When instability has effected internal economic development, its impact on economic activities of other countries in Nepal will also be naturally felt. In this context, this section briefly looks at the Indo-Nepal relations and the manner in which the internal conflict poses a challenge to it.

India and Nepal share close economic relations. These are guided by the Treaty of Trade which spells out the preferential treatment to Nepali manufactured goods in Indian market; the Treaty of Transit which spells out the various provisions and facilities while third country goods are imported into Nepal as it is a landlocked country; the Treaty on Unauthorized Trade has provisions to prevent entry of third country goods and other activities which hamper each other's economic relations.

India is an important economic partner for Nepal. The following trade figures show this very clearly.[167]

---

[166] For details refer, "Central Bank Paints Bleak Picture of the Economy", *Nepalnews.com,* May 26, 2010, http://www.nepalnews.com/main/index.php/business-a-economy/6344-central-bank-paints-bleak-picture-of-the-economy-.html http://www.nepalnews.com/main/index.php/business-a-economy/6344-central-bank-paints-bleak-picture-of-the-economy-.html; Also see, "Economy Heading Towards Crisis",*Nepalnews.com,* http://www.nepalnews.com/main/index.php/business-interview/3166-economy-heading-towards-crisis-dr-mahat-html.

[167] India is Nepal's largest trading partner. Of the Rs 6, 078.7 crore in total exports by Nepal in 2007-08 (15-14 July), India accounted for 63.53 percent, or Rs3, 862 crore. Similarly, of Rs22, 611.6 crore of the country's imports, exports from India were to the tune of 63.91percent, or Rs14, 452.4 crore. The value of unofficial trade, too, is pegged at similar levels.

Trade with India (Including Petroleum Products)

Figures in Million NRs

Fiscal Year	Export to India	Import from India	Trade Defict with India
1997-98	8,794.40	27,331.00	(18,536.60)
1998-99	12,530.70	32,119.70	(19,589.00)
1999-00	21,220.70	39,660.10	(18,439.40)
2000-01	26,030.20	45,211.00	(19,180.80)
2001-02	27,956.20	56,622.10	(28,665.90)
2002-03	26,430.00	70,924.20	(44,494.20)
2003-04	30,777.10	78,739.50	(47,962.40)
2004-05	38,916.90	88,675.50	(49,758.60)
2005-06	40,714.70	107,143.10	(66,428.40)
2006-07	41,728.80	115,872.30	(74,143.50)
2007-08	38,626.40	144,524.10	(105,897.70)

Source: www.nicci.org

Top 20 Items of Import from India

S.No.	Major Commodity	2007/08	2006/07	2005/06
1	Diesel	16988.3	12635.0	12843.3
2	Transport Vehicles & Spare Parts	11873.8	9794.5	5213.7
3	Kerosene	11236.2	10275.2	11995.8
4	Petrol	6999.6	6675.8	5813.6
5	Medicine	5434.1	4442.4	4389.0
6	Other Mach. Equip. & Spare Parts	4673.6	3530.5	3509.4
7	L.P. Gas	4216.6	2989.2	2351.1
8	Electrical Equips & Goods	3584.8	2360.1	1570.9
9	Chemicals	2693.9	2567.5	3281.4
10	Cement	2100.2	2327.9	1933.6
11	Agricultural Equipment & Parts	1482.4	1073.1	671.6
12	Synthetic Thread	1218.5	2190.9	1536.4
13	Vegetable	1210.9	834.5	1139.6
14	Glass Sheet & Glassware	1075.2	481.9	454.9
15	Other Thread	1062.2	342.1	182.8
16	Pipe and Pipe fittings	1028.7	246.3	261.3
17	Coal	905.9	940.8	1193.5
18	Wire Products(Nails, nut & bolts etc)	891.7	138.3	298.8
19	Readymade Garments	865.4	727.8	1083.4
20	Rice	784.0	1505.0	2309.8

Source: www.nicci.org

Top 20 Items of Export to India

S.No.	Major Commodity	07/08	06/07	05/06
1	Other Threads	4134.5	4055.9	1898.3
2	Polyster Yarn	2617.7	2240.4	3476.3
3	Banaspati Ghee	2132.3	4136.5	3861.7
4	Textiles (Cotton, Synthetic & Others)	2113.9	3056.9	2154.6
5	Juice	1836.4	1591.3	1139.6
6	Other Wire	1546.7	1610.7	1504.1
7	Sacks	1219.9	1408.6	1265.4
8	Cardamom	1034.8	848.1	608.1
9	MS Pipes	979.5	761.9	105.7
10	Twines	833.8	973.1	906.9
11	Copper wire & Rod	617.4	206.0	305.8
12	Cateche	543.7	542.8	382.4
13	Ginger	543.2	541.3	275.2
14	Noodles	532.9	237.4	414.7
15	Hessain	528.8	375.1	464.5
16	Readymade Garments	478.1	765.0	1137.3
17	Tooth Paste	475.6	663.4	730.8
18	Toilet Soap	424.2	502.7	363.6
19	Oil Cakes	404.7	318.1	291.6
20	Hide & Skins	346.0	363.1	334.8

Source: www.nicci.org

The huge trade deficit is indeed a major cause of concern. However, it needs to be noted that more than 45 percent of the trade deficit with India is on account of petroleum and electricity imports. Of the balance close to 2/3rd is paid back to Nepal by excise duty refund (about 200 crores per year); remittances from Nepalese working in India (about 1209 crores in 2005-06); payment of pensions by India to Ex-servicemen (Rs 830 crores in 2006-07); Indian investments (Rs 291 crores in 2006-07) and spending by Indian tourists. The largest numbers of tourists to Nepal originate from India. In addition, India's current assistance outlay is more than Rs 2100 crores. Thus it is an important source of development assistance in Nepal providing budgetary support as well. This comes out from the fact that there are 265 projects having an outlay of more than 21 billion (2006-07) reflecting the drastic upsurge of Indian assistance. India maintains that Nepal has a very favorable trade treaty with India and that since 1996 bilateral trade has had an impressive growth. Since 1996, 96 percent of increase in Nepal's exports has been on account of India's purchase from Nepal and that India is improving trade related infrastructure and enhancing cross-border connectivity. [168]

While these arguments are accepted by Nepal, they do specify that until Nepal has a huge flow of Indian investment it cannot increase its exports to India. Income from services sector like tourism and remittances is too small a factor to bridge this huge trade gap. Some of the problems they face concern rules of origin, informal trade, non-tariff barriers etc: the state governments in India impose unnecessary taxes on Nepali goods, illegal trade continues to be a problem and efforts need to be made to control organized smuggling in large commercial volumes through better enforcement, there is no major investment by India in Nepalese private sector in recent years, the present system of export procedure does not facilitate export of primary goods and agricultural products, handicrafts which are Nepal's strength, 30 percent value addition is another deterrent which discourages Nepali export to India, Indian producers make hue and cry to obtain protection against Nepali manufactured goods through political intervention.

Thus an important question arises as to how to bridge this trade gap?

The general consensus in both India and Nepal is that hydropower is one of the areas which can address this trade deficit. Nepal has also realized the significance of hydropower for leapfrogging its economy, bridging the

---

[168] For details see Interview with Ambassador Shiv Shankar Mukherjee, NICCI Newsletter, April-September, 2008, http://www.nicci.org/includes/downloads/newsletter/newsletter2.pdf,11

trade deficit and to turn the country from being energy scarce to energy surplus. It has targeted production of at least 10,000 MW hydropower in 10 years for speedy acceleration of overall economy of Nepal. It is aware that due to many social, political and other seen and unseen reasons Nepal has not been able to harness hydropower. With its abundant water resources Nepal is an ideal destination hydropower projects.[169]

Until recently, India's interest in Nepal's hydropower sector was said to be motivated by the huge energy demands in the Indian market.[170] To remove these misconceptions India has clarified that Indian investment in power sector will first target to fulfill Nepal's domestic consumption the surplus will be exported to India for revenue generation. India is not relying primarily on power export from Nepal in its National Policy and now is the time to re-look at hydropower in view of Nepal's own huge and rapidly growing power deficit and its acute dependence on imports from India.

Investments in hydro-power will be large and long term. Nepal would require around $ 20 billion to generate 10,000 MW of power which will be possible only through public private partnership and foreign direct investment will enter Nepal only if there is political commitment to all stakeholders involved in the hydro sector.[171] This commitment is different from the issue of providing security. Even prior to Maoist insurgency, Indian cooperation in the water resources of Nepal had become a politically sensitive issue. Thus the business community in Nepal opines that joint ventures should not be made a politically hot potato to achieve some vested interests. On the security front Nepal's political leaders maintained that they were contemplating to review existing law to give security guarantee to big projects.

The business community in Nepal is questioning the need to ponder over the lack of adequate foreign investments especially from India. They feel that the momentum seen on entry of Nepal-India Joint venture after the Trade Treaty of 1996 faded away after 2000 and the established ones

---

[169] NICCI Newsletter, October 2008- March 2009, http://www.nicci.org/includes/downloads/ newsletter/Oct_%20March_2009.pdf.

[170] Ibid.

[171] Ibid.

have been shifting from Nepal. They say that the security situation within Nepal is responsible for this for it is not congenial for economic activity. The Maoist insurgency has had a definite adverse impact on economic activity in general which included Indian investments. Maoists had in 2001 in a 13-point memo to industrialists called upon them to get rid of Indian employees. Also in the first spate of renewed strikes by the Maoists in 2001, a bomb was found outside the Nepal Lever factory in Heutada.[172] Many trucks with Indian number plates were being attacked and burnt by the Nepalese insurgents and some major Indian joint venture industrial enterprises were being closed down as a result of attacks or threats issued by the Maoists. Some joint venture establishments in Nepal have been relocated to Indian cities closer to Nepal. The relocation of Colgate Palmolive Plant from Hetauda (Nepal) to Shimla (Himanchal Pradesh) is an example. Similarly, the closure of the Nepal Unilever Company, the bomb blast in the Nepal Bottlers Company, and other acts of industrial sabotage have deterred potential foreign investors in Nepal. This situation has provoked India to blame Nepal for not providing enough security to its people and their socio-economic activities in Nepal.[173]

After the conclusion of the CPA in November 2007 too, Indian industry has been targeted. The multinational Dabur Nepal has decided to shut down its Greenhouse Project in Banepa due to Maoist threats and 'unnecessary demands.'[174] Earlier in May 2006, amid huge 'extortion threat' by a trade

---

[172] Rita Manchanda, "The Future of the Indo-Nepal Preferential Trade Treaty Hangs in the Balance", *Frontline* 18 no. 25 (2001).

[173] Shiva K Dhungana ed., *The Maoist Insurgency and Nepal –India Relations*, (Kathmandu, Friends of Peace: 2006), http://www.friendsforpeace.org.np/images/pdf%20files/Nepal_India_Relations.pdf, The book opines that , the issue of the open border, the proliferation of small arms and light weapons, the issues of water resource development and sharing are all directly concerned with the security, political stability and socio-economic development of both countries.

[174] "Dabur Shuts Down its Greenhouse Due to Maoist Threats", *Nepalnews.com,* January 4, 2007, http://www.nepalnews.com/archive/2007/jan/jan04/news02.php. According to this report, the company had been running the nursery as a Corporate Social Responsibility project with the investment of Rs 100 million and employed 60-80 women. The company has already notified the governments of Nepal and India about the situation. The company's annual transactions crosses Rs 3 billion and has been paying revenue of Rs 250 million to the government every year.

union wing of the Maoists, it is seen that Dabur Nepal Pvt. Ltd. (DNPL)—
one of the largest joint venture companies in the country—has closed down
its manufacturing unit at Rampur Tokani of Bara district in southern
Nepal.[175]

After the CA elections and with the launch of the fourth phase of the
protest movement by UCPN (M), the Indian industries are again facing
insecurity. Officials in India and Nepal are both apprehensive about the
future. The political turmoil in Nepal may hurt the ambitious plans of Indian
power generation firms such as Satluj Jal Vidyut Nigam Ltd, or SJVNL,
Bhilwara Energy Ltd, or BEL, and GMR Infrastructure Ltd, to set up
hydroelectric projects with a combined capacity of 1,124MW in that country.
While SJVNL is building the 402MW Arun-III project, GMR is developing
the 302MW Upper Karnali and the 250MW Upper Myarsangdi projects
and BEL is constructing the 120MW Likhu and 50MW Balathi projects.
While all these projects are commercially viable, the insecurity and
uncertainty due to political turmoil may be a deterrent. India's Federation
of Indian Chambers of Commerce and Industry (FICCI) in a survey report
said: "A pall of gloom has enveloped Indian investors and the business
community doing business in Nepal as the country drifts towards political
turmoil and strikes, extortion, threat to life and property becomes the order
of the day."[176]

It stands established that the internal conflict has affected economic
activities and the importance of the environment of peace. If such a state
of affairs continues indefinitely the increasing hardships with continued
instability will only push the people towards anti–social and criminal activities.
Whichever government comes to power in Nepal, economic reconstruction

---

[175]"Dabur Nepal Closes Down its Factory", *Nepalnews.com,* May 19, 2006, http://
www.nepalnews.com/archive/2006/may/may19/news15.php, According to this report,
Dabur Nepal is an FMCG (Fast Moving Consumer Group) company, which caters to Nepali
markets besides exporting its products to India. Dabur Food, Dabur Nepal and Dabur
Balsara are owned by Dabur India Ltd. that sells its products in over 50 countries around
the world.

[176] Utpal Bhaskar, " Crisis in Nepal may affect Plans of Indian Power Generation Firms",
livemint.com, The Wall Street Journal, May 7, 2009, http://www.livemint.com/2009/05/
07214700/Crisis-in-Nepal-may-affect-pla.html

will be a huge task. Political consensus across the board is required so that economic activity will remain immune to political differences. Indian foreign policy has limited influence in such a scenario.

Understanding the Unpredictable Trajectory of the Peace Process

The deadlock which apparently began under the UCPN (M) government following the differences on the issues concerning the army remains unresolved. There was no consensus among the political parties for a resolution regarding the President's action on the Army chief issue in spite of the UCPN (M) led government's reservations. This eventually led Prime Minister Prachanda's resignation in 2009. New issues of civilian supremacy and national sovereignty have been introduced into the national agenda by the Maoists sidelining Constitution drafting and the peace process through the four phase protest movement. The High Level Political Mechanism (HLPM) had also failed to garner consensus.[177] The Maoists then demanded for the resignation of Prime Minister Madhav Kumar Nepal as a pre-condition for any forward movement. The other political parties put forward their demands on the Maoists which stated that some contentious issues like the number and modalities of the Maoist combatants to be integrated into the security forces, dismantling of the Young Communist League (YCL), statute writing and the returning of property seized during the conflict should be addressed first.[178] To press its demands, the UCPN (M) called for an

---

[177] The High Level Political Mechanism (HLPM) was led by late Nepali Congress President Girija Prasad Koirala. The other two members were UCPN (M) Chairman Prachanda and UML Chairman Jhala Nath Khanal with the Prime Minister as an invited member. HLPM was expected to pave the way for smooth peace process, constitution drafting and ending the months long political uncertainty. This mechanism had come in for criticism and rightly so by elements in all the political parties. It too failed to resolve the deadlock and build consensus. For details see "Three Major Parties Declare High-Level Political Mechanism", *Nepalnews.com*, January 8, 2010, http://www.nepalnews.com/main/index.php/news-archive/1-top-story/3334-three-major-parties-declare-high-level-political-mechanism.html

[178] "Fulfill Past Pacts for Unity Govt.: NC, UML to Maoists", *ekantipur.com*, May 12, 2010, http://www.ekantipur.com/2010/05/12/top-story/fulfill-past-pacts-for-unity-govt-nc-uml-to-Maoists/314177/ ; Phanindra Dalal, "Parties Enmeshed in Age-old Game of Chicken-and-Egg- Integration & Rehab of Combatants", *ekantipur.com,I* May 11, 2010, http://www.ekantipur.com/2010/05/11/editors-pick/parties-enmeshed-in-age-old-game-of-chicken-and-egg/314057/;

indefinite national strike from May 1ˢᵗ 2010, but had to soon call off following pressure from civil society's call for peace.[179] The last minute Three Point Agreement concluded among the major political parties -NC, CPN (UML) and UCPN (M) - which indirectly incorporated both these views extended the term of CA for another one year on May 28th 2010.[180] Following, differences over interpretation of the Three Point Agreement, Madhav Kumar Nepal finally resigned on June 30th 2010[181]. Whether a national consensus government comes or a majority government, the peace process has become unpredictable and the possibility of deadlock always remains. Why is this so? Can it be overcome?

Some studies have shown that irrespective of underlying causes, objectives or ideology, once levels of violence increase and general civil administration collapses they set into motion dynamics that are entirely autonomous and independent of the antecedent or 'triggering' mechanisms and motives. Unless these new set of events are understood and analyzed and responded to, peace becomes evasive. [182]

---

[179] "Prachanda Apologises for Khullamanch Remarks; Urges Civil Society to Push PM Nepal to Quit", *ekantipur.com,* May 12, 2010, http://www.ekantipur.com/2010/05/12/top-story/prachanda-apologises-for-khullamanch-remarks-urges-civil-society-to-push-pm-nepal-to-quit/314169/

[180] "Crisis Averted with Passage of Eighth Amendment Bill", *Nepalnews.com,* May 28, 2010, http://www.nepalnews.com/main/index.php/news-archive/1-top-story/6402-crisis-averted-with-passage-of-eighth-amendment-bill.html; "Big Three Resume Talks for Consensus", *Nepalnews.com,* May 30, 2010 http://www.nepalnews.com/main/index.php/news-archive/2-political/6427-big-three-resume-talks-for-consensus.html. The three points of the agreement are as follows: i) We are committed to moving ahead with consensus and cooperation to take the peace process to a meaningful conclusion, to carry out all the remaining works related to the peace process, and to accomplish the historic responsibility of completing the task for writing the new Constitution. ii) Though a significant progress has been made in the Constitution-writing process, it has not been completed yet. Therefore, we have agreed to extend the tenure of the Constituent Assembly by one year. iii) Based on the agreement to fulfill these responsibilities and works as soon as possible, we are ready to form a national consensus government and for that, the prime minister of the incumbent coalition government is ready to resign without delay.

[181] "Prime Minister Madhav Kumar Nepal Resigns", *Nepalnews.com,* June 30, 2010, http://www.nepalnews.com/main/index.php/news-archive/1-top-story/7218-pm-nepal-announces-his-resignation.html.

[182] Ajai Sahni & J.George, "Security and Development in India's Northeast :An Alternative Perspective" , *Faultlines,* 4 (2000), http://www.satp.org/satporgtp/publication/faultlines/

In this context this paper raises the question – What are the new sets of events which have arisen in the peace process in Nepal? The paper argues that at each stage since Jana Andolan II began, unexpected developments have resulted in the peace process and have gotten more complex and unpredictable by the day. A series of events over a period of time led to consequences and these became causes for other unforeseen events. Thus, the chain reaction continued. For example, one of the consequences of Jana Andolan II was the unanticipated rise and assertion of the marginalized sections and the beginning of identity politics in a major way. The unexpected violent developments resulted in grave law and order issues and rise of many criminal groups, one of the consequences of which was increased security problems in the open Indo-Nepal border. Another consequence of the agitations by the marginalized especially the Madhesi agitations, was the assurances given on federalism and major changes made in the election system. These changes which included proportional representation and quota system ensured that the CA elections resulted in

---

volume4/Fault4-JG&ASf1.htm . This section draws from some of the analyses of the authors regarding their case study in India's North East trying to understand why peace is elusive there despite the enormity of funds. They question widely held assumptions that massive investment in developmental projects in affected regions would magically eliminate both the source and all violent manifestations of discontent and thereby eliminate terrorism. Though Nepal and North East are two completely different case studies, this chapter uses some of the questions raised by these authors to understand why peace is elusive in Nepal ? These authors state that, "the dynamics of terrorism, however, acquire a character and autonomy entirely divorced from the paradigms of such naïve determinism, resulting in high rate of failure for all initiatives based on the conviction that terrorism can be made to disappear through developmental investment." Their analysis is based on the "assumption that irrespective of underlying causes, objectives or ideology, once levels of violence and of general civil administration collapse or have exceeded certain parameters, they set into motion dynamics that are entirely autonomous and independent of the antecedent or 'triggering' mechanisms and motives." Having gone into the root causes of the conflict in Nepal and seen that a certain measure of success in having political representation of the widest possible nature till now in the CA elections in Nepal, this section questions if certain new dynamics have developed into the conflict situation in Nepal that are entirely autonomous of the root causes of conflict. Do these issues need to be addressed before getting back to the peace process? This paper does not claim to have the answers for these questions, but nevertheless attempts to understand if certain complex linkages have developed under the shadow of the peace process which need to be first understood and entangled to take the peace process ahead.

Nepal having its most representative assembly so far. The consequence of all these series of events was, that the scenario wherein the Maoists were considered as the major champion of the grievances of the marginalized no longer held true. The Maoists became one among the many new forces which had arisen sharing the same agenda. The consequence of all this is the multiplication of the stakeholders and discussions, debates and consensus building had to involve these new stakeholders.

The unexpected results of the CA elections which overhauled power equations soon became the cause which took the peace process off track bringing in not only new issues but modes of protest too which became inimical to peace and stability. These new issues became the cause of problems both within the country and bilaterally especially with India. Drafting the Constitution no longer held priority. All the political parties and leaders of Nepal and the external stakeholders including its most influential one – India– did change their strategies. As a result, a deadlock situation emerged wherein the Constitution was not drafted by its stated deadline of May 28th 2010.

As the peace process stretches without any substantial progress, it also becomes the breeding place and a cause for intra-party differences, as seen in Nepal. This may lead to splits in the party too. The consequences would be new influential groups within the party or new political parties itself. Personal ambitions for power dominate over everything else, in the absence of statesmen who would have prioritized the goals of the peace process. Stalemate gives rise to certain vested interests, including non-state actors, who revel in deadlock. The result is that all activities centre around secondary issues and not on discussing and debating the real issues such as drafting the Constitution and the integration and rehabilitation of the Maoist combatants. The number of meetings the leaders of the three main political parties has had with each other, right throughout the tenure of Madhav Kumar Nepal to discuss these secondary issues has indeed been amazing.

The study of Nepal helps to understand that building peace is a difficult process. The trajectory of the peace process cannot be pre-defined. A certain degree of unpredictability will be there as these are dynamic situations. The question then arises – How to maintain the priority of the real issues for which the conflict began initially, while simultaneously responding to the secondary issues? For, these too are real and need to be addressed. The context in which the peace process is being conducted should have the following aspects.

i) Need for statesmen who can see the whole picture and have a larger vision. They will ensure that new dynamic developments which will necessarily arise will be incorporated keeping in view the larger goals of the peace process.

ii) The impartial vigilant media which puts pressure on the stakeholders consistently and continuously by highlighting issues which need to be focused and the cost of moving away from peace

iii) The civil society which through their pressure groups monitors every move of the political leaders and reacts not on certain rare occasions but on a continuous basis

iv) The NGO's who continuously educate the people and bring out the consequences of delay in implementing the agreed goals and how finally the people will have to bear the brunt of any failure

The above will ensure accountability of those at the helm in the peace process, be it internal or external stakeholders. Also specifically the new leaders too who have arisen with great promises will be monitored. It will help to change the context in which the peace process is being conducted by conveying to them that they are being continuously monitored; expectations are high; and goods need to be delivered. The chances of peace become substantially higher than a reversal to a conflict situation while both could be a real possibility.

Conclusion: Future Scenarios

Nepal has been in a state of conflict and instability for most of the past two decades, moving from one form of instability to another and bringing changes – both positive and negative – at each stage. Jana Andolan I very significantly spelt out the issues, the Maoist insurgency did the same violently and the agitations post-Jana Andolan II are being carried with violence and assertion. The CPA might have ended the war with the Maoists but multiple conflicts permeate the Nepalese society even now. As the conflict moved from one level to another it provided enough opportunities for conflict prevention which when overlooked led to conflict escalation. Efforts at conflict management and resolution have turned out to be controversial themselves deepening the conflict rather than resolving them. This provides conflict prevention lessons to all countries. Post CA elections, there is an acceptance of an inclusive agenda but the intent is not matched with actions on the ground.

The continuous instability has put immense stress on Indian foreign policy which has had to be changed over time. Internal security issues of Nepal and their fallout on India have formed a major issue in bilateral relations for the past 15 years. However, India and Nepal share a special relationship of interdependence which has not been eroded. There have been attempts to revise the relationship without relegating its importance. While Nepal continues to improve relations with China the political leadership acknowledges that India-Nepal relations are completely different and their significance will not decline. Indian influence is clearly visible in the 12 Point Agreement and in the events post CA elections. It is , however, important to see how India will utilize the influence it enjoys as it can no longer continue to use its traditional approach while the situation in Nepal changes.

This chapter notes that despite the tremendous discussion and debate on the root causes of conflict, the real issues have been left out. There is a need to revisit the debate and also a need to focus efforts on the drafting of the Constitution. Depending on the manner in which the peace process proceeds, many possible scenarios emerge for Nepal. The following paragraphs discuss these scenarios and their likely impact on India:

a) The best possible scenario would be one where a national government is formed without attaching any conditionality. The leadership of the national government can be under rotation and if there are irresolvable differences among the major parties, then a leader from the marginalized parties can lead the government. Also, India and UCPN (M) should build cordial relations for the stability and peace of both the countries. This would also enable India to be constructively influential and have a meaningful role to play in Nepal. An Indian foreign policy towards Nepal which is not able to build constructive relations with the Maoists will have only limited success in fulfilling India's interests. The UCPN (M) will be equally influential whether in power or in opposition. It is essential that the experiment of bringing UCPN (M) succeeds so that it demonstrates to similar elements in India and the sub-continent that democratic politics is the best option.

b) A second scenario emerges where the political parties and groups of the marginalized sections, the various organizations representing the indigenous and ethnic communities and the civil society are able to exercise enough pressure and fill the vacuum of consensus politics to find middle ground and help completing the peace process and the transitional phase. This could happen for Jana Andolan II was a people's movement and the people could rise above divisive politics to build a consensus where the leaders failed. In this scenario India's influence will be marginal and reactionary.

c) If consensus completely fails, there could be a scenario, where violence and protests break out by not only the Maoist combatants but the other armed groups that emerged Post Jana Andolan II 2006. These groups could include marginalized groups and youth wings of political parties like Young Communist League (YCL) and the Youth Force. In the absence of stabilizing forces a military option will be called for. India would then have to help the Nepal Army through arms and training but its influence may still be limited due to the presence of multiple actors. The instability would also spill over into India's border areas. In this scenario India will not be able to play the critical role it did to help the Maoists and the established political parties come together in the 12 Point Agreement of 2005 and start the peace process. The failure of the democratic forces will only increase the role of the Army leading to long term negative effects. This scenario should be avoided.

Even in a scenario where the transition phase concludes and a temporary consensus is arrived at to complete the peace process, politics in Nepal will be divided and polarized if events of 2009 are any indication. The political parties and their leaders in Nepal have been divided earlier too as was seen in the decade following the Jana Andolan I of 1990. The situation now is further polarized with the UCPN (M) as a legitimate mainstream political party along with the other identity based political parties representing aspirations of the marginalized groups. Hopefully the Constitution should provide a mechanism to address these issues. Also some of the political parties will have new leaders with whom India would have to build relations for mutual benefit. India should be prepared for the change and should not cling on to the past. Even if the peace process is concluded, once the transitional phase ends Indo-Nepal relations will be entering a difficult terrain. India would have to maintain close relations with all the political parties, implement programmes which directly benefit the people and focus on economic development. India will have to learn to handle these divisive politics and support issues and not persons.

The study has brought out the limited success of Indian foreign policy in Nepal. India-Nepal relations did not gain substantially either under the Maoist led government or the Madhav Kumar Nepal government. Irrespective of the scenario, Indian policy towards Nepal especially in this transitional period should be based on – i) the twin pillars of building consensus among the political parties of Nepal and adopting measures which will fulfil the goals of Jana Andoaln II *i.e.* furthering the inclusive agenda; ii) take a holistic picture of balancing its strategic interests with those of state transformation in Nepal; iii) consciously build its political relations with the UCPN(M), the established political parties and the parties championing the cause of the marginalized in a manner where it is primarily committed not to any political party but to the agenda of change. This will help it to shed rigidity and infuse flexibility thereby providing choices in fluid situations; iv) concentrate more on the inherent strength and depth of Indo-Nepal relations than on Nepal's relations with China at least till the Constitution is drafted and the peace process is concluded; and v) be prepared to face the consequences of economic challenges that Nepal will face irrespective of peace.

The paper argues that the Maoists have wasted the very impressive mandate they got in the CA elections. Their protest movements have done them the most harm. They need to change their methods of protest and give priority to the peace process in order to maintain and expand their political space.

Finally, the paper argues that the trajectory of the peace process is / will be highly unpredictable. Consequences of a set of actions have become the causes for another set of unexpected events and the chain continues. In such a dynamic situation, the challenge lies in creating an environment which will respond to secondary issues without losing focus of the main causes of the conflict. The onus of doing this, however, lies primarily on the media, civil society and the NGO's.

INTERNATIONAL IMPACT OF CONFLICT IN NEPAL

Nihar Nayak

Apart from Nepal's strategic location, political instability and Maoist insurgency has caused external forces to engage directly and indirectly in Nepal's internal affairs. Throughout the decades external forces have been taking an interest in Nepal, but the last decade has seen Nepal emerge as a strategic factor for powers like the US and UK apart from India and China. Amidst a tumultuous political evolution, these powers have taken efforts to secure their strategic objectives, which might have directly and/or indirectly influenced the evolutionary process within the country. The increasing influence of external actors has reasonably enhanced an uncertain prospect of long term peace in the country and their divergent interests have complicated the matter further. The political parties and the domestic politics are divided on the basis of the external forces' interests in Nepal. Most importantly, the two neighboring countries-China and India- recently have become more concerned about the pro-active role of western influences in the domestic politics of Nepal, leading them to rethink their existing foreign policies towards the 'New Nepal.'[1]

This chapter focuses on the involvement of major powers, in particular China, the United States, India and the European Union, in Nepal since 2006. While analyzing their interests in Nepal, the paper also covers in brief their past engagements with Nepal and focuses on the interests of the

---

[1] The reference 'New Nepal' has been coined to describe the transformed political structures and dynamics in the past few years, when Maoists waged a war against the Monarchy and managed to assimilate into the political mainstream of the country.

external powers, their stakes in its political transformation and the extent of their influence.

Strategic Relevance of Nepal

Both India and China view Nepal as strategically important. India considers Nepal as a buffer country and shares an open border with strong ethnic, social, cultural and economic relations. It is natural that political instability in Nepal would have an imminent spill over effect in India. Recently, there was evidence of anti-India elements having taken advantage of chronic political instability and poor governance in Nepal. Of late, another major concern of India was the growing triangular relationship between Pakistan, China, and some groups in Nepal identifying India as their common enemy. Massod Khalid, additional secretary, Ministry of Foreign Affairs, Pakistan, in charge of South Asia, said that 'both Nepal and Pakistan attach(ed) greater importance to the relations with that giant neighbor [China] to the north'.[2] Articulating India's strategic interests in Nepal, Jawaharlal Nehru in December 1950 said "From time immemorial, the Himalayas have provided us with a magnificent frontier... We cannot allow that barrier to be penetrated because it is also the principal barrier to India".[3] This natural frontier might lose its relevance now, in an era of Nuclear weapons, globalization, and growing Sino-India relationship in recent years.

China, on the other hand, wants to ensure that Nepal is not used as a base for anti-China activities by Tibetan separatists. For China, Nepal also acts as a geographical and cultural buffer between Tibet and Tibetan refugees living in India. It feels insecure over India's leverage as well as the presence of the United States, the United Kingdom and the European Union. Therefore, China always looks for a credible nationalistic force in Nepal, amenable to its influence for political stability.[4] Second, following an

[2] Yuba Nath Lamsal, "Steady Growth of Nepal–Pakistan Ties", *The Rising Nepal,* Gorkhapatra Sansthan, May 21, 2008; http://www.gorkhapatra.org.np/detail.php?article_id =541&cat_id =7 (Accessed July 13, 2008).

[3] Ministry of Information and Broadcasting, "Jawaharlal Nehru's Speech in Parliament, December 6, 1950", *India's Foreign Policy: Selected Speeches- September 1946-April 1961,* (Delhi: The Publication Division, Government of India, August 1961),   436.

[4] Nihar Nayak, "Involvement of Major Powers in Nepal since the 1990s: Implications for India", *Strategic Analysis,* 33 no. 1, (January 2009).

active policy of strategically encircling India with the 'string of pearls', it is trying to increase its influence in Nepal. Third, Chinese analysts believe that US presence in Nepal is part of its larger strategy of encircling China. Beijing may also be interested in protecting Nepalese territorial integrity to maintain its buffer status. In fact, recently, Mr. Liu Hong Chai, the International Bureau Chief of the Chinese Communist Party, assured Nepalese people that 'any foreign conspiracy to disintegrate Nepal will be appropriately dealt with by China'.[5]

During the Cold War, the United States had identified Nepal as a strategic location to prevent the spread of communism to South Asia. When the Maoists began their armed struggle in 1996, the United States declared that 'it has a strong interest in helping the people of that country overcome the serious political problems they face, and the developmental problems from which much of their current political crisis derives'.[6] Bruce Vaughn observed that 'American foreign policy interests in Nepal seek to prevent the collapse of Nepal which, should it become a failed state, could provide operational support or territory for terrorists'.[7] Washington also considered Nepal as the ideal listening post to monitor relationship between India and China and their influence in South Asia. Importantly, from US point of view, Nepal could also be an ideal place to extend support to the Tibetan refugees.

EU members do not seem to have a major strategic interest in Nepal, but they did have strong sympathy for Tibetan refugees. Some EU members, like the United Kingdom usually follow the US line on Nepal. Since 2005,

---

[5] "We Will not Tolerate Any Foreign Interference in Nepal: China", *The Telegraph Nepal*, November 5, 2008. He made this statement during an interaction with some Nepali journalists in Beijing on November 4, 2008. http://telegraphnepal.com/test/news_det.php?news_id=4302&PHPSESSID=80e05039d4a7289f008cf74a2f1cc0be (Accessed November 10, 2008).

[6] Donald Camp, Principal Deputy Assistant Secretary, "United States Interests and Goals in Nepal", Statement before the US House of Representatives Committee on International Relations, Washington, DC, March, 2, 2005, http://www.nepalnews.com/archive/2005/mar/mar07/news02.php. (Accessed on September 15, 2010)

[7] Bruce Vaughn, "Nepal: Background and U.S. Relations", Congressional Research Service, Report for Congress, The Library of Congress, February 2, 2006, 17, http://www.fas.org/sgp/crs/row/RL31599.pdf (Accessed on August 30, 2010)

the EU members are mostly involved in humanitarian programs and conflict resolution in Nepal.

India-Nepal Relations

A peaceful and stable Nepal is always in India's interest. India's Foreign Secretary, Shiv Shankar Menon, said, for example: "We [India] want to see a peaceful periphery around so that we can concentrate on our primary task, which is eradicating poverty, developing our economy, bringing prosperity to our own people."[8] Though political instability in Nepal is a major concern for India, it cannot intervene much in Nepal due to strong anti-India feeling among the various groups in Nepal.

Of late, India has been blamed for excessive intervention in the internal affairs of Nepal and encouraging encroachment of Nepalese territory, both by the UCPN-Maoist party after Prachanda's resignation on May 2009, and by the common people. This anti-India feeling has affected India's economic relations with Nepal. A Federation of Indian Chambers of commerce and Industry (FICCI) survey highlighted that "Industries [in Nepal] are badly hit by acute shortages of power and raw materials, petrol and diesel supply has run out and the labour unrest has struck at the very heart of businesses."[9]

There are also concerns of delay in the implementation of hydro projects like the proposed 6000 MW Pancheshwar dam. Quoting one India official a media report said, "We view the developments in Nepal very disturbing as far as the Pancheshwar dam is concerned."[10]

This combination of anti-India feeling and political instability will benefit anti-India elements on Nepalese soil. In recent years, Nepal is believed to have become a haven for terrorists, smugglers and anti-India elements

[8] Prerana Marasini, "Nepal is in India's Interest: Menon", *The Hindu,* February 19, 2009, http://hindu.com/2009/02/19/stories/2009021954861300.htm

[9] "Nepal events hitting India Inc: Ficci", *The Hindustan Times*, May 6, 2009, http://www.spacenepal.com/forum/index.php?showtopic=24945

[10] Shishir Prashant, "Nepal crisis may hit Pancheshwar dam", *The Business Standard*, May 7, 2009, http://www.business-standard.com/india/news/nepal-crisis-may-hit-pancheshwar-dam/357257/

sponsored by Inter-Services Intelligence (ISI). The increase in Islamic seminaries on the India–Nepal border is also a major concern for India.

Despite an unfavorable situation in Nepal, India cannot ignore the present situation due to the vulnerable strategic importance of Nepal for its own security. However, India does have certain strategic leverages in Nepal. These strategic leverages put India in a more advantageous position than other countries. The Government of India can use these leverages, mostly geographic location, trade and commerce, and cultural and people-to-people relations, to resolve differences of opinion in bilateral relations.

India's Perception on External involvement in Nepal

India has been apprehensive about major powers' involvement in Nepal owing to many reasons. First, due to India's geographical, historical and cultural linkages with Nepal, India would prefer to take note of the developments in Nepal and have the privilege of be 'consulted' by external powers before involving themselves in Nepal. Though India seems to be following a non-intrusive foreign policy in South Asia, at no point would India prefer to lose its existing leverage over crucial neighbors like Nepal to any other external actor.

Second, Beijing has already flexed its relations with all of India's South Asian neighbors and has enhanced its political and military presence in the Indian Ocean Region. With this vulnerability already reflecting on India's South Asia policy, Nepal would be among the last few frontiers where India would compete with China for sustaining its political sway.

As the Maoists are known to have blossomed with strong anti-India feelings, New Delhi would attempt to constrain possibilities of any future dispensation in Nepal which can cultivate negative sentiments against India at the government level. Significantly, with a presence in Nepal, they can have easy access to separatist and Maoist outfits operating within Indian territory. These groups can foment anti-India activities. There are concerns that Chinese presence in Nepal may leverage Pakistan to carry out anti-India activities from Nepalese soil. For example, around 20 terrorists entered into India from Nepal using the open border and fake Indian currency worth almost Rs 2 crore was seized in 2009.[11]

Recent media reports reveal that radical Islamic groups operating within India (like Indian Mujahedeen) are using Nepalese territory as a haven in recent days, especially after Bangladeshi security forces launched action against their bases in Bangladesh.[12] In June 2009, Mohammad Omar Madani, alleged Lashkar-e-Taiba (LeT) head in Nepal, was arrested in Delhi. According to media reports Madani had set up a madrassa in the jungles along the India-Nepal border from where newly trained militants could be sent to India. On 15 March 2010, a 55-year-old Pakistani woman was arrested at the Tribhuvan International Airport in Kathmandu with fake Indian currency worth Rs.3 million.[13] On April 4, 2010, sources in the Ministry of Home Affairs, India, said the Nepalese police arrested a LeT cadre, who was instructed by Lashkar to be part of the outfit's larger plan to carry out attacks on India's mainland.[14] Therefore, India has genuine security concerns regarding the issue of open border with Nepal.

Fourth, India feels that a democratic, stable and peaceful Nepal will be in India's interest. As a result since February 1, 2005, India has been playing major role in resolving the conflict. In fact India has been an important player in the present peace process since November 2005. Hence, any external forces acting as spoiler would be intolerable for India. India's perception on Nepal will be somewhat different from other countries,

---

[11] "Nearly 20 Terrorists Entered India via Nepal: Indian Envoy," *NDTV.com*, April 29, 2010, http://www.ndtv.com/news/india/nearly-20-terrorists-entered-india-via-nepal-indian-envoy-21997.php (accessed on August 30, 2010)

[12] Caesar Mandal, "IM has Shifted to Nepal after Bangladesh Crackdown", *Times of India*, March 10, 2010. http://timesofindia.indiatimes.com/india/IM-has-shifted-to-Nepal-after-Bangladesh-crackdown/articleshow/5665538.cms

[13] "Pakistani woman nabbed with fake Indian currency in Nepal", *The Thaindian News*, March 16, 2010. http://www.thaindian.com/newsportal/south-asia/pakistani-woman-nabbed-with-fake-indian-currency-in-nepal_100335185.html. (Accessed on September 15, 2010). Also see http://sify.com/news/pakistani-woman-nabbed-with-fake-indian-currency-in-nepal-news-international-kdqmEcddagd.html. (Accessed on September 15, 2010)

[14] "ISI-backed bombing plot by Khalistan Group Foiled", *The Times of India*, May 5, 2010. http://timesofindia.indiatimes.com/india/ISI-backed-bombing-plot-by-Khalistan-group-foiled/articleshow/5891417.cms

because of India's comprehensive relationship with Nepal.[15]

Finally, China's growing influence in Nepal could come at the expense of India and key Western players, such as the United States and the United Kingdom.[16] Some Nepalese scholars argue that UN role in Nepal could promote Chinese role in Nepal. Most of the countries view the UN as an extension of US foreign policy and the Chinese, aware that Nepal is the easiest route to Tibet would be wary of the UN. It would be a prudent decision for the Indian policy makers to consult China before taking major decisions on Nepal.[17] The competition for leadership between major powers in South Asia in general and Nepal in particular may disturb the regional peace and stability.

Nepal in China's Foreign Policy

Nepal may not have prominently figured in the broad foreign policy of China, but it certainly occupies an important position in its neighborhood policy. China believes that this region is extremely significant for its security along its vulnerable Tibet border. Since 1950s, China has been consistently worried of Nepal being used by external powers to challenge China's strategic interests. Its vulnerability increased when it lost its traditional influence in Nepal with the demise of Monarchy in 2008. The year also witnessed the increase in anti-China protests by Tibetan refugees in Nepal during the interim government led by G P Koirla. Professor Wang Hongwei, a Chinese Nepal expert believes that India and the US are using Nepali soil against China.

Since then China has been adopting a four-fold policy to strengthen its bilateral relations with Nepal: "First, accommodate each other's political

[15] Dishanirdesh, "His Excellency Shyam Saran's Interview", July 12, 2004, Nepal Television, http://www.nepalpoll.com.np/ntv/dishanirdesh/videos.asp?id=63 (Accessed on October 26, 2007)

[16] David G. Wiencek, China's Geopolitical Manoeuvring in the Himalayas, Association *for Asian Research*, 7/5/2005, available at http://www.asianresearch.org/articles/2649.html, (Accessed on October 26, 2007)

[17] Suman Pradhan , "Long and Winding Road to UN Mediation", *South Asia Intelligence Review*, 4 (2), 25 July 2005, http://www.satp.org/satporgtp/sair/Archives/4_2.htm, (Accessed on October 29, 2007)

concern. Second, enhance the economic cooperation on the basis of mutual benefit. Third, boost people-to-people and cultural exchanges. Fourth, strengthen the coordination and cooperation in international and regional affairs."[18]

Political Engagements

China was left with little option when the Maoists emerged victorious in the April 2008 elections. Initially, China suspected the Maoists' intentions and adopted a wait and watch policy. This was based on an impression that the Nepalese Maoists were backed by India because Maoists were catapulted to the political centre stage only after a comprehensive peace agreement where India had played a substantial role behind the scene. However, media reports reveal that after several interactions with Maoists leaders, China felt comfortable with the Maoist-led government. Their ideological similarities with China and their keenness to neutralize India's influence in the region would have made Maoists look for China in the changed circumstances.

During their interactions, the Maoists leaders reportedly gave an impression that the future democracy of Nepal could be guided by the example of the Communist Party of China (CPC). In fact, some hard-line leaders of the party have suggested a people's republic similar to China on a number of occasions even after Maoists have joined multi-party democracy in Nepal. These ideas might have encouraged China to consolidate its position in Nepal by continuously engaging the Maoists at the political, economic, military and social levels, to secure its strategic interests in the region.

China also wants to keep good relationship with other political parties. It is open to work with any dispensation in Kathmandu subject to a guarantee of taking strong action against Tibetan refugees. It has penetrated into the Nepalese political system by gaining the confidence of hard-line communist leaders both in the CPN-UML and the CPN-Maoist. China is known to have played major role in facilitating the alliance between the CPN-UML

---

[18] Qiu Guohong, "Nepal and China have Win-Win Ties", *Nepali Times* no.448 (24 April 2009 - 30 April 2009).

and the Maoists. Prior to Jhala Nath Khanal becoming UML Chief, a four-member Chinese delegation visited Kathmandu on May 10, 2008 and met Mr Khanal and other Maoist leaders. A senior delegation from the Communist Party of China led by vice Minister Liu Hongcai was also in Kathmandu in February 2009 to attend the inaugural ceremony of the 8th national convention of the UML. Khanal's victory as chairman of the UML was crucial for the survival of the Maoist-led coalition government. Khanal is close to Prachanda.

During Prime Minister Madhav Kumar Nepal's visit to China in December 2009, Nepal and China agreed to further strengthen political and economic ties. Both the sides agreed to further promote exchange of high-level visits and contacts at all levels and make full use of the existing mechanisms.[19]

Significantly, China has also begun taking interest in Terai politics. There are reports of a high level Chinese delegation visited the General Convention of the Madhesi People's Rights Forum in early 2009. According to Bhim Prasad Bhurtel, the executive director of the Nepal South Asia Centre, Kathmandu, "more recently 33 China Study Centers have been established in southern Nepal adjoining the Indian border."[20]

Exchange of High Level Visits

A number of Chinese delegations, including military teams, visited Nepal during 2008-2009. During these visits, China repeatedly assured economic, technological and military aid to Nepal. The then Maoist-led government was also asked to adopt the 'One-China' policy, i.e., not to allow use of Nepalese land for anti-China activities, take strong action against Tibetan refugees and grant special facilities for Chinese investments in strategic

---

[19] Joint Statement between the People's Republic of China and the Federal Democratic Republic of Nepal on December 31, 2009, http://www.china-un.ch/eng/xwdt/t649608.htm (Accessed on August 25, 2010)

[20] Abanti Bhattacharya, "China's Inroads into Nepal: India's Concerns", *IDSA Comment*, May 18, 2009, http://pakistanpal.wordpress.com/2009/05/19/china's-inroads-into-nepal-india's-concerns/ (Accessed on August 25, 2010)

sectors. Beijing has also initiated Track-II diplomacy with Nepal and invited Nepalese scholars to undertake visits to Chinese think tanks in recent days.

Nepal's engagement with China has also increased manifold with the visit of delegations both at State[21] and non-state levels. Apart from the visits at the official levels, the private visits by political leaders, journalists and academicians are also sponsored by China as part of the public diplomacy exercise. During these State visits Chinese authorities had reportedly assured all kinds of support to the Nepalese leaders in their efforts aimed at laying the foundation for a 'New Nepal'.[22]

Strategic Partner

The nature of Chinese engagements in Nepal goes beyond the political domain. During a meeting in Kathmandu between Nepal Defense Minister Ram Bahadur Thapa and the deputy commander of China's People Liberation Army, Lieutenant General Ma Xiaotian in December, 2008, China pledged to provide US $2.6 million as military assistance for modernization of Nepal Army. Earlier in September 2008, China had announced military aid worth $ 1.3 million, the first such assistance to the Maoist government in Nepal. In recent times, Beijing has shown keen support for the Maoist governments' proposal to integrate some 19,000 Maoist guerrillas with the Nepal Army. In fact, China has reiterated its interest in military modernization assistance to Nepal during Nepal's Defense minister Bidya Devi Bhandari visit in March 2010.

One Nepalese scholar observed that China has been trying to match India in Nepal by extending scholarships on National Defense Course (NDC) to Nepal Police and Armed Police Force (APF) officers, besides their regular quota to a Nepali Army (NA) officer. For the first time, China granted a

---

[21] Prime Minister Prachanda and Madhav Kumar Nepal visited China in September 2008 and December 2009 respectively. Defence Minister Ram Bahadur Thapa and Bidya Devi Bhandari under took official trip to China in September 2008 and March 2010 respectively. Home Minister Bhim Rawal visited China in February 2010.

[22] Nihar Nayak, "Nepal: New 'Strategic Partner' of China?", *IDSA Comment*, March 30, 2009, http://www.idsa.in/idsastrategiccomments/NepalNewStrategicPartnerof China_NNayak_ 300309 (Accessed on August 25, 2010)

scholarship to a civilian officer — then Kathmandu CDO Jaya Mukunda Khanal. In April 2009, Chinese authorities took a 10-member team of Nepal Police, Armed Police Force and National Investigation Department to China on a 15-day tour. A 20-member Nepali team comprising bureaucrats and security officials visited Lhasa in August 07, 2009 by Chinese sponsorship.[23] Objective of this initiative could be to owe the officials of security agencies to quell the anti-China activities in Nepal and influence the deployment of security forces in the northern districts to curb Tibetan movement in that region.

The increasing level of bilateral engagement between the two countries indicates that China is wooing Nepal as a new strategic partner. This has been confirmed by the statements of various Chinese officials. For example, on 16 February 2009, Chinese Foreign Minister Yang Jiechi said in Beijing that China would prefer to work with Nepal on the basis of a strategic partnership. Recently, during Prime Minister Madhav Kumar Nepal's visit to Beijing, President Hu Jin Tao vowed to enhance the bilateral relations to a 'Comprehensive Partnership of Cooperation'.

Economic and Trade

China is leveraging its economic power to secure its strategic interests in Nepal. China has expanded its financial assistance to Nepal in several parts of the country. It announced a doubling of aid to Nepal amounting to $21.94 million. The trade volume between the two countries currently stands at $401 million with China selling goods worth about $386 million, and Nepal exporting a mere $15 million. To bridge the trade deficit, China agreed in April 2009 to provide duty free access to 497 Nepali goods in the Chinese market. As part of promoting Nepal's hydro-power projects, in 2008, China's Assistant Minister for Foreign Affairs, He Yafei, pledged to provide Nepal a loan of $125 million for Upper Trishuli 3 'A' and $62 million for Upper Trishuli 3 'B'. The plants would start operating from 2012.[24]

---

[23] Kosh Raj Koirala, "China Trying to Match India in Nepal", *Republica*, August 18, 2009, http://www.myrepublica.com/portal/index.php?action=news_details&news_id=8755 (Accessed on August 25, 2010)

[24] Nihar Nayak, "Nepal: New 'Strategic Partner' of China?" *IDSA Comment*, March 30, 2009.

People to People contact

China has also expanded its relationship from State to State level to people to people level in Nepal. China has started encouraging, and in many instances funding, the establishment of front organizations[25] in Nepal to spread Chinese language and culture. Latest in a series is the establishment of Nepal China Himalayan Friendship Society (NCHFS) and Nepal-China Media Forum. "Objective of the NCHFS is to expand its network in 15 mountainous districts sharing border with China in the first phase".[26] Moreover, China has been funding several social development projects including construction of schools, hospitals and other basic necessities to build favorable constituency. China has also come up with special the package of economic development of northern part of Nepal that borders with China.

United States

While Chinese engagement with Nepal is obvious, involvement of major powers like the US is driven by divergent political objectives. US policy towards Nepal since 1950 is supported by three objectives — containment of the 'Domino' effect of Communist permeation in South Asia; Nepal's strategic location; and emergence of China and India as economic and military powers. The fist two factors dominated the US policy towards Nepal since 1950.

Although US supported the nascent democratic movements, it continued to tacitly back the Monarchy after 1996 when the Maoists came into the scene. The Maoist surge since 1996 had forced the US to re-look its Nepal policy. The Maoists declaration of strategic equilibrium phase in 2001 and followed by 9/11 led to a major policy shift towards Nepal. US Secretary of State, Colin Powell's visit to Nepal in January 2001 was the first high-level diplomatic trip by a US official in 30 years, which signaled the mounting

---

[25] China Study Centre, China Information Center, Nepal-China Mutual Cooperation Society, Nepal-China Executive Council, Nepal-China Friendship Association, Nepal-China Youth Friendship Association, Nepal-China Investment Promotion Centre, Nepal-China Himalayan Friendship Society and Nepal-China Media Forum.

[26] Kosh Raj Koirala, "China Trying to Match India in Nepal", *Republica*, August 18, 2009.

concerns in the US on the emergent Nepalese political changes and prompted new political and military support to crush the Maoist-led struggle.

In fact, since 2002, the US had given assistance of $20 million to train the former Royal Nepal Army (RNA), along with 12,000 US M-16s submachine guns as well as military advisers to King Gyanendra to aid him in fighting 'terrorism.' The external support emboldened the King to suppress democratic movement in Nepal. Taking it further, the US has added the Communist Party of Nepal-Maoist (CPN-Maoist) to its terrorist watch list, next to Al Qaeda, Hezbollah, and other terrorist groups.[27] The US in fact opposed peace talks between the Government and Maoists in 2003. The resumption of the people's war in 2003 marked the high point of US involvement in Nepal.[28] Although the US had admonished King Gyanendra's declaration of emergency in February 2005, it did not put pressure on the King to restore civil liberties.

However, the US is aware of its limited choices in curbing the increasing Maoist surge in Nepal. Being quite aware of the rising resistance to the Monarchy, Washington worked with New Delhi and other powers to counterbalance the Maoists by supporting other political parties and their faster accession to power. After the Monarchy abdicated power in April 2006, then US Ambassador to Nepal, James Moriatry, told the media that the King has no choice but to give into the opposition's demands for a return to democratic rule.[29] Secretary of State Condoleezza Rice acknowledged that the US is working "very closely with the Indian government" to resolve the crisis in Nepal. However, wary of the American manipulation, the Maoists observed that this maneuvering was not about

---

[27] David Baake, "After the Coup: 'Humanitarian Abyss' in Nepal", *Upside Down World,* April 26, 2005, http://upsidedownworld.org/nepal-coup.htm (Accessed on October 12, 2007)

[28] John Mage, "The Nepali Revolution and International Relations", *Monthly Review,* 59 no.1 (2007):1834-1839. This also appeared in the May 19, 2007 issue of *Economic and Political Weekly,* Mumbai.

[29] Nihar Nayak, "Involvement of Major Powers in Nepal since the 1990s: Implications for India", *Strategic Analysis,* 33 no.1(2009), http://www.idsa.in/strategicanalysis/InvolvementofMajorPowersinNepalSincethe1990_nnayak_0109 (Accessed on August 25, 2010)

bringing democracy to Nepal. Rather, it is about trying to ensure that the "resolution of the current crisis" will be in the interest of the US and India and will not lead to any gains by the Maoists.[30]

In fact, analysts had noted this US position as being adamant that the Maoists should not be allowed to win. Ambassador James Moriarty had then repeatedly urged the king and parliamentary parties to work together in order to defeat the People's War, while criticizing the opposition parties for working in tandem with the Maoists. In fact, before the Monarchy withdrew from power, the US Assistant Secretary of Central and South Asian Affairs, Richard Boucher, had remarked:

> "We need to work as much as we can to pressure the King to restore democracy, to encourage the parties to stay together and to come up with a workable, functioning democracy. And be able to expunge the Maoists from Nepali society. What the U.S. cannot accept is a revolution that takes up arms in order to overthrow a regime that serves U.S. interests. What the U.S. cannot allow is a revolution which aims to fundamentally change the current economic, political, and social relations under which the masses of Nepalese people are oppressed."[31]

The US activities in Nepal are basically driven by its strategic interests in the region than any liberal ideology. Nepal's location is of extreme strategic importance. Nepal is a vital element in this scheme considering its proximity with Tibet. US want to maintain a psychological pressure on China by engaging itself in Nepal. Having a friendly regime in Kathmandu is therefore of highest priority to any US administration. Therefore, there is marked change in US policy towards Nepal since the assumption of Scott H DeLisi as ambassador of US to Nepal. Instead of looking at Nepal through an Indian perspective, the US has decided for deep engagements in Nepal. In fact, the US suddenly found the Maoists are most reliable partner. During a discussion with vice chairman of the UCPN-Maoist Party Naryan Kaji

---

[30] Li Onesto, "Upsurge Continues in Nepal: US interests, Plots and Intrigues", *Revolution*, http://revcom.us/a/045/nepal-upsurge-continues.html (Accessed on October 19, 2007)

[11] Ibid,

Shrestha, Ambassador DeLisi said the "US was "positive" towards formation of a National Unity Government under the leadership of Unified Maoists' Party."[32] Interestingly, the Maoists are still listed in the US terrorists list.

European Union

Unlike the US, European Union countries are actively involved in conflict resolution, and restoration of democracy in Nepal. The European Commission to Nepal has been functioning in Nepal since 1977 and a total of Euro 130 million was granted up to 2002 in areas such as irrigation, watershed management, livestock, reproductive health, primary education, refugees and institutional capacity building.[33] EU countries are also, engaged in human rights assistance (energy, food, elections) and supporting civil liberty and democratic movements since 2001 with approximately yearly budget of 30 million Euro.

Another important contribution from Europe are the Non Governmental Organizations (NGO) co-funded projects on family health, literacy and poverty eradication along with campaigns on prevention of human trafficking. The European Commission (EC) has also contributed to conflict mitigation through support to core legal institutions, improving peace research capacities and assistance programs to victims of Maoist insurgency.[34] The EC is supporting the Office of the High Commissioner for Human Rights (OHCHR) mission with a contribution of E5 million (around 30 percent of the budget). The first EU Troika was held in Nepal on 13-15 December, 2004 mandated in Nepal with the aim to offer EU support to all efforts aimed at promoting multi-party Democracy –within the framework of a constitutional monarchy-and Human rights.[35] In September 2007, the European Parliament (EP) launched the "Friends of Nepal Group" - a

---

[32] "US Envoy Changes Stance, says Unity Govt. Under Maoist Command Positive", *The Telegraph Nepal*, May 14, 2010. http://www.telegraphnepal.com/news_det.php?news_id=7680

[33] "The EU's Relations with Nepal-An Overview", www.ec.europa.eu, (Accessed on September 12, 2007).

[34] "European Initiative for Democracy and Human Rights / Non Governmental Organizations", www.ec.europa.eu, (Accessed on October 24, 2007)

[35] "The EU's relations with Nepal-An Overview", www.ec.europa.eu

political campaign to improve parliamentary dialogue between the EP and the Nepalese parliament. Earlier, the EP has conducted several missions to Nepal over the two years to support the new democratic reconstruction movements.[36]

Apart from the massive humanitarian assistance from Europe, some EU countries, like UK, France, and Belgium, had supplied arms to fight the Maoists. In fact, this caused consternation within the EU, as many other members condemned the arms supply alleging that these arms might possibly be responsible for killing thousands of Nepalese caught in the crossfire. However, the EU in general endorsed such transfers affirming that "Nepal was a democratic state fighting an illegal Maoist rebellion, not a country engaged in civil war."[37] It also upheld Nepal's right to defend its newly established democracy in countering insurgency. The EU also noted that the democratic state has the sole right to use legitimate force to preserve the rights and security of its citizens.[38]

However, unlike the EU approach in general to Nepal, the United Kingdom has adopted an independent policy on Nepal, almost in line with the US policies. The UK shares the US concern on the internal security situation and has provided valuable military assistance to fight the Maoists. Like the US, UK was also one of the leading arms suppliers to Nepal and strong supporter of the Monarchy. In 2001, the UK supplied 6,780 assault rifles to Nepal. Subsequently, in 2003, the UK provided two MI-17 helicopters to the Royal Nepal's Army and two Islander short takeoff and landing aircraft in the year 2004. Whitehall's official export figures say Britain exported only £110,000 worth of military equipment to Nepal between 2001 and 2003. It also points out that a number of senior Nepalese army officers, including the commander in chief, were trained at Sandhurst.

---

[36] "MEPs Give Nepal a Helping Hand, New Europe", *The European Weekly*, http://www.neurope.eu/articles/MEPS-give-Nepal-a-helping-hand/78032.php, (Accessed on September 30, 2007)

[37] "Belgium Arms Sale Row Deepens", August 27, 2002, http://news.bbc.co.uk/2/hi/europe/2220116.stm, (Accessed on October 24, 2007)

[38] Ministry for Foreign Affairs , "Nepal-EU Relations", Europe America Division,Government of Nepal, http://mofa.gov.np/bilateralRelation/nepal-eu.php (Accessed on August 26, 2010)

Although the government suspended all military assistance to Nepal after the King captured power in February 2005, a statement by the British Foreign Secretary then on arms supply to Nepal has created controversy over UK's approach in Nepal. After the King lifted the state of emergency in April 2007, the then foreign secretary, Jack Straw, had announced a review of security assistance to Nepal, while hitting out at the human rights record of the RNA.[39]

Moreover, the UK policy has been diametrically opposite to that of the EU policy, which places greater emphasis on a negotiated settlement. Despite that the UK is the second largest bilateral donor to Nepal after Japan and fourth overall after the World Bank and Asia Development Bank. The bilateral aid program for 2004/05 was around £32m and aimed to reduce poverty and social exclusion, and establish the basis for lasting peace.[40] The UK has also invested significant political and financial resources in conflict prevention and resolution.[41]

The EU members are concerned about delay in the writing of the new constitution and political instability in Nepal. The member countries have taken several attempts to forge a consensus between the major political parties to form a national unity government. However the European efforts have been criticized both by the government and some political parties for their proactive role in the internal affairs of Nepal. Non-Maoists parties have alleged that the EU members are sympathetic to the Maoists. Nationalists groups in Nepal alleged that some EU affiliated INGO's indulged in religion conversion.

United Nation's Mission in Nepal (UNMIN)

According to conflict resolution steps prescribed by the UN, to bring peace

---

[39] Richard Norton-Taylor, "British Arms Supplies Fuelling Abuses in Nepal, says Amnesty", *The Guardian*, June 15, 2005, http://www.guardian.co.uk/world/2005/jun/15/armstrade.foreignpolicy , (Accessed on October 24, 2007)

[40] British Embassy in Kathmandu, http://ukinnepal.fco.gov.uk/en/

[41] "Nepal Crisis: Mobilising International Influence," *Crisis Group Briefing*, 19 April, 2006, International Crisis Group, 5, http://www.crisisgroup.org/en/regions/asia/south-asia/nepal/B049-nepals-crisis-mobilising-international-influence.aspx (Accessed on August 26, 2010).

and stability in a county affected by civil war, there has to be a clear-cut disarmament, demobilization, and rehabilitation programme. In Nepal, the disarmament process is not complete. There is a mismatch between the number of arms registered with the UN Mission in Nepal and the arms held by the UCPN-Maoist. Similarly, there exists a huge gap between the number of armed cadres registered and number of arms surrendered. There is also difference between the UNMIN registered combatants and Prachanda's discloser on PLA strength at Shaktikhor cantonment in January 2008.[42] According to the UNMIN, the types of weapons registered so far are: 91 mortars (of which 55 are locally made), 61 machine guns, 2403 rifles, 61 automatic weapons (sub-automatic guns – SAGs), 114 side-arms, 212 shotguns, 253 miscellaneous and 233 home-made weapons. Against 61 SAGs that the Maoists have declared, the Army's official statistics show that during the course of the insurgency, the security forces lost 121 SAGs. Interestingly, Prachanda in an interview in 2008 disclosed that on November 23, 2001 in an attack on the army barrack in the Dang district, the PLA seized more than 12 trucks of sophisticated arms and ammunition.[43] According to the PLA commanders they have not surrendered their arms. They have just kept their arms in the container.[44] The UNMIN also says that there has been no disarmament.[45] Interestingly, the DDR programme is not part of the UNMIN mandate in Nepal. The UNMIN mandate is to monitor the peace process.

The unclear position of the UNMIN on the Peace Process (PP) has deepened the mistrust between the Maoists, Nepal Army and political parties. Political parties perceive that the UNMIN is biased towards Maoists and has failed to monitor the PP effectively. In fact, the recent "non-paper" prepared by the UNMIN proposing a 60-week time plan for the integration

---

[42] In January 2008, at Shaktikhor PLA cantonment of Chitwan district, Prachanda said that the PLA combatants' strength was 9,000 by the time the party entered into the peace process with the government in 2006.

[43] Anirban Roy, "Prachanda: The Unknown Revolutionary",(Kathmandu: Mandal Book Point, 2008), 71-72.

[44] Author's interaction with PLA commanders in the Shaktikhor cantonment on June 27, 2009.

[45] Author's interaction with a senior UNMIN officer in Kathmandu on June 19, 2009.

and rehabilitation of Maoist combatants has surprised the government about UNMINs intention in Nepal.

Conclusion

The delayed Peace Process in Nepal has both external and internal dimensions. The divergent interest of the external forces and lack of unanimity to find a solution to the problem has complicated the matter further. Even as Nepal passes through a difficult transitional phase, all the international stake holders are obliged to support it in nation building rather pushing it further towards uncertainty. It is illogical to say that the Nepalese people and political leaders are responsible for not making the peace process successful. As a dependant country riddled with poverty and a fragile political system, donor countries' influence matters greatly for any major political decisions. Nevertheless, Nepal should behave as a responsible country without attempting to take vicious advantage of the counterbalance bargain.

Despite the comprehensive peace agreement in November 2006, arrival of the United Nations as an observer and the Maoists joining in the interim government, uncertainty prevails in Nepal. Increasingly external interventions and their conflicting political interests have also added to the worsening of these uncertainties. Continuous engagements of US, UK and other western powers and their support for the revival of the Tibetan movement would virtually convert Nepal from a peaceful to conflict riddled region. UNMIN's flawed verification process has further widened the distrust between major political parties. In this scenario, India as the biggest stakeholder should pursue the external forces to cooperate with the Nepalese establishments to draft the constitution under a national consensus government.

CONTRIBUTORS

Brig. K. Srinivasan (Retd) a defence and security analyst, while in service has been involved in addressing internal conflcirs in Jammu and Kashmir. At Centre for Security Analysis, he guides and supervises the work of research fellows. His areas of interests include conflict resolution & peace building, disaster management and role of civil society in conflict situations. He is an active member of the working group on non-traditional security of Regional Network of Strategic Studies Centres set-up by NESA Centre, National Defence University, Washington.

Mr. Yubaraj Ghimire is Editor of the popular 'Samay' newsweekly and recently launched English news tabloid 'Newsfront'. He is among the few Nepali journalists who honed their skills abroad and eventually returned home to practice the craft.

Mr. Chiran Jung Thapa holds Masters Degree in International Affairs (MIA) with a specialization in international security policy, UN studies and conflict resolution from Columbia University, New York and Bachelors Degree in International Relations from State University, New York at Geneseo, New York. He is presently Civil-Military Relations/Security Sector Consultant at the Asia Foundation and Senior Research Fellow at the Centre for South Asian Studies. He has worked with the Permanent Mission of Singapore to the United Nations in New York, Permanent Mission of Nepal to the United Nations and IFC/World Bank – Macedonia International Institute of Education (Fulbright Commission). His research interests include national security, civil-military relations, security sector reform including Disarmament, Demobilization and Reintegration.

Ms. Indra Adhikari is Director, Nepal Red Cross Society. She writes on politics, economy and Bhutanese refugees. She has been associated with Nepalnews.com and South Asian Media Solidarity Network. Ms. Adhikari is also life Member of the International Nepali Literary Society in Washington DC.

Mr. Uddhab Pyakuryel a Research Scholar at the Center for the Study of the Social Systems (Sociology), School of Social Science Jawaharlal Nehru University and political analyst writing on the conflict related issues of Nepal.

Brig Gen (Retd.) Keshar Bahadur Bhandari, is a staff college graduate and a defense & security analyst. He holds Masters Degree in Management Studies from Osmania University, Hyderabad, India and Masters Degree in Sociology from Tribhuvan University, Nepal. He also has a degree in 'Civil Engineering' from the College of Military Engineering, Pune, India. Brigadier General has a long and distinguished career with the Nepal Army spanning over 33 years during which he has commanded an Infantry Brigade in the Central Development Region of Nepal; headed the R & D division of National Security Council Secretariat and worked as Deputy Director of Planning & Policy at the Army HQ. He has written several high level policy documents on national security and national interest. He has served as the Military Secretary and the Engineers Director as well as the Engineers' Advisor to the army. Brig Gen Bhandari has also served as the United Nations Military Advisor in Afghanistan & Pakistan and led the Military Advisory Unit of Pakistan. He has also served the UNIFIL mission in Lebanon.

Professor Bhuwan Chandra Upreti is Professor of Political Science and Director of South Asia Studies Centre, University of Rajasthan, Jaipur. He has been a keen observer of South Asian affairs in general and Nepali & Bhutanese affairs in particular. He has a research experience of over three decades and his research interest include political development, foreign aid, migration, water resources development, conflict and peace studies, foreign policy and regional cooperation. He has to his credit 22 books and more than 100 research papers in national and international journals and is a regular contributor to news papers and magazines. Prof. Upreti's publications include *Politics of Himalayan River Waters* (2003), *Nepal: Democracy at the Cross Roads: Post 1990 Dynamics, Issues and*

Challenges (2007), *Maoists in Nepal, From Insurgency to Political Mainstream* (2008) and *Nepal, Transition to Democratic-Republican State* (2010). He has also written articles in several journals such as the Economic and Political weekly, Seminar and Contemporary South Asia.

Professor Anjoo Sharan Upadhyaya is Professor of Political Science & coordinator of the Centre for the Study of Nepal at the Banaras Hindu University (BHU) in Varanasi, India. Her teaching experience spans a period of over three decades where she has been the Dean, Faculty of Social Sciences, Head, Department of Political Science, and Director of Center for Rural Development, BHU. Prof. Upadhyaya has also has been Research Director, UNU/Ulster University INCORE (Institute of Conflict Resolution and Ethnicity),UK; Fellow at the Department of International Relations, London School of Economics & Politics (LSE); Scholar-in Residence at the Woodrow Wilson Centre for International Scholars, Washington DC; and Fellow at Henry L. Stimson Center, Washington DC. She has also served as a member/consultant at UN University's International Planning Study Team; Academic Council of the United Nations System (ACUNS), Commission on International Conflict Resolution at the Council of the International Peace Research Association (IPRA); International Alert and the Ministry for Nationalities and External Relations, Republic of Daghestan (Russian Federation) as a subject expert.

Ms. Padmaja Murthy is an independent researcher working on South Asia and is currently based in Visakhapatnam, Andhra Pradesh. She was formerly a Fellow at Institute for Defence Studies and Analyses (IDSA), New Delhi and also a Visiting Research Fellow at United Nations Institute for Disarmament Research (UNIDIR), Geneva. She has an MA in International Studies and M.Phil in South Asian Studies from the School of International Studies, Jawaharlal Nehru University. Her particular area of focus is on issues concerning India's relations with its immediate neighbours and she is the author of *Managing Suspicions -Understanding India's Relations with Bangladesh, Bhutan, Nepal, Sri Lanka* (New Delhi: Knowledge World, 2000). She has also extensively written on SAARC and issues relating to regional groupings.

Dr. Nihar Nayak holds a Ph.D. from the School of International Studies, Jawaharlal Nehru University, New Delhi. He is currently Associate Fellow at Institute for Defence Studies and Analyses (IDSA), New Delhi. Dr Nayak was visiting fellow to the International Peace Research Organization (PRIO), Oslo and has a degree on Peace Research from University of Oslo, Norway. He is currently working on the project "Maoist Movement in Nepal: Security Implications in South Asia". He worked as Research Associate at the Institute for Conflict Management, New Delhi, before joining the IDSA. His research area is Nepal and Maoist Insurgency in South Asia. He has a number of national and international publications to his credit and has written extensively in the media.

CSA PUBLICATIONS

CONFLICT RESOLUTION AND PEACE BUILDING

1. Conflict Resolution and Peace Building in Sri Lanka

2. Federalism and Conflict Resolution in Sri Lanka

3. Peace Process in Sri Lanka: Challenges & Opportunities

4. Conflict Over Fisheries in the Palk Bay Region

5. Conflict in Sri Lanka: The Road Ahead

6. Peace and Conflict Resolution: Emerging Ideas

7. From Winning the War to Winning Peace: Post War Rebuilding of the Society in Sri Lanka

8. Internal Conflicts in Myanmar: Transnational Consequences

SECURITY STUDIES

9. US and the Rising Powers: India and China

10. Maritime Security in the Indian Ocean Region: Critical Issues in Debate

11. Public Perceptions of Security in India: Results of a National Survey

12. Essential Components of National Security

13. Economic Growth and National Security

14. Security Dimensions of India and Southeast Asia

15. India & ASEAN: Non-Traditional Security Threats

16. Emerging Challenges to Energy Security in the Asia Pacific